CASES IN PUBLIC POLICY-MAKING

CASES IN PUBLIC POLICY-MAKING

edited by JAMES E. ANDERSON
UNIVERSITY OF HOUSTON

PRAEGER PUBLISHERS   NEW YORK

Published in the United States of America in 1976
by Praeger Publishers, Inc.
111 Fourth Avenue, New York, N.Y. 10003

CI OCT. 1 7 1978

Library of Congress Cataloging in Publication Data
Main entry under title:

Cases in public policy-making.

Includes bibliographies.
CONTENTS: Problems and agendas: Cobb and Elder.
Participation in American politics: the dynamics of agenda-
building.—Nadel. Politics of Consumer protection.—
Kingdon. Congressmen's voting decisions. [etc.]
1. United States—Politics and government—1945–
—Addresses, essays, lectures. 2. Policy sciences—
Addresses, essays, lectures. I. Anderson, James E.
JK271.C35   32C'.2'0973   74–30994
ISBN 0–275–85230–X

Printed in the United States of America

Contents

Introduction   1

part one PROBLEMS AND AGENDAS   7

1 Issue Creation and Agenda-Building   10
Roger W. Cobb and Charles D. Elder

2 Consumer Protection Becomes a Public Issue
(Again)   22
Mark V. Nadel

3 Dynamics of Agenda Formation in Congress
35
John W. Kingdon

part two POLICY FORMULATION   51

4 Speculative Augmentation in Federal Air
Pollution Policy-Making   54
Charles O. Jones

5 Policy Formulation in the Executive Branch:
Central Legislative Clearance   80
Robert S. Gilmour

6 The Presidency and Policy Formulation: The
Use of Task Forces   97
Norman C. Thomas and Harold L. Wolman

Contents

part three **POLICY ADOPTION** 119

7 Congressional Voting Decisions 122
Leroy N. Rieselbach

8 Coalition-Building in the United States House of Representatives: Agricultural Legislation in 1973 141
Weldon V. Barton

9 Selective Service and Draft Protestors: A "One-Man" Policy Decision 162
Larry L. Wade

10 Congress Adopts Medicare: The Politics of Legislative Certainty 173
Theodore R. Marmor

part four **POLICY IMPLEMENTATION** 193

11 Beyond the ITT Case: The Politics of Antitrust Enforcement 196
Harlan M. Blake

12 Implementing Presidential Foreign Policy Decisions: Limitations and Resistance 208
Morton H. Halperin

13 Civil Rights Policies and the Matter of Compliance 237
Charles S. Bullock, III, and Harrell R. Rodgers, Jr.

part five **POLICY EVALUATION** 259

14 Political Feasibility 262
Ralph K. Huitt

15 What Does the Most Good? 279
Alice M. Rivlin

16 The Politics of Evaluation: The Case of Head Start 292
Walter Williams and John W. Evans

17 The Politicization of Evaluation Research 310
Carol H. Weiss

Bibliography 323

Introduction

Political scientists have usually focused their
attention on the description and analysis of
political institutions (for example, legislatures),
on processes (for instance, how bills become
laws), and on behaviors (for example, how
congressmen make their voting decisions).
During the past decade or so, a major
expansion of interest by political scientists in
the analysis of public policy has resulted in a
proliferation of books and articles, college
courses and programs, and university institutes
and schools concerned with public policy.

Just what does the analysis of public policy
entail? Or to put it somewhat differently, what

is policy analysis? Generally, policy analysis is concerned with the systematic examination and explanation of the formation of public policy, its substantive content, and its impact and consequences. However, those concerned with policy analysis have not abandoned their concern with political institutions, processes, and behaviors. Rather, they are concerned with them to the extent that they are more or less directly related to the formation and implementation of public policy. Whereas, for example, the prime concern of the student of congressional voting behavior is to explain how congressmen make voting choices, the policy analyst is more likely to want to know what caused Congress to adopt or reject a particular piece of legislation. To illustrate further, the policy analyst will seek answers to such questions as: Why does government act on some public problems and not others? How do pressure groups and public opinion affect the formation of public policy? To what extent is the substance of public policy shaped by administrative agencies? What are our national priorities in the area of foreign policy? What impact does fiscal policy have in maintaining economic stability? Why do people comply with public policies? Does antitrust policy really help to maintain economic competition?

Policy analysis should be differentiated from policy advocacy. In contrast to policy analysis, with its focus on systematic inquiry, explanation, and the development of theoretical and factual knowledge, policy advocacy is concerned with what government ought to do, with the generation of support for particular policies, with political activism. Examples are the presidential candidate calling for welfare reform, the socialist orator declaiming on the need to abolish capitalism, and the citizens' group urging the need for better police protection. Policy advocacy may or may not be based upon much policy analysis.

We have said that public policy is the focal concern of policy analysis; what then is a public policy? A useful definition holds that it is a purposive course of action followed by government in dealing with some topic or matter of public concern, such as unemployment, economic monopoly, housing, the use of the national forests, crime in the streets, or the external activities of the Soviet Union. Notice particularly that, defined as a course of action, a public policy involves more than a decision by some governmental body to act or not to act on some matter. Especially assuming the decision involves some kind of positive action, what is done or not done to carry out the decisions helps give form to the policy. A policy, in short, usually involves a series of decisions. The word "purposive" indicates that the policy involves deliberate, goal-oriented behavior and not simply random or chance behavior. (I would not, however, deny that some policies may have their origin in such behavior, though most will not.)

The vast number and variety of public policies to be found in the United States can be categorized in several ways. They can be classified by subject matter, as foreign policy, labor policy, civil rights policy, energy policy, and so on. Or they can be classified on the basis of the number of people affected and their relationships with one another. Using these criteria, Professor Theodore Lowi has depicted public policies as being either distributive (problems involving individuals or small numbers of people), regulatory (demands by one group that the activities of another be restricted), or redistributive (calling for transfer of resources among large groups, or classes, in society).[1] To this another scholar has added the category of self-regulatory policy,[2] which entails control of a group, often by itself, to increase its options, as in the case of most professional licensing programs. Policy analysis is, as we have indicated, concerned with more than the study and classification of policy content. If it were not, it would be essentially a descriptive activity lacking much challenge or vitality. In the past, policy analysts have concentrated primarily on the *formation* of public policy. However, in the last few years, policy analysts have also become considerably involved with the systematic evaluation of policy impacts.

The task of understanding public policy is further complicated by the fact that there are myriad centers or arenas of public policy-making in the United States. Policy is made by all branches of government—legislative, executive, judicial, and administrative—if one wishes to follow the practice of those who designate the administra-

---

[1]For a discussion see Theodore J. Lowi, "American Business, Public Policy, Case Studies, and Political Theory," *World Politics* 16 (July 1964): 667–715.

[2]Robert H. Salisbury, "The Analysis of Public Policy: A Search for Theories and Roles," in Austin Ranney, ed., *Political Science and Public Policy* (Chicago: Rand McNally, 1968).

tion as the fourth branch of government.[3] Moreover, policy is made by all levels of government—national, state, and local—sometimes cooperatively, sometimes independently of one another. The political decision-makers in these various arenas are subject to a variety of environmental and political forces and influences. There is, in my view, no single policy process but rather a wide variety of processes by which public policies are made. Thus policies emanate from the United States Supreme Court, the Federal Power Commission, the California state legislature, the Chicago City Council, and Deaf Smith County (Texas). The processes by which these and other entities make policies may differ in terms of such factors as participants, procedures, influencing factors, levels of public awareness, and institutional contexts.

Given the complexity of public policy-making in the United States (and other developed, pluralistic societies), how should the task of policy analysis be approached? Let us first dispatch with a couple of intellectual straw men. Overly simple or glib explanations should be avoided, such as the popular Marxist view that public policy in capitalist countries simply reflects the interests of the bourgeoisie. On the other hand, one should not despair of imposing any order or understanding on what is often a complicated and confusing situation. What we need are models or concepts of policy-making which can be used to organize and clarify our thinking about and inquiry into the formation of public policy.

Political scientists have developed or co-opted a number of theories, concepts, and models which can be employed in the study of public policy. These include group theory, systems theory, institutional analysis, incrementalism, game theory, public choice theory, and elite theory.[4] Each of these theories or models has its adherents and critics. Each also has its utilities and shortcomings. Thus, for example, while group theory alerts us to the important role played by interest groups in the formation of public policy, its attempt to explain

---

[3] E.g., Peter Woll, *American Bureaucracy* (New York: Norton, 1963).

[4] For discussion of some of these, see James E. Anderson, *Public Policy-Making* (New York: Praeger, 1975), ch. 1, and Thomas R. Dye, *Understanding Public Policy*, 2d ed. (Englewood Cliffs, N.J.: Prentice-Hall, 1975), ch. 2.

all important political activity in terms of the group struggle over-states the role of groups and understates the importance of other factors in policy formation.

Rather than employ one or more of the theories or models enumerated in the preceding paragraph, I have chosen to organize this book of readings on the basis of yet another conceptualization of the policy process, namely, that it can be viewed as a sequential pattern of activity (that is, a process) in which a number of functional categories of activity can be distinguished.[5] The various categories, briefly set forth, are:

1. Problem formation and agenda-setting. What is a policy problem? What makes it a public problem? By what means does it get onto a governmental agenda? Why do some problems not get to a governmental agenda?
2. Policy formulation. What alternatives are there for dealing with a policy problem? How are they developed? Who participates, and with what effect, in policy formulation?
3. Policy adoption. How is a policy alternative adopted or enacted; that is, how is it legitimized? What requirements must be met? Who adopts policy?
4. Policy implementation. Unless a policy is self-executing (and relatively few are), what if anything is done to carry it into effect? Who is involved? What procedures or techniques are used? What impact does implementary action have on policy content?
5. Policy evaluation. What impact does a policy have on the problem at which it is directed? How is the effectiveness or impact of a policy measured? Who evaluates policy? What are the consequences of evaluation? Does it produce feedback, for example, demands for change or repeal of the original policy?

This sequential process approach has a number of advantages as a tool for public policy analyses. In actuality, policy-making often

---

[5]This discussion is based on Anderson, *op. cit.*

does follow in sequence the pattern of activities listed above. It is, in short, realistic, which is a quality not especially abundant in some approaches (game theory, for example). Second, it provides a dynamic and developmental rather than static or cross-sectional view of the policy process. Third, the sequential process approach is open to change and adaptation. Additional stages can be added if experience indicates they are needed for analytical or descriptive clarity. Various forms of data collection and analysis—whether quantitative, institutional descriptive, or normative—are compatible with it. Fourth, the sequential process approach is not "culture bound" and hence can be used to study policy-making in foreign political systems as well as at all levels in the United States. Finally, it lends itself to manageable comparisons and to the development of "middle-range" theories. Thus one can ask, and compare, how policy problems reach the policy agenda in various countries. Or one can compare the processes of policy formulation within various institutional settings, such as those provided by a number of administrative agencies in a single country, or the legislatures in a number of countries.

The selections in this book have been chosen to provide the reader with a basic understanding of the various functional activities involved in the sequential policy process. By examining what happened to a number of recent, substantive issues at various points in the national legislative and administrative arenas, it is hoped that the reader will glimpse the complexity and uncertainty—and the occasional drama and intrigue—of the public policy process.

part one PROBLEMS AND AGENDAS

The formation of public policy begins with the development of a public problem and its appearance on the agenda of government. This seems like a rather commonplace and obvious statement. However, policy analysts have tended to take public problems as given and to begin their inquiry and analysis at the point at which a problem appears on the agenda of a governmental body such as a legislature or executive department. But if we examine why some conditions or situations in society give rise to policy problems and, in turn, why some of these problems reach the agenda and others do not, we can gain substantial insight into the operation of the political system. We will also acquire some understanding of how the unequal distribution of governmental benefits and costs in a society comes about.

A problem can be defined as a condition or situation which produces a human need, deprivation, or dissatisfaction. It becomes a public problem when many people become involved in it or perceive themselves as being affected by it. Problems give rise to issues when conflict develops over what should be done, if anything, to alleviate or resolve the problem. For example, inflation (rapidly increasing prices) is perceived as a public problem by most people. Whether government should become at all involved in trying to control inflation was once a major public issue. Since World War II the need for governmental action to combat inflation has become widely accepted and this aspect of the issue has disappeared, but has been replaced by many other questions about what the substance of government intervention ought to be; for example, should taxes be increased to combat inflation? Should price and wage controls be imposed?

Not all public problems, or issues, reach the agenda of some governmental body. A governmental agenda should not be thought of as a formal list of matters to be dealt with by a set of decision-makers. Rather, it simply designates those problems or issues to which the members of a governmental body feel compelled to give active and serious consideration. For some people, the graduated income tax is a serious public problem, and at times it becomes an issue between some groups. However, because of the wide public acceptance of the graduated income tax, and the need for the revenue it produces, it has not occupied a place on the congressional policy agenda in recent years.

There are, at any given time, many public problems in existence in our society. Only some of them appear on a governmental agenda. The readings in this part are intended generally to illustrate the nature of public problems and to help explain how they reach a governmental agenda. Cobb and Elder provide an overview of concepts of issue and agenda and of agenda formation. Then a particular public problem is considered—the need to protect consumers against deception, harmful products, and other evils. This issue appeared on the congressional policy agenda early in this century and again in the 1930s, but at other times, such as during the 1940s and 1950s, it was not an active agenda item. Mark Nadel seeks to explain why consumer protection became a major agenda item again during the 1960s. John Kingdon deals specifically with the question of how issues or problems come to the attention of members of Congress and reach the congressional agenda.

1. Issue Creation and Agenda-Building

Roger W. Cobb
Charles D. Elder

WHAT IS AN ISSUE? WHAT MAKES AN ISSUE?

*An issue is a conflict between two or more
identifiable groups over procedural or
substantive matters relating to the distribution
of positions or resources.* Generally, there are
four means by which issues are created. The

From Roger W. Cobb and Charles D. Elder, *Participation
in American Politics* (Baltimore, Md.: The Johns Hopkins
University Press, 1975), pp. 82–93. Copyright © 1972 by
Roger W. Cobb and Charles D. Elder. Reprinted by permission of the Publisher.

most common method is the manufacturing of an issue by one or more of the contending parties who perceive an unfavorable bias in the distribution of positions or resources. For example, in 1950 truckers in Pennsylvania thought the railroads had an inherent advantage in carrying freight over long distances and sought to create an issue to redress this imbalance. Such initiators are labeled "readjustors."

Another form of issue creation can be traced to a person or group who manufacture an issue for their own gain; for example, individuals who want to run for public office and are looking for an issue to advance their cause. Such individuals may be labeled "exploiters." As Herbert Blumer has written:

> The gaining of sympathizers or members rarely occurs through a mere combination of a pre-established appeal and a pre-established individual psychological bent on which it is brought to bear. Instead the prospective sympathizer has to be aroused, nurtured and directed.[1]

Hans Toch echoes a similar sentiment when he writes:

> People are brought into social movements through the skills of leaders and agitators rather than because of pre-existing problems. ... Appeals seem to originate with people who are primarily interested in other ends than the solution of the problems of potential members.[2]

Another means of issue initiation is through an unanticipated event. Such events could be called "circumstantial reactors." Examples include the development of an oil slick off the California coast near Santa Barbara in early 1969 that led to a reconsideration of the whole question of offshore drilling regulations. Other examples are the assassination of President Kennedy, which led to the gun control issue, and Eisenhower's heart attack in the mid-1950's, which raised the question of presidential disability.

---

[1]Herbert Blumer, "Collective Behavior," in J. B. Gittler (ed.), *Review of Sociology* (New York: Wiley, 1957), 148.

[2]Hans Toch, *The Psychology of Social Movements* (Indianapolis: Bobbs-Merrill, 1965), 87.

Issues can be generated by persons or groups who have no positions or resources to gain for themselves. Often, they merely acquire a psychological sense of well-being for doing what they believe is in the public interest. These initiators might be called "do-gooders." The efforts to support Biafran relief programs fall in this category.

The above categories are not mutually exclusive, as an individual or group may have more than one motive for a particular action. For example, some people supported civil rights legislation because they felt it was humanitarian, while others supported it because they sought personal or collective gains.

Triggering Devices

At least two classes of triggering mechanisms, or unforeseen events, help shape issues that will be defined by the initiators. These can be subdivided into internal and external events that correspond to the domestic and foreign spheres.

Within the internal subdivision, there are five types of triggering devices. The first is a natural catastrophe, such as a mine cave-in, air inversion, flooding, and fire. The second is an unanticipated human event, such as a spontaneous riot, assassination of public officials, air hijackings, and murder of private individuals. The third is a techno-logical change in the environment that creates heretofore undiscussed questions. It might involve mass transportation, air and water pollu-tion, or air travel congestion. The fourth category is an actual imbal-ance, or bias, in the distribution of resources leading to such things as civil rights protest and union strikes. A fifth type is ecological change, such as population explosion and black migration to North-ern cities.

There are four types of external trigger mechanisms. The first is an act of war or military violence involving the United States as a direct combatant. Examples include the Vietnam war, the Pueblo seizure, and the dropping of atomic bombs on Hiroshima. The second cate-gory includes innovations in weapons technology involving such things as arms control, the Hotline between the Kremlin and the White House, and the deployment of an anti-ballistic system. The third type is an international conflict in which the United States is not a direct combatant, such as the conflicts in the Middle East and the

Congo. The final category involves changing world alignment patterns that may affect American membership in the United Nations, troop commitments in the North Atlantic Treaty Organization, and the American role in the Organization of American States.

Issue Initiation and Trigger Mechanisms

The formation of an issue is dependent on the dynamic interplay between the initiator and the trigger device. For example, a mine disaster itself does not create an issue. Many times in the past such an event has occurred with no ameliorative action. A link must be made between a grievance (or a triggering event) and an initiator who converts the problem into an issue for a private or a public reason.

In a system perspective, the inputs consist of the initiator and the event, or triggering mechanism, that transform the problem into an issue. The output is the agenda, which will be the focus of the next section.

AGENDAS: WHAT ARE THEY?

In general terms, we have identified two basic types of political agendas. The first of these is the systemic agenda for political controversy. *The systemic agenda consists of all issues that are commonly perceived by members of the political community as meriting public attention and as involving matters within the legitimate jurisdiction of existing governmental authority.* Every local, state, and national political community will have a systemic agenda. The systemic agenda of the larger community may subsume items from the systemic agendas of subsidiary communities, but the two agendas will not necessarily correspond. For example, the systemic agenda of Boston may include items on the national agenda of controversy, such as pollution and crime in the streets, but will also include such items as the need for a new sports arena.

There are three prerequisites for an issue to obtain access to the systemic agenda: (1) widespread attention or at least awareness; (2) shared concern of a sizeable portion of the public that some type of action is required; and (3) a shared perception that the matter is an appropriate concern of some governmental unit and falls within the bounds of its authority. The terms "shared concern" and "shared perception" refer to the prevailing climate of opinion, which will be conditioned by the dominant norms, values, and ideology of a community. An issue requires the recognition of only a major portion of the polity, not the entire citizenry.

For an item or an issue to acquire public recognition, its supporters must have either access to the mass media or the resources necessary to reach people. They may require more than money and manpower; often the use of action rhetoric is essential. For example, use of terms such as *communist-inspired* or *anti-American* is a useful verbal ploy in attracting a larger audience than the original adherents of a cause.

In addition to gaining popular recognition, the issue must be perceived by a large number of people as both being subject to remedial action and requiring such action. In other words, action must be considered not only possible, but also necessary for the resolution of the issue. To foster such popular conviction, the mobilization of a significant number of groups or persons will normally be required.

Often, the fate of an issue in gaining systemic agenda status will hinge on whether or not it can be defined as being within the purview of legitimate governmental action. Perhaps one of the most devastating tactics that may be used to prevent an issue from reaching the systemic agenda is to deny that it falls within the bounds of governmental authority. For example, equal access to public accommodations was kept off the systemic agenda for some time because opponents successfully argued that the grievance fell outside the proper bounds of governmental authority.

The second type of agenda is the institutional, governmental, or formal agenda, which may be defined as *that set of items explicitly up for the active and serious consideration of authoritative decision-makers.* Therefore, any set of items up before any governmental body at the local, state, or national level will constitute an institutional agenda.

Two clarifications are in order regarding key terms in the above definition of a formal agenda. "Explicitly" refers to an issue involving action or policy alternatives or involving simply the identification of a problem requiring some action. An example of the former would be a proposal to raise the minimum wage to a specific level per hour. An illustration of the latter would be a reconsideration of certain restrictive loan practices of savings and loan institutions in the ghetto.

"Active and serious" are used to distinguish formal agenda items from what might be called "pseudo-agenda items." By pseudo-agenda, we mean any form of registering or acknowledging a demand without explicitly considering its merit. Decision-makers will often use such an agenda to assuage frustrations of constituency groups and to avoid political ramifications of a failure to acknowledge the demand. This typically occurs in a legislature where bills are placed in the hopper to placate some groups of activists with no real chance of action being taken.

Policy-makers will participate in the building of both systemic and institutional agendas. However, the natures of the two agendas are substantially different. The systemic agenda will be composed of fairly abstract and general items that do little more than identify a problem area. It will not necessarily suggest either the alternatives available or the means of coping with the problem. For example, it might include a vague item like "ending discrimination."

An institutional agenda will tend to be more specific, concrete, and limited in the number of items. It will identify, at least implicitly, those facets of a problem that are to be seriously considered by a decision-making body. An example would be a city council's consideration of alternative forms of local taxation for the support of public schools. It is possible for an item to get onto the formal agenda without having been a part of the systemic agenda. Each year, Congress considers many private bills of little social import or concern. However, it is unlikely that any issue involving substantial social consequences will gain standing on a governmental agenda unless it has first attained systemic agenda status.

Content of Formal Agendas

Formal agenda items can be divided into two major categories: *old items* and *new items*. *Old items* are those that have action alternatives delineated. They are predefined in most instances, except in specific cases (for example, the issue may not be whether workers will receive a 5 percent or a 10 percent raise, but whether they will get a raise at all).

There are two agenda components under the general heading of *old items*. Habitual items include those that come up for regular review. Examples would be budget items such as personnel pay and fights between existing agencies for a larger slice of the federal budget.

Recurrent items are those that occur with some periodicity, but need not appear at regular intervals. Examples would include governmental reorganization and regulation arising from a concern for efficiency or economy or both, rules changes in the legislature (for example, the filibuster in the Senate), Congressional reform, tariff items, tax reform, and social security increases or extensions.

The second general heading, *new items,* refers to those components that have no predetermined definitions, but are flexible in their interpretation or development. The first subdivision would include automatic or spontaneous issues appearing as an action or reaction of a key decision-maker in a specific situation. Examples include public employee or major industry strikes with a substantial impact on the economy or our military strength, the steel crisis under President Truman during the Korean War, foreign policy crises (e.g., Korea, Cuba, and the Dominican Republic), and innovations in foreign policy (e.g., American entrance into the United Nations, the test ban treaty, and the nuclear proliferation treaty).

A second component of *new items* is channeled items, those issues channeled to the agenda by the mobilization of mass support or by the activation of significant public groups (e.g., unions). Examples of issues with mass support include the civil rights issues of the 1960's and the gun control issue. Illustrations of issues backed by significant public groups include the Taft-Hartley repeal effort and the farm parity program.

An issue need not be static or confined to one category throughout its existence. At any point in time, it may be redefined. An example of a dynamic issue is the Vietnam policy. Initially, it became a spontaneous issue when President Eisenhower committed several hundred advisers in the late 1950's. The issue of expanded commitment became recurrent under Presidents Kennedy and Johnson. By 1963, the dispute appeared on the docket with great regularity. It continued in this form until opposition to the war—a channelized item begun by peace groups—raised the question of the legitimacy of American involvement. The peace groups expanded concern with American involvement until it became the policy stance of a major presidential candidate in 1968.

The Form of an Institutional Agenda

The explicit form of the formal agenda may be found in the calendar of authoritative decision-making bodies such as legislatures, high courts, or regulatory agencies. Unless an item appears on some docket, it will not be considered to be an agenda item. Agenda composition will vary over time. However, recurrent or habitual items will be the most numerous. They tend to receive priority from the decision-makers, who constantly find that their time is limited and that their agenda is overloaded. Spontaneous, or automatic, items take precedence over channeled items, so it is very difficult to get new issues on the agenda. Decision-makers presume that older problems warrant more attention because of their longevity and the greater familiarity officials have with them.

DIFFERENTIAL ACCESS TO INSTITUTIONAL GATEKEEPERS

The content of a formal agenda will tend to reflect structural and institutional biases found within the system. These biases arise from differential resources among individuals and groups and concomitant differences in access. For an issue to attain agenda status, it must command the support of at least some key decision-makers, for they are the ultimate guardians of the formal agenda.

Political leaders are active participants in the agenda-building process, not simply impartial arbiters of issue disputes. As Bauer, Pool, and Dexter note:

> Congress is not a passive body, registering already-existent public views forced on its attention by public pressures. Congress, second only to the president, is, rather the major institution for initiating and creating political issues and projecting them into a national civic debate.[3]

---

[3]Raymond Bauer, Ithiel Pool, and Lewis Dexter, *American Business and Public Policy* (New York: Atherton Press, 1963), p. 478.

The strategic location of these leaders assures them of media visibility when they want to promote an issue and places them in an excellent position to bargain with other decision-makers over formal agenda content. Because they have fairly direct control over what will appear on the formal agenda and considerable freedom to choose among the plethora of issues competing for attention, they can insist that an issue of concern to them be considered in return for agreement to consider an issue that is salient to another decision-maker or set of decision-makers.

It is easy then to understand why access to one or more key officials is so important to political groups. As one commentator noted,

> The development and improvement of such access is a common denominator of the tactics of all of them, frequently leading to efforts to exclude competing groups from equivalent access or to set up new decision points access to which can be monopolized by a particular group.[4]

Some groups have a greater ease of access than others, and are thus more likely to get their demands placed on an agenda.

The differential responsiveness arises from a variety of factors. First, the decision-maker may be indebted to a particular group or identify himself as a member of that group. Second, some groups have more resources than others or are better able to mobilize their resources. Third, some groups are located so strategically in the social or economic structure of society that their interests cannot be ignored (for example, big business and agriculture). Fourth, some groups (such as doctors, lawyers, and church leaders) are held in greater esteem by the public than others and thus can command greater access to decision-makers. As a consequence, certain groups are more likely than others to receive attention from decision-makers when they come up with new demands. Farmers have an inherent advantage over many other groups in obtaining action on their needs because there are many decision-makers who identify themselves with farm groups and because agriculture occupies a pivotal position in the American economy.

---

[4]David Truman, *The Governmental Process* (New York: Knopf, 1951), p. 264.

A group may encounter different types of responses from different levels or branches of the government. When the National Association for the Advancement of Colored People first started to press its demands, it focused on the Congress and the presidency, but received no support. However, the group was much more effective when it focused on a judicial strategy of making gains in civil rights through a series of court cases. Thus, differential responsiveness may result from the type of governmental unit petitioned as well as from differences among groups themselves.

Political parties also play an important part in translating issues into agenda items. To assure support, they will often seek out and identify themselves with issues that are salient to large portions of the populace. Typically, these issues are identified in the party platform in general terms and with considerable ambiguity. However, as Truman notes:

> The significance of preparing a platform lies primarily in the evidence that the negotiations provide concerning what groups will have access to the developing national party organization. ... Interest group leaders are aware that the real settlement of the issues they are concerned with ... will take place later; in the platform, they seek tentative assurance of a voice in that settlement. To maximize this assurance, political interest groups normally seek recognition in the platforms of both major parties.[5]

Certainly recognition on a party platform is at least indicative of an issue attaining standing on the systemic agenda of political controversy.

The media can also play a very important role in elevating issues to the systemic agenda and increasing their chances of receiving formal agenda consideration. Certain personages in the media can act as opinion leaders in bringing publicity to a particular issue. Examples of individuals who have gained a larger audience for a dispute include Walter Lippmann, Jack Anderson, and Drew Pearson. Individuals who have acquired an audience simply by constantly appearing in the news can also publicize an issue. Ralph Nader has a ready-made

---

[5]Truman, *op. cit.*, p. 285.

constituency stemming from his many attacks on various inefficient and unscrupulous business practices.

DIFFERENTIAL LEGITIMACY

While most observers grant that there are inequalities in access to decision-makers, they argue that the existence of multiple points of access owing to different levels and branches of government has the net effect of insuring widespread contacts. Further, the existence of dispersed inequalities (that is, the fact that groups having great resources in one area may not have comparable resources in other areas) supposedly assures that no group will be without political influence in some areas. However, this argument fails to consider the relatively stable pattern of differential legitimacy accorded various social groupings. Differences in accessibility to decision-makers are a function of the relative legitimacy of various groups. For example, a proposal advanced by a group of businessmen to improve traffic flows into the downtown business area is more likely to receive the attention of decision-makers than a counterproposal by ghetto residents to develop more extensive and effective mass transit systems.

The problem confronted by any newly formed group is often how to legitimize the group and the interest represented rather than how to legitimize a particular issue position. The legitimacy of the group will be greatly enhanced by the status and community standing of its members. In other words, people without resources (for example, lower-income groups) will have greater difficulty attaining legitimacy than their higher-income counterparts. For example, the anti-war movement initially promoted by student groups who traditionally have little political standing received little public support until more socially prominent persons and groups entered the fray on their behalf (for example, business groups, military leaders, clergymen, and senators).

SYSTEMIC CONSTRAINTS ON AGENDA ENTRANCE

Even if an issue is promoted by a group that is perceived to be legitimate, its appearance on a formal agenda may be problematic owing to cultural constraints on the range of issues that are considered legitimate topics for governmental action. Any institutional agenda will be restricted by the prevailing popular sentiment as to what constitutes appropriate matters for governmental attention. For example, federal aid to education was long considered by many to be an inappropriate area for federal governmental action, a fact that precluded active and serious consideration of the merits of the issue for decades. Legitimizing issues that are considered outside of the governmental realm is difficult and normally takes a long time. The net effect of this is that new demands of particularly disadvantaged or deprived groups are the least likely to receive attention on either the systemic agenda of controversy or the institutional agenda.

2. Consumer Protection Becomes a Public Issue (Again)

Mark V. Nadel

THE BEGINNINGS OF THE PRESENT

Like much of the rest of the New Deal, interest and activity in consumer issues was a casualty of World War II. The consumer issues of the war years were unique to the times as Americans had to cope with rationing and other dislocations of the consumer goods economy.

From Mark V. Nadel, *The Politics of Consumer Protection* (Indianapolis, Ind.: Bobbs-Merrill, 1971), pp. 31–43. Copyright © 1971 by The Bobbs-Merrill Company, Inc., and reprinted by permission.

In the remaining years of the 1940s, consumer issues still tended to be related to the economic problems caused by the war and reconversion. In those years, there was a tone to consumer issues which was entirely different from the previous and later eras of "consumerism." Public attention was focused on such consumer problems as inflation and price stabilization, housing shortages, rent control, and proposed social security legislation. This conception of consumer protection can be seen in the "Program for Action" recommended to Congress by *Consumer Reports* in 1949. The recommendations included a cut of military spending, price and rent controls, an excess profits tax, an improved farm price program, new antitrust laws, and others.

During the late 1940s, and through the 1950s, the only consistent voice of consumer interests was Consumers Union which published *Consumer Reports*. While *Consumer Reports* began to run articles on chemicals in foods, meat inspection, and finance rackets, it was largely a voice in the wilderness and the period was one of general quiescence for consumer protection (as well as many other later reform issues) until the early 1960s.

One intervening issue during those years is the exception that proves the rule—automobile safety. Auto safety emerged in 1965 as a major consumer issue which, in the opinion of many consumer activists, was the "breakthrough" issue. Yet it was also an issue on the congressional agenda, although with much lower public visibility, in the 1950s. From 1956 until his defeat in 1964, Congressman Kenneth Roberts, Democrat of Alabama, held hearings on automobile safety. During those years, however, Roberts was the only consistent advocate of federal safety standards for automobile design. From 1956 until 1966, congressional response consisted of passing three piecemeal auto safety bills, all of them in the years from 1962 to 1964. The most important bill of those years required the General Services Administration to set safety standards for all cars purchased by the government. (Twice previously the House had passed this bill sponsored by Roberts, but the Senate did not act until 1964). Nonetheless, this legislation and the years of hearings went forth with no fanfare; there was practically no publicity given to Roberts' hearings. . . .

The real origins of consumer protection as an important congressional political issue at the present time are to be found in the hearings on the prescription drug industry held by Senator Estes Kefauver's Antitrust and Monopoly Subcommittee. The hearings were held intermittently from 1959 through 1962. Although the original focus of the hearings was drug prices, the revelation that Americans had narrowly missed the mass marketing of thalidomide, a drug which produced birth defects when taken by pregnant women, turned the hearings around, brought widespread public attention, and caused a previously emasculated bill to emerge in reasonably effective form. As in the previous two eras of consumer protection activism, drug safety was a central issue touching on public emotion and creating a public demand for action. The drug amendments of 1962 became law on December 10, 1962. However, these events did not lead directly to an increased consumer activism or the expansion of a generalized consumer protection issue. There was no presidential package of consumer proposals until 1965 and no outpouring of legislation until 1966.

The one issue which both preceded the late 1960s period of consumer activism and was also a link with it was truth-in-lending, originally championed by Senator Paul Douglas. Senator Douglas began hearings on a bill to require full disclosure of interest costs in 1960, but it did not become law until 1968—two years after Douglas was defeated for reelection. The chronology of truth-in-lending is illustrative of the development of consumer protection as an issue although there are unique reasons as well for the length of time it took for the bill to pass. Nonetheless, while it had not even been able to get out of committee for eight years, by the time it passed in 1968, the bill was actually more comprehensive and stronger than the one which had originally been introduced.

In general, the years 1966 through 1968 were the major years of congressional action. Table 1 shows the development of the congressional issue.

In the two major consumer eras of the past, the President was prominently associated with the consumer issue at hand. While the relative degree of support varied, there was no question that Presidents Theodore Roosevelt and Franklin Roosevelt publicly supported the food and drug measures under consideration. In the development of the present era, varying degrees of presidential support are also seen. However, Lyndon Johnson was the first President to adopt a set of legislative consumer protection proposals as his own and make them a major part of his overall legislative program.

The examination of the role of the President as proponent of consumer protection starts with John Kennedy. It is an understatement to say that consumer issues were not among the major concerns of his predecessor's administration. President Eisenhower fully shared the congressional apathy and negative attitude toward consumer protection. The administration took no position on the Roberts auto safety proposals and, in 1960, opposed the Douglas truth-in-lending bill. Thus the Democratic administration inherited a tradition of the President sharing the general indifference to the issue and potential of consumer protection.

The first major presidential articulation of the consumer interest since the New Deal was President Kennedy's 1962 consumer message to Congress, the first such message delivered by any President. Although, in that message, President Kennedy proclaimed four "rights of consumers" and announced his commitment to consumer protection, his only major intervention in consumer politics was to aid in opposing some sections of Senator Kefauver's original drug amendments—an effort which was quickly reversed in the wake of the thalidomide episode.

Regardless of the specific instances of support and opposition to legislation, from 1965 onward, consumer protection had become an issue on the public agenda which was legitimated by annual presidential messages to Congress and legislative proposals. Indeed, President Johnson made consumer protection a major part of his legislative program and, in 1968, included consumer proposals in his state-of-

Table 1 Number of New Consumer Protection Laws Enacted by Congress

1962	1
1963	0
1964	1
1965	0
1966	5
1967	4
1968	6
1969	1
1970	2

the-union address. By 1969, the legitimacy of a governmental role and the need for further action was so widely accepted that a conservative Republican President, Richard Nixon, delivered his own consumer message.

While there is no available survey data to permit a precise analysis of the growth of the consumer protection issue in the public mind, we can at least establish a rough measure of public exposure to consumer protection issues simply to illustrate the growth of consumer protection as a *public* political issue. Table 2 lists the number of general consumer protection stories in popular magazines from 1963 through 1970. While it is hazardous to infer from these figures the state of public awareness, at the very least media exposure makes public awareness possible, and it is possible to see the chronology of that potential awareness.

Table 2 Number of Consumer Protection Articles in Popular Magazines

1963	4
1964	9
1965	6
1966	14
1967	24
1968	24
1969	32
1970	48

SOURCE: *Readers Guide to Periodical Literature,* for the years indicated. (Includes only stories listed under general heading of "consumer protection.")

In general, the present era of consumer protection began slowly with two specific issues in the early 1960s. Presidential support, congressional action, and public attention converged in 1966, by which time one could speak in terms of consumer protection itself as a general issue. Perhaps the event which most dramatically symbolized this maturing of the issue was a *Newsweek* cover story which proclaimed Ralph Nader as "Consumer Crusader." Just as with Ralph Nader, the issue was no longer automobiles or other separate issues, but was consumer protection as a generalized category of issues.

WHY NOW?

In discussing the background of the present focus on consumer protection, one major unanswered question is why this should become an issue at the present time after it was a "non-issue" for so long. While it may be impossible to resolve this problem definitively and to assign the precise weight to each causal factor, still something can be said about the causes which will satisfy our present purposes. Beyond being interesting in their own right, the causes behind the present concern with consumer protection are significant because they are important ingredients in determining the shape of policy outcomes. Policy emerging from a cluster of causes labeled "A" will be different from policy emerging from cluster of causes "B" if A and B differ from each other.

We can view the making of an issue from two perspectives: the perspective of the participants in the policy, or a more detached perspective based on the investigator's own assessment. Taking the former first, several of the interview respondents were asked to make their own assessment of why the consumer issue developed. Although this group consisted of only eleven persons, it was a carefully selected group of consumer activists who themselves participated in making consumer protection a political issue. Their responses are summarized in Table 3. The response "good politics" usually meant that the political climate was now able to sustain the issue and to profit those who were active in it. The category of "necessity" generally referred to the increased complexity of the marketplace and the relative powerlessness of individual consumers. "Consumer demand" was a judg-

Table 3 Activists' Perception of the Rise of Consumer Protection as an Issue

CAUSE	NUMBER OF RESPONSES
Good Politics	8
Necessity	5
Need for low-cost program	3
Consumer demand	3

N = 11

ment that the issue arose in response to a spontaneous public demand for government action. "Need for a low-cost program" is closely related to "good politics" but more specifically indicates a belief that some sort of liberal or reform program was desired by the administration, and consumer protection was pushed because it had the advantage of low cost to the government. The responses total to more than the number of respondents because most individuals cited more than one major factor.

As can be seen, most participants felt that the fact that the issue was profitable politically was a major factor in its rise to prominence. This does not imply a cynical attitude—few people are so cynical about their work. Rather, it simply is a recognition by political realists that a good cause is helped if it is also good politics. Indeed, many a worthy cause will get nowhere if it is not good politics. On the other side of the spectrum, it is interesting that so few participants attributed the issue to public demand. Apparently, the champions of this cause view themselves as being in the business of generating that public demand.

But the story does not end there. While the participants directly involved are in the best position to assess the causes, it may be that they cannot see the forest for the trees. In any case, a more detached perspective is useful not only to assess the validity of the participants' judgments but to elaborate upon them.

Perhaps the most basic cause of consumer protection becoming an issue was that this was an area where government intervention was necessary and, more importantly, was perceived as necessary by the public and policy makers alike. In a variety of important ways, the marketplace had become more complex and more removed from control by the consumer. In the 1960s there was a greater number of new or modified products of greater complexity than ever before. This increased complexity meant that there was more that could go wrong and that the consumer was less knowledgeable about each product. Poorly made electric can openers were not an irritation in the early 1950s. Service problems with color television sets were of a complexity and cost unknown in the 1950s. A myriad of examples point to consumer confusion arising from increased complexity. Nor are they limited to relatively trivial consumer goods. Prescription drugs also became more complex, more potent, and, hence, more dangerous.

The need for rigorous FDA regulation was greater than ever before. In the purely financial sphere, the 1960s brought to fruition a host of new consumer problems. The use of consumer credit increased greatly with the introduction of bank credit cards and the widespread distribution of unsolicited credit cards. Outstanding consumer installment credit rose from $21.5 billion in 1950 to $56.0 billion in 1960 and to $87.9 billion in 1965. In the face of increased traffic and soaring court judgments, automobile insurance rates continued to rise and coverage was restricted. One of the most frustrating developments of the decade was the rise of computerized billing. No longer could the consumer obtain direct redress from human error by a human billing clerk. The impersonality and intractability of computers became the subject of many a magazine article replete with horror stories of people whose credit ratings were ruined by a random hole in an IBM card and who could not obtain redress for years.

Both the complexity and the increased impersonality of a computerized market certainly created a need for a regulatory system more in tune with the times. However, while there was widespread consumer frustration with various aspects of the modern market, it is interesting that so few of the participants viewed public demand as a causative factor in creating the issue. Indeed, necessity was only the second-ranked factor. This leads to the second type of cause—the politics of the situation. There is a difference between societal needs and public issues, and there are many needs which are not issues or which do not become issues for a long time. The question then becomes: Granted that there was a need for consumer protection legislation, why did it, out of all the other needs, become an issue on the public agenda?

The modern Presidency has been the single most important factor in defining the national political agenda; thus the political factors behind the issue can best be seen in light of presidential action. Basically, presidential activity in behalf of consumer protection from 1966 on can be seen as a presidential response to a need for a new issue. The condition of the President's program and relations with Congress are relevant in this regard.

The impressive legislative outpouring of the 88th and especially the 89th Congresses in 1964 and 1965 is well known. President Lyndon Johnson was lavish in his praise of the progress and programs of the first session of the 89th Congress. In those two years Congress completed favorable action on much of the original program of the late President Kennedy—most notably in the form of the Civil Rights Act of 1964. Furthermore, with the help of substantial congressional majorities, in 1965, President Johnson largely realized his goal of completing enactment of programs long on the agenda of goals of the (Northern) Democratic party—some since the New Deal. Thus the "Fabulous 89th" enacted Medicare, aid to elementary and secondary education, voting rights, immigration reform, establishment of the Department of Housing and Urban Development, and the poverty amendments. This was a dramatic and impressive record but it presented the proverbial problem of being a hard act to follow.

Nor was President Johnson content to rest on his laurels even if he was presented with that opportunity. The same 89th Congress, however, became recalcitrant in 1966, and the President fared poorly in comparison with the preceding session. He was defeated in his attempt to secure passage of the District of Columbia home rule bill and to repeal the right-to-work section of the Taft-Hartley Act. Several other of his measures were passed in very diluted form.

In 1967, the President had a still harder time with the 90th Congress and its reduced Democratic majorities. Although his requests were generally more modest, he met with less success than previously. His *Congressional Quarterly* legislative success "score" (the percentage of presidential requests enacted by Congress) declined from 68.9 percent in 1965 to 47.6 percent in 1967.

In addition to the decreasing success with Congress, although related to it, was the war in Vietnam and the resulting economic problems. Throughout 1965 and 1966, the conflict in Vietnam escalated into a full-scale American war. This was clearly reflected in the January, 1966, budget presentation in which President Johnson called for an appropriation of $15.2 billion to finance the expansion of the war in fiscal year 1966–67. At that time there was almost no slack left in the economy and the inflationary pressure of new war-related spending was reflected in an increase in the consumer price index of 2.9 percent during 1966 (compared to 1.7 percent during 1965). By the end of 1967, the index had hit 117.5. Although most economists advised that a tax increase was essential to stem the inflationary tide, the President resisted such a measure and continued to conduct the war without wartime economic controls. In spite of the pledge of the President in the state-of-the-union message in early 1966 to provide both guns and butter, it was apparent by year's end that the war and related inflationary pressures had made costly domestic programs a luxury whose implementation was highly improbable.

In short, during 1966, two factors converged which created a need for a new domestic issue. First, while the President had already enacted a substantial program of major domestic reform legislation, he was facing an increasingly recalcitrant Congress as he desired to push forth with new programs. Second, it was clear that the war and inflation dictated that no *costly* new programs be enacted. Consumer protection fit these two needs precisely. While it was not a brand new issue at that time, it had never been seriously pushed by the administration beyond a recitation of legislative endorsements in the consumer messages of 1962 and 1964. This is borne out by the fact that there was no consumer message in 1965—the year of the "Fabulous 89th." During that time, the President still had bigger fish to fry. Thus, while consumer protection was already on the presidential agenda, its elevation as a public issue and increased administration activity on its behalf came at the same time that the need for a new such program was developed.

Furthermore, the type of legislation being pushed was extremely cheap compared to such programs as the War on Poverty or pollution control. No major new government bureaucracies were to be created nor was substantial revenue sharing with the states contemplated. The new agencies which were created had budgets so modest they created no noticeable dent in the federal budget. For example, in fiscal year 1968, the National Transportation Safety Board received an enacted appropriation of $4,050,000, and the President's Committee on Consumer Interests received a mere $345,000. New programs such as expanded federal inspection of meat processors could be accomplished by relatively modest increments to the already small budgets of the relevant inspection agencies. In the main, the costs of these programs would eventually be absorbed by consumers or industry and would not be reflected in a noticeable increase in the federal budget.

As an issue, consumer protection had one important advantage in addition to novelty and low cost: it is a "consensus" issue. At a time when divisions were beginning to appear on the Vietnam War and the poverty and civil rights issues were becoming subject to increasing tension, consumer protection presented itself as a reform issue not subject to those same divisions. Merely to state the fact that poultry should be safe and wholesome is to gain overwhelming public support for that position. To champion an issue as inherently popular as consumer protection was an irresistible opportunity for a President concerned both with getting new programs and with achieving consensus.

The political appeal and political dividends of the issue went beyond the White House, of course. . . . The Congress was a major center of activity and there the issue also filled political needs. For now, suffice it to say that several members of Congress who were to become key activists seized upon the issue to broaden their base of support by being identified with an issue with wide public appeal and reap a good deal of personal publicity by bringing forth dramatic problems or incidents the resolution of which also had wide public appeal.

Looked at from another perspective, in saying that congressmen were attracted to consumer protection because it was good politics, we are really saying that the issue coincided with their career maintenance needs. From that same perspective it becomes more clear why the issue achieved a fair amount of publicity. Publicizing it was not only good for politicians, it was also good for the journalists who brought the news directly to public attention. The issue was the source of many important exclusive stories which furthered the careers of reporters. In short, just as with the members of Congress, the consumer issue filled the career maintenance needs of several reporters all of which increased the coverage of the issue.

Given the appeal of the consumer issues, initial success in pressing one issue led to more activity and further success on other issues. While it may be impossible to pinpoint one "breakthrough" issue which led to increased activism on other issues, most activists are probably correct in assigning this role to the auto safety bill. In passing legislation to specifically regulate an industry which had never before known government regulation specifically aimed at it, Congress dramatically proved that it could be done—which had previously been in doubt. The auto safety legislation demonstrated that a powerful industry could be defeated in Congress, that the public supported such legislation, and that political careers could be enhanced by championing such causes. One important element in the auto safety case which made it a breakthrough was the involvement and rise to fame of Ralph Nader. Having come to prominence by playing a major part in enacting auto safety legislation, Nader was able to work for legislation in other consumer areas more effectively. This brings us to yet another factor behind the development of the issue—the rise of Nader himself.

Ralph Nader quickly became a personal symbol of the drive for consumer protection policy. He has been extremely effective in getting his message across to the public as well as to governmental decision makers. His role in the auto safety bill was largely one of spearheading a successful drive toward enactment of legislation, and he was clearly the most important individual participant. However, the question of whether there would have been a consumer movement without Ralph Nader is analogous to the classic historical question of whether great men make events or whether events make great men—and perhaps as unanswerable. Clearly Nader had a major role in developing the issue and bringing it to public attention. However, he came along at a time when other conditions also pushed the issue forth. Whether Nader could have done it without the coincidence of other factors is an unanswerable question. Suffice it to say that the other factors discussed above made the success of individual activists like Nader possible—or at least much more probable.

All the above factors are specific to the current interest in consumer protection. But there are deeper contextual reasons which lay behind the emergence of consumer protection as an issue. While consumer protection became an issue essentially because it was good politics, there are underlying reasons why it was good politics. These factors are found in the fact that beyond all the groups and individuals involved, consumer protection was one part of a much larger reform movement. Some scholars have argued that such periods are cyclical and culminate in new policy after a long period of agitation and gradual public acceptance. While the years of the Kennedy administration may be seen as the final stages of building support, the first part of the Johnson administration was the culmination of that cycle. Public support existed for Johnson's version of completing the New Deal, and he had the political resources equal to the task. Consumer protection must be seen in the context of this larger scene. It was not on the agenda of the Eisenhower administration because major reform legislation in general was absent. The reasons underlying the growth of reform movements themselves is beyond the scope of this study, but the relation between the issue of consumer protection and those movements is relevant.

This situation is of course parallel to the earlier major episodes of consumer protection policy making which occurred during the Progressive era and the New Deal. Those previous eras like the short-lived era of the "Great Society" were periods of popular support for an expanded or different government role in economic, political, and social life. It was this underlying base of support which made consumer protection good politics and politically feasible then and now. In short, the most fundamental reason for the emergence of consumer protection was most likely the "temper of the times." The specific factors outlined above can only account for the development of the issue when the temper of the times is such as to make those factors important components in the rise of any public policy issue.

3. Dynamics of Agenda Formation in Congress

John W. Kingdon

AGENDA-SETTING

Decisions on questions of public policy do not simply involve the final decision on the floor of the legislature. There are a number of steps both antecedent and subsequent to the floor vote. One of the most important of these other steps is the determination of the public agenda, or the list of subjects which will come up for

From John W. Kingdon, *Congressmen's Voting Decisions* (New York: Harper & Row, 1973), pp. 206–10, 261–71. Copyright © 1973 by John W. Kingdon and reprinted by permission of Harper & Row, Publishers.

decision in the public arena and those that will not. There are a number of ways in which the mass media play a highly central role in the structuring of this agenda.

First, congressmen often initially hear of a given item for decision from the mass media. Given the severe constraints on time and attention span under which they operate, anything which simply catches their eye is of great importance. Congressmen are fond of using the phrase "brought to my attention," to describe this process—a problem, fact, or interest group viewpoint is "brought to my attention." Often, the agent which accomplishes this attention-getting is the media. One congressman, when asked how he first became aware of the ABM issue, replied in the following semibewildered fashion: "I first became aware of it when it appeared in the papers and on television, and people in the street started to discuss it. Is there some other way I should have become aware of it? Anything I missed? That's always the way it is." Another acknowledged the importance of newspaper reports on financing of slum real estate in Washington in precipitating a congressional inquiry: "We have been told that the information in these articles was old stuff. But it was the first most of us who write housing laws knew of these situations."

Another congressman furnished a kind of case study in this attention-getting process. He laid out in great detail for me his experience in trying to get committee hearings on a certain subject, which he regarded as highly important. He had been making speeches on the floor and writing the committee chairman for months, to no avail. Then an editor for a minor magazine noticed it and asked him to write an article. When the article, drawn from his speeches, appeared, the editor of an important newspaper in the district of a senior committee member picked it up and wrote a prominent editorial. That committee member, in turn, inquired of this congressman and became a leading advocate of hearings. Then the editor of another newspaper, this time in the district of another committee member, also picked it up and wrote a prominent story. That committee member called the congressman, asking for a copy of his bill, and eventually introduced it. Finally, after the chairman's initial reluctance, hearings were scheduled. As is so often the case, nothing happened until well-placed media decided to play up the story, which in turn forced congressmen to respond in some fashion.

A second way in which media play a part in the agenda-setting process is by stimulating constituency interest and resultant mail. Congressmen, while expressing disdain for "stimulated" mail, do pay attention to what appears to be a spontaneous outpouring of mail from their constituents. One agent in the system, perhaps the only one, that is capable of stimulating such a "spontaneous" outpouring is the mass media. Continuous or prominent coverage of a given story ensures that congressmen will have it constantly before them, partly because they read it themselves and partly because it stimulates constituents' interest and even their action. Because of this sort of coverage, there are some issues which congressmen find it virtually impossible to ignore.

Examples of mail outpourings related to the media coverage are not hard to uncover. Many congressmen noted the dramatic difference between the votes on the seating of Adam Clayton Powell during the session under study as compared to two years previous. This time, there was hardly a ripple in the public, and the House voted to seat him. But earlier, it had been an entirely different story, because of the repeated stories about various Powell activities which had appeared in the press over several months, resulting in a public outcry. One congressman, describing the difference, said, "Last time, there had been a long period when the disclosures were in the papers every day, and people got stirred up." The fierce mail which congressmen received on the pay raise bill is another example of prominent media coverage resulting in a public outcry.

Perhaps the most pronounced instance of such mail during the session under study, however, was the mail regarding taxes. When asked why tax reform had come up this year rather than at some other time, congressman after congressman referred to the importance of the heavy volume of "spontaneous" mail which had poured in from the constituencies. Many attributed this outpouring in the first instance to several recent tax raises at all governmental levels experienced by their constituents, including very prominently the federal surcharge. This general dissatisfaction, however, would probably not be enough in and of itself to start a strong public reaction. However, the fact that a number of wealthy people were escaping taxation altogether was prominently displayed in media all over the country. This relative deprivation apparently offended many people's sense of fairness, and they wrote and talked to their congressmen in great volume and with great heat. One congressman exclaimed, "They read in the papers about some millionaires, and they hit the ceiling." Said another: "I got volumes of letters, as did everybody else, and then you'd go back to the district and all they'd talk about was taxes, taxes, taxes, and cost of living too. The pressure from the public was really on and Congress had to respond." Finally, congressmen who had always been aware of the inequities in the tax system now had to respond in some way. It became impossible to explain inaction in view of the public pressure. This need to do something was translated into a tax reform bill, although it could have taken another form. One congressman summarized the process in this fashion:

> These people got a surtax on top of high taxes. Local and state taxes were raised, so they got it socked to them again. Then Drew Pearson starts hammering away at oil depletion and a lot of people read him. On top of it, Barr testifies to a "taxpayer revolt" and talks about millionaires who aren't paying. Well, the public rose up in outrage and letters started pouring in. It was just like the flood of letters over Adam Clayton Powell. And Congress responded to the public outcry.

A third way in which the media are important in agenda-setting is that they tend to structure the public discussion. The ways in which issues are reported, and the terms in which stories are phrased tend to establish the dimensions along which congressmen and others think about the policy questions involved. One unusually introspective congressman said of his thinking on the ABM:

> I'm reading everything I can get my hands on. The president's message, newspaper articles, magazines, mail, everything. Look at this ad. "It won't work." Well, will or won't it? "Takes money away from domestic programs." See, this sort of thing gives me the outlines of the argument. Then it's a question of tracking down the technical details. The public arguments sort of set the parameters. Now I have to fill in the details and answer the specific questions.

Perhaps the best instance of the media's power in structuring discussion was their coverage of campus unrest early in 1969 and the resultant dimensions along which congressmen and others tended to think about campus problems. Many newspapers took to publicizing the most major campus disruptions, such as the guns on the Cornell campus, and then printing a virtual box score of other campus disruptions, that is, a short paragraph on each of five or six problem campuses describing the latest act of disruption or riot. These reports were characteristically very shallow, concentrating on the "riot" itself and saying little else. This sort of reporting left the unmistakable impression, day after day, that most of the campuses of the country were beset by rebellion from all sides. Many congressmen, like everyone else, flew into a rage. One said, "We have to get tough with these militants. Here I read about them taking over a building with bullets and guns. We can't have that. I'm a real hardliner on this, and this is a common sentiment." It is important to note that for most congressmen, this box score approach in media coverage was the only information about the campuses that they had, and the only information on which they and their constituents were relying. It undoubtedly affected the ways in which they thought about the campus unrest, blinding them to complexities, concentrating their attention on the violent acts themselves, and, in more general terms, structuring the discussion of the issue.

Finally, in addition to noting how important the media are in bringing subjects, facts, and interpretations to congressmen, it is also important to mention that the media also play some part in determining which pieces of information will *not* be brought to congressmen. It is already customary to think of the media's effects on the general public in these terms. But the same applies to some degree with congressmen as well. Congressmen follow the mass media, and for many issues, especially on the floor, their sources of information are not necessarily much broader than that. In structuring what congressmen will not hear, therefore, the media play a central role. This is true in part because the media themselves do not bring some things to the congressmen's attention, and in part because media tend to divert their attention from other sources of information. Furthermore, because of media effects on attentive publics, the congressman will not tend to hear from his constituency in any volume unless the subject is reported prominently in the mass media. Probably one reason that congressmen follow home district newspapers is that they can implicitly assume that if the local media are not covering a story, the chances are that district attentive publics have not heard of it. This assumption rules out a good deal of territory as a subject for political concern, and gives them some clue as to the subjects on which the public is likely to be concentrating its attention. . . .

THE AGENDA AND ALTERNATIVES

Throughout most of this book, we have concentrated on the final step in the decision process: choice. Actually, one can conceive of two previous steps which are also highly important in terms of understanding the outcomes of the legislative process. The first step is the setting of the agenda for decision, that is, the collection of topics which become subjects for governmental policy. Then within these topics or policy concerns, the second step is the specifying of the alternatives among which a choice is to be made. In the third and final step, a choice is made among the alternatives. The processes by which the agenda and alternatives are determined, and which actors in the political system have a primary role in these processes, are as crucial to an understanding of governmental policy-making as the choice processes themselves.

It is important to keep in mind that in the process of setting the agenda and specifying the alternatives, a good many policy options are eliminated from consideration. There is a myriad of subjects that could conceivably be decided by Congress or by any other authoritative decision body. Governmental decision-makers, particularly congressmen, cannot attend to them all or even to a very large fraction of them. The subjects that do become part of the decisional agenda, therefore, represent only a part of the population of subjects that are potential agenda items. This selection of which subjects to address and which ones to overlook is a kind of structural "decision" of major consequence. In the process, a goodly number of potential agenda items are left untouched. Similarly, once a matter does reach the decisional agenda, the process by which alternatives are evoked and seriously considered is also crucial. At this stage, many alternatives will be eliminated from serious consideration, and only a few are left for the final-choice stage. Many of the decisional possibilities, both in terms of subjects to be considered and alternatives to be weighed, are screened out before the final choice stage is reached.

ATTENTION-GETTING

The first agenda process in the legislative case is what I choose to label "attention-getting." There are so many people, events, and pieces of information that compete for a congressman's attention, that his conscious or unconscious choice about which matters will receive his attention is a decision of great moment. Apart from the congressman's choices about attention, furthermore, the communication net which brings certain things to his attention and screens out other things is also of crucial importance in determining which matters will be left untouched, which problems will be left unsolved.

Congressmen themselves continually refer to the mechanisms by which information penetrates their consciousness and thus has some potential for an impact on their decisions. They themselves use the phrase, "bringing it to our attention." One said of a doctor's testimony about the terrible shortages of supplies and personnel at D.C. General Hospital, "If people don't bring these problems to our attention, we never hear about them." Another said about his relationship with a member of the Ways and Means Committee, "Every now and then someone would write me with some problem they were having, and if I thought it was something that should be brought to his attention, I'd send him a copy." Another referred to the tax reform bill: "Bolling caught this thing on the rate structure, or whoever brought it to his attention." An unusually reflective congressman, after having described his considerable efforts to study the antiballistic missile issue, mused, "One interesting question: Why am I studying *this?* What made me pick it? Usually, this would just zip through—another piece of hardware for the military—what else is new? I don't know the answer."

It is difficult to exaggerate the importance of attention-getting. If a matter is not brought to congressmen's attention, it will not become a subject of legislative action, in statute or otherwise. In an effort to conserve time and handle an impossible job, congressmen often start by assuming implicitly that if a problem is not brought to their attention, then the problem does not exist. The intensity with which people hold their attitudes is often measured by contact with the congressman. If constituents do not contact him, for instance, he assumes they have little interest. Or if the administration is not actively lobbying for its position, he assumes the administration regards the matter as being of low priority. In other words, unless something is forcibly brought to his attention and kept there, it tends to be shunted aside in the terrific press of other business.

There appear to be several agents of attention-getting, that is, several sources of agenda items. First, the mass media appear to be highly important in setting the agenda. Printed and broadcast media are capable of the kind of continuous and prominent coverage of a story which makes it virtually impossible for a congressman to ignore. Since congressmen follow the media, they themselves do not escape such coverage. But indirectly as well, there is no other actor in the system which is in quite the same position to arouse the attention of constituents or to stimulate the avalanche of "spontaneous" mail as is the media. Conversely, the media also play a prominent part in selecting *out* the subjects which fail to appear on the agenda. There are surely many congressmen and other political actors who have abandoned attempts to get subjects considered for want of media attention.

A second actor in the system which appears to have a negligible independent effect on the final choice, but which has a rather more important effect on the agenda, is the collection of Washington-based policy elites. Many authors have discussed their importance. The boundaries of such an elite are not particularly well defined, but they include lobbyists, academics, think-tank members, and governmental officials. A good bit of lobbying may not have much effect except to keep a subject on the agenda, but in view of the competition for a place on the agenda, this is no mean accomplishment.

Another attention-getting force is the congressman's own colleagues. A few particularly innovative or ambitious congressmen are acutely aware of the importance of the agenda, and participate actively in its definition. They take on causes, and by repeated and insistent talking in various forums, through which they communicate directly with their colleagues and indirectly through the media, they manage to force other congressmen to pay attention to what they are saying. One Northern Democrat reflected: "This notion of national priorities is catching on, I think. (Kingdon: It's almost a cliché.) Well, sometimes you have to repeat things and repeat and repeat until you almost gag on the words before people will finally grasp it. You may be up to your nose in the water, but it's barely washed over their boots. This is one of those cases." Media coverage patterns enhance the importance of these congressmen in affecting the public agenda, since they capture headlines by virtue of the journalists' tendency to display congressional activities prominently.

Finally, it should not be forgotten that inescapable turns of events that are not particularly under the control of any identifiable set of system actors often structure the agenda, perhaps more than anything else. A mine disaster at Farmington, West Virginia, placed the subject of coal mine safety on the agenda in a forceful way, and resulted finally in new safety legislation. The 1968 presidential candidacy of George Wallace threw a scare into leaders of the two major parties both in and out of Congress, resulting in active interest in electoral college reform. As one congressman wryly observed, "I've always favored reform, whenever it would come up. Now that it was forcibly brought to our attention, it is up." Congressmen and others may seize upon such events to dramatize the need for governmental attention to a problem. A group of congressmen waged a fight early in 1969 to refuse the counting of a North Carolina Republican elector's vote for Wallace, not so much to affect that vote as to dramatize the need for electoral reform. But crisis events are often important in and of themselves, and not particularly controllable.

One kind of event which is worth notice is what I call a "focusing event." Once a matter is in the congressman's attention field, events may take place which have a powerful focusing effect. A former Treasury Secretary's comment that there was a "taxpayer revolt" in progress, for instance, obviously summarized the experience of many congressmen in talks with their constituents, and was repeatedly cited in interviews on tax matters. Or Senator Eastland's substantial agricultural payment came up over and over again in my interviews about the farm payment limitation. Or the Ford Foundation grants to aides of the late Senator Robert Kennedy symbolized to many congressmen everything that they had found wrong with foundations. It is not clear that this sort of event has an effect on legislative outcomes independent of other factors at work. But such a focusing event often does serve as an important catalytic agent. It strikes a responsive chord in congressmen because it symbolizes something in their own experience. They pick it up, and from then on the focusing event proves to have a dynamic of its own.

THE LEGISLATIVE AGENDA

Once a subject is on the public agenda, the focus of attention in a rather wide circle of attentive people, it must still be placed on the legislative agenda. In this substep of agenda-setting, the standing committees and the party leadership, particularly of the majority party, are of major importance. Some of this influence on the legislative agenda has to do with the scheduling function, through which the timing of votes can be manipulated to maximize the chances that the view of the leadership will prevail. The committees also serve as legislative agenda-setters, particularly through their power to block legislation and prevent it from ever reaching the floor. Many subjects never reach the whole House because of the influence of the standing committees, party leaders, and the Rules Committee on the legislative agenda, and those that do are affected by the timing of their consideration.

Decision-making changes in several respects as a congressional session progresses, due in part to committee and leadership timing. It is possible to divide the issues which form the core sample of this study according to the time of the session in which they were considered: the first five as being at the early part of the session, the middle five votes at midsession, and the last five at the end of the session. As the session moves along, two features of congressmen's decisions change markedly. First, decisions become less routine. At the beginning of the session, there is more voting by previous history, less search for information, and less uncertainty about the decision than there is later in the session. Second, more information and more varieties of information are brought to bear on later decisions than on those made earlier in the session. Congressmen go outside their state delegation more, receive more conflicting cues and fewer strictly procedural cues, receive more information from their constituency and more mail, and increase their supply of information from staffs and reading. As the session proceeds, then, decisions become less routine and more information-laden.

Reasons for these changes are rooted in the behavior of House agenda agents. The committees and the leadership tend to get routine and minor pieces of legislation out of the way early in the session and take longer to consider the more major bills in committee. This tendency was exacerbated in the session under study because it was the first term of a new administration, though it probably is true of most sessions to some extent. To this natural rhythm of committee consideration of legislation, which may have no necessary conscious design, should be added an explicitly strategic possibility: Committee and party leaders may delay some of the legislation for which they anticipate trouble on the floor until later in the session, in the hope that the committee bill and the conference report encounter fewer serious attempts at amendment at the end of the session. This would presumably occur since in the rush for adjournment, the legislative process often becomes terribly confused; congressmen's attention is much more diffused and less focused on particular features of given bills, and the chances are better then, than they would have been earlier, for a committee bill or conference report to come through floor consideration unscathed.

ALTERNATIVE SPECIFICATION

After the agenda has been set, the alternatives among which the final choice will be made are specified. In this step, members of the standing committee that consider the bill assume a primary importance, at least in terms of setting the alternatives for floor choices. Congressmen largely leave to committee members these choices about which alternatives to pose. If they are not presented with the alternatives they would ideally prefer, they feel nearly powerless to change them. They can, of course, choose fairly freely among the alternatives presented by majority and minority members of the committee. But they find it very difficult to change those alternatives or to generate new ones. One congressman said, "You just take what you're presented with."

In this process of structuring the alternatives which will be presented to their colleagues for ultimate decision, the committee members engage in a number of crucial behavior patterns in addition to simply deciding which alternatives will and will not be presented. They may paper over their differences in the committee, for instance, and never present alternatives to the whole House at all. They are also instrumental in translating the concern which placed a subject on the agenda into concrete proposals. This translation process does not always accurately mirror the original concerns. In the tax reform case, for instance, it was public outcry at the level of taxes which played a large part in placing the item on the agenda, but this outcry was translated, not only into simple tax cuts, but also into a degree of tax reform. In other words, the committee members evoke the alternatives to be seriously considered. Finally, in the alternatives which they do present, committee majorities and dissenters who offer amendments often package their amendments in such a way as to prevent congressmen from picking and choosing among provisions as they see fit. The Joelson amendment to the Health, Education, and Welfare appropriations bill was a classic case in point: The popular impacted aid was joined to the unpopular education programs, many of which if considered separately would go down to defeat. Or on occasion, if a package approach appears unlikely to succeed, the proposers of amendments may break up a package in order to salvage what they can from it.

DECISION BOUNDARIES

In the entire discussion of the importance of agenda-setting and alternative-specifying agents in the political system, it is well to keep in mind that rank-and-file congressmen deciding how to vote on the floor of the House are not without their own influence on the prechoice processes. Alternatives are not simply presented to congressmen. Instead, committee members' and others' calculations about "what will go," based on congressmen's preferences, play a vital part in structuring the alternatives in the first place. Agenda- and alternative-setters find that they are obliged to operate within the boundaries set for them by the whole House. Thus, the Ways and Means Committee members calculated the effects of various tax reform provisions on floor votes, Appropriations Committee members were continually concerned about "getting rolled" on the floor, amendment-writers would ask themselves whether or not they could "sell" a given amendment on the floor, and so forth.

The consequences of failing to anticipate floor reactions adequately are painfully evident. The Appropriations Committee's failure to build sufficient impacted aid funds into the education appropriation, for example, resulted in getting rolled to the spectacular tune of about one billion dollars. The move of the Education and Labor Committee majority to extend the Elementary and Secondary Education Act for five years went down to decisive defeat. By contrast, Wilbur Mills's reputation for care in anticipating floor reaction was repeatedly confirmed through the session under study.

The notion that committees must operate within the boundaries set for them by the whole House, of course, has been discussed in several other legislative studies. A major theme of Fenno's work on the Appropriations Committee, for instance, is that even as powerful a committee as Appropriations finds that it must make decisions within the constraints set by the parent body. And as Manley has convincingly argued, one key to Wilbur Mills's reputation for power in Congress is his ability to anticipate the reactions of his colleagues and take account of their preferences. It has in fact long been argued in the legislative literature that the whole House sets boundaries which the committees transgress at their peril, and within which they must exercise the discretion left to them by the whole House.

Furthermore, a congressman's constituency sets boundaries within which he is obliged to stay without risking serious political trouble. The boundaries set by the mass public in the district, of course, are quite vague and allow the congressman a good deal of discretion. Those set by elites in the district, however, particularly the elites that form his supporting coalition, are better defined and allow him less discretion as compared to the mass public's constraints. Once again, this notion that a constituency sets boundaries for a legislator is not new to the literature of political science.

This entire line of argument leads us to a general model of the political system which I call the model of "successively narrowing boundaries." According to this notion, one could conceive of a full range of possible alternatives in given arenas of public policy. A congressman, however, is not entirely free to select any of these alternatives. The distribution of attitudes within the mass public in his constituency sets (admittedly broad) boundaries within which he is able to choose among the alternatives remaining after the mass public has effectively eliminated several alternatives from serious consideration. Similarly, within the range of alternatives still permitted by the mass public, elites in the district further constrain the congressman by not tolerating some alternatives that were tolerated by the mass. Basically, these elite and mass attitude distributions make up the congressman's decision parameters. He still has a range of choice available, but it is considerably narrower than the full range of conceivable policy options.

Within these boundaries, there is a distribution of congressmen's attitudes in the whole House. The committees are obliged to make their choices from among the range of alternatives which would be permitted in the whole House. Just as in the case of constituency constraints on individual congressmen, committees do have discretion, but it is limited by the whole House. The Appropriations Committee may be able to report out a bill containing anywhere from $600 million to $1 billion in funds for water pollution abatement, for instance, but they would not be permitted to report only $200 million and expect that figure to stand. Of the original full range of conceivable options, furthermore, the committees seriously consider only a rather narrow set, since decisional boundaries have been successively narrowed through a number of steps.

This notion of successively narrowing boundaries is similar to a notion of sets and subsets. Out of the total range of all conceivable policy options (i.e., the full set), the mass public makes some of these options politically improbable, and allows only a subset to be seriously considered. From that mass public subset, constituency elites constrain congressmen further to an elite subset of policy alternatives. From that elite subset, congressmen themselves choose the alternatives which they will allow to be seriously considered, leaving a comparatively narrow whole-House subset of alternatives from which the committees are free to choose.

This conceptual framework is a model which emphasizes constraints on decision, rather than causes. Instead of saying that constituents influence or cause some configuration of congressmen's behavior, for instance, we say that constraints set by constituents make certain congressional behaviors highly *un*likely. Similarly, instead of saying that the distribution of attitudes in the whole House determines committee behavior, we would say that the distribution of attitudes in the whole House makes certain committee behaviors highly *im*probable. Note too that this is a kind of *negative* model. It would be difficult according to this notion of successively narrowing boundaries to determine precisely which behaviors will occur. But we can say something about which behaviors are *un*likely or *im*probable. This notion, therefore, essentially narrows the range of the behaviors that are likely to occur.

This whole discussion, of course, is only suggested by this study and must remain highly speculative. Some interesting further possibilities for research, however, do come to mind. How much of the range of conceivable alternatives is rendered unlikely at each stage, for instance? I would conjecture that the mass public rules out rather few possible alternatives, but that elites rule out rather more. To cite another interesting question, are alternatives from the Left of the ideological spectrum made improbable as additions to public policy more than alternatives from the Right, or vice versa, and at what step in the process? More possibilities could suggest themselves.

Finally, the interpretations which one attaches to these speculations constitute another interesting aspect. The concept of successively narrowing boundaries emphasizes the limits placed on elites. At each stage, I would hypothesize, the narrower set of people is limited by the broader set. But one interpretive question is whether the limits are important. Are they true limits on behavior, or are they so vague as to be meaningless? And conversely, are the more narrow questions mere details, or are they the guts of the issue? If leaders really do lead their followers, furthermore, what influence do they themselves have on the attitudes that would presumably define their constraints? It would be difficult to resolve such questions here. But one can still postulate that the boundaries at each stage do exist and are definable, and that behaviors outside these boundaries are improbable.

part two POLICY FORMULATION

Policy formulation involves the development of appropriate and acceptable means for dealing with public problems and issues. Assuming the desire for positive governmental action (doing nothing, of course, is always an alternative), there are two distinguishable aspects of policy formulation. First, decisions must be made as to what kind of action is needed for a particular problem. What kind of activity is necessary to guarantee equal employment opportunities? What sorts of changes should be made in welfare programs to eliminate abuses while meeting the real needs of the poor? Answers to questions such as these must then be converted into a form—legislation, administrative rules, court opinions, or whatever—that, when adopted, is designed to accomplish the course of action decided upon.

Many political actors are involved in the formulation of public policies, either directly or indirectly. Participants may include the chief executive and staff agencies; administrative officials, special study groups, commissions, or task forces created by the executive; legislators and legislative staff; pressure group representatives and unorganized citizens. Political science literature has emphasized the role of the executive in policy formulation at the national level. Thus, the President is often referred to as "chief legislator," and initiative in the legislative process is said to rest with the executive. Indeed, two of the selections in this part discuss the roles of executive staff agencies, especially the Office of Management and Budget and the White House Office, and presidential task forces in policy formulation. Nonetheless, the important roles played by others in policy formulation should not be neglected. In the area of environmental pollution control, the formulation process has really been dominated by Congress, which has also been the source of much of the initiative in this area. This is indicated by Charles Jones's article dealing with federal air pollution policy-making.

Although policy formulation and policy adoption are analytically distinguishable activities, in practice they are often blended. Policy formulation is not simply a process in which means for dealing with a problem are developed and an effort is then made to see whether the proposal as developed can win adoption. Rather, formulators will be influenced in what they do by the need and desire to win support for their handiwork. What they can get adopted by Congress, for instance, may not be what they would like if they had their "druthers." Political feasibility must be taken into account. The situation involving air pollution policy in 1970 where, according to Jones, "rather than having to find a coalition for policy ... air pollution policy-makers had to find a policy for a coalition," is not a normal occurrence.

The fact that many participants are involved in the formulation of policy proposals, especially on complex or major problems, means that a considerable amount of bargaining and compromise may be necessary in order to arrive at a generally acceptable proposal. Gilmour's article on central legislative clearance helps illustrate this point. Formulators may also be influenced in what they do by how they think their proposed policy, once adopted, will be treated by administrative agencies and courts during implementation.

Finally, we should note that a major task confronting policy formulators is the need to deal with the causes and not just the symptoms of a problem. Inflation is a problem, which is manifested in rising prices and wages, but what causes them to rise? Excessive demand? Inadequate supply of goods and services? Inflationary psychology? In many instances policy formulators may be hard put to decide what conditions or actions they must treat in order to deal effectively with a policy problem. If causes were more easily perceived and undisputed, their task would be easier. Imagine that your problem is to formulate and secure adoption of a policy to eliminate poverty in the United States. What causes poverty in American society?

4. Speculative Augmentation in Federal Air Pollution Policy-Making

Charles O. Jones

Don K. Price, among others, has spoken of the challenges to political institutions resulting from the scientific revolution. The public and private sectors are less distinguishable, administration of public affairs is increasingly complex, checks and balances are not in their original order. These developments, according to Price, make "our traditional reactions" less reliable. He might have added, as he surely implies, that they make traditional political analysis less reliable as well.

This article treats an issue-area in which science and technology have major impact on

Reprinted from *Journal of Politics* 36 (May 1974): 438–64. By permission.

both cause and cure. Air pollution is a rather recent addition to the federal domestic agenda, dating from the mid-1950s. Though a more or less traditional "majority-building incrementalist" model adequately explains federal air pollution policy development before 1970, the dramatic surge in public concern for and interest in environmental issues in 1969–70 makes generalizations based on the model less durable. I develop an alternative "public satisfying-speculative augmentation" model of policy development that I hope has utility beyond this particular case.

The processes of policy development for each model are compared by examining the characteristics of the issue-area itself, the institutional units responsible for action, decision-making, and the resulting policies. I then turn to consider some of the broader implications of the second model. Demands for increased public involvement producing large change in nominations, elections, and public policy-making have become commonplace in recent years. In issues of technical complexity, as with most environmental matters, various publics may know what they want but lack knowledge of realistic alternatives (given scientific, technological, and economic realities). As attractive and contemporary as "satisfying the public" may seem on the surface, this alternative model of policy development creates costs and makes demands we may not be willing to meet.

MAJORITY-BUILDING INCREMENTALISM, 1955–67

The majority-building incrementalism model of policy development, which is principally based on pluralistic assumptions, is familiar to students of American politics. It features a set of expectations about the characteristics of issue-areas, institutions, decision-making, and politics. For example:

(1) Issue-areas will be characterized by multidimensional complexity, groups seeking support and access for their special interests, low general public opinion thrust.

(2) Institutions will accommodate the multiplicity of special interests and thus will be characterized by highly specialized organization. Assigning responsibility for new issue-areas will be circumstantial until institutional adjustments are made.

(3) Decision-making in policy development will be characterized by "tapering demands from the optimal down to the acceptable" so as to insure majority support in Congress.[1]

(4) Policy output will be in "the form of an indefinite sequence of policy moves" which "rarely solve problems but merely stave them off or nibble at them, often making headway but sometimes retrogressing."[2]

The sets of expectations regarding decision-making and policy are of particular interest here. Lindblom identifies four quadrants of political decisions based on the dimensions of understanding and the volume of change: (1) high understanding, large change; (2) high understanding, incremental change; (3) low understanding, incremental change; (4) low understanding, large change.[3] The third quadrant is typical of most political decision-making in his judgment. He describes it in more detail as follows:

> It is decision-making through small or incremental moves on particular problems rather than through a comprehensive reform program. It is also endless; it takes the form of an indefinite sequence of policy moves. Moreover, it is exploratory in that the goals of policy-making continue to change as new experience with policy throws new light on what is possible and desirable. In this sense, it is also better described as moving *away* from known social ills rather than as moving *toward* a known and relatively stable goal.[4]

Given pluralist assumptions, one could hardly expect it to turn out differently very often. Analysis of federal air pollution policy development, 1955–67, shows a reasonably close fit between these projections and reality.

---

[1]William J. Keefe and Morris S. Ogul, *The American Legislative Process: Congress and the States* (Englewood Cliffs, N.J.: Prentice-Hall, Inc., 1968), 13.

[2]David Braybrooke and Charles E. Lindblom, *A Strategy of Decision: Policy Evaluation as a Social Process* (New York: Free Press, 1963), 71.

[3]*Ibid.,* 67.

[4]*Ibid.,* 71.

Issue-Area Characteristics

Our expectations about the nature of the issue—principally its multidimensionality—are unquestionably met. In fact, comprehensive decision-making for air pollution control is obviated by the immense information problem characterizing the issue-area. Suppose, for example, one concentrated just on the public health aspects of air quality (ignoring for the moment the economic, social, and aesthetic aspects). The following scientific and technical data would seem to be essential as a base for decisions:

(1) Air composition.

(2) Synergistic effects of various mixes of gases and particulates.

(3) Photochemical effects.

(4) Sources of pollution.

(5) Variation of sources, including various industrial processes.

(6) Meteorological and topographical effects on air and its components.

(7) Health effects of various pollutants for people with differing physical characteristics.

(8) Acceptable limits of pollutants, given health data.

(9) Developments in control technology for various industrial processes and motor vehicles.

If available, these data would permit one to define objective problems resulting from dirty air. Seldom is it possible in the American democratic policy process to act on the basis of objectively determined problems, however. We also pay heed to the preferences of groups affected by policy. Indeed, this attention is a central theme of the majority-building model. Such groups have had both expertise and access to (in some cases control of) decision processes. The complexity of the issue-area itself was to industry's advantage while early policy sought to define specific problems. Those debilitated or otherwise offended by foul air lacked organization or precise information on their condition and its causes. Even as late as 1967, a news account observed that "national air-pollution-control efforts seem caught in a smog of political expediency thickened by public indifference. In

Washington, reports are that the President's air-pollution-control bill faces emasculation, if not demise."[5] In fact, therefore, a national air pollution issue could hardly be said to have existed before 1969.

Institutional Characteristics

The institutional expectations of circumstantial jurisdiction for air pollution as a new issue-area are also fulfilled—both in the executive and in Congress. Administrative responsibility for air pollution policy was logically set in the Public Health Service, Department of Health, Education, and Welfare during the initial research phase. But as research inevitably led to control, it became obvious that an air pollution agency located in PHS was an organizational contretemps. Rather than shift the agency, however, frequent attempts were made to reorganize for increased effectiveness. These reorganizations were not likely to enhance the power of a fledgling agency. By 1968, the National Air Pollution Control Administration (NAPCA) was, through certain nonhierarchical arrangements, beginning to develop strength in organization, leadership, and executive support despite being administratively remote from the secretary of HEW. An NAPCA official explained as he discussed problems in implementing the Air Quality Act of 1967.

> Our organization was so small, so under-financed, so bureaucratically dominated by layers up to the secretary, that we could not achieve what was set forth as highly desirable in the 1967 Act until Secretary [John] Gardner developed a direct pipeline communication with us and he said to Under Secretary [Wilbur] Cohen, "Look, I want you to take over the air pollution control program and see that it floats." At that point, we got the first substantial administrative support for air pollution control.[6]

Thus, throughout its decade of existence, the national air pollution agency was extremely weak by almost any of the accepted measures

---

[5] *Christian Science Monitor,* June 26, 1967.

[6] I conducted interviews with over 30 key policy actors in the Senate, House, and executive. Name anonymity was guaranteed.

of power. Only the "soft" arrangements under Secretary Gardner (dependent as they were on the individual preferences of the incumbent secretary rather than any permanent organizational commitment), had bolstered NAPCA.

In Congress, committee jurisdiction was circumstantial and expertise was limited. Legislation dealing with this subject was assigned to the Committee on Interstate and Foreign Commerce in the House of Representatives because of its jurisdiction over "public health and quarantine" matters. This prestigious House committee has extensive jurisdiction, a busy membership, and a small staff. "We handle more domestic legislation probably than anybody but Ways and Means," noted a staff member. Because of its jurisdiction, the committee works with five departments and oversees six regulatory commissions. It may hold conferences with four different Senate committees: Commerce, Labor and Public Welfare, Public Works, and Judiciary. The result is, of course, that very few of its members or its staff have had time to devote to an emerging issue-area with little apparent national public interest. Even in 1970, only one member, Paul G. Rogers (D-Fla.), exhibited much interest or expertise in air pollution. Commerce committee staff was allocated to air pollution only on a part-time basis—typically part-time of just one man.

Senate jurisdiction for "public health and quarantine" matters is assigned to the Committee on Labor and Public Welfare. Air pollution legislation is assigned to the Committee on Public Works, however. In 1955, the Subcommittee on Flood Control of the Public Works Committee devoted a part of one day's hearings to air pollution—a task they justified by the fact that the subcommittee already had jurisdiction over water pollution. In 1963 a Subcommittee on Air and Water Pollution was established, chaired by Edmund S. Muskie (D-Me.).

Characteristics of the Senate Public Works Committee contrast sharply with those of the House Commerce Committee. It is a low-prestige committee with limited jurisdiction and a sizable staff. Having established a subcommittee with exclusive jurisdiction over pollution, however, Public Works became a center of air pollution policy development. Chairman Muskie developed considerable interest and expertise in the area, as did three or four other subcommittee members; staff was specifically assigned to the pollution subcommittee; and extensive hearings were held on air pollution (17 days of hearings in 1967—nearly 2,700 pages of testimony, statements, debate, and reports; over 150 persons representing 143 industries, associations, citizen groups, unions, and government agencies appearing before the subcommittee). Muskie's interest and resourcefulness must be credited for the success of the subcommittee.

Decision-making Characteristics

"Tapering down" did indeed characterize federal air pollution policy development from 1955 to 1970—logically so, given the knowledge and organizational capabilities in this issue-area at the federal level. Limited capabilities surely explain the research emphasis in the initial phases of federal policy (see Table 1). For example, in 1958 when Paul F. Schenck (R-Ohio) introduced legislation directed against interstate use of motor vehicles emitting dangerous amounts of unburned hydrocarbons, the surgeon general, who would be made responsible for setting standards, objected. He argued PHS did not have "available the scientific knowledge needed to carry out the purposes of the act." The Schenck Act as eventually passed merely required the surgeon general to begin identifying the health problems of automotive exhaust.

Randall B. Ripley's description of the passage of the Clean Air Act of 1963 suggests a process of indifferent or circumstantial bargaining. Conflict developed over federal enforcement power—not in regard to "how much" but on the more basic question of "whether." Before the president endorsed the idea, both the Public Health Service and the Bureau of the Budget opposed federal enforcement. The issue did not require extensive bargaining, in part because the proposal itself included only mild authority (to be implemented only after special conditions were met), and because industrial groups were neither unified nor all that committed to do battle on this legislation.

Policy development in 1967 well illustrates the process of tapering down and its preconditions. The Johnson administration had been convinced by Vernon MacKenzie, then deputy director, Bureau of Disease Prevention and Environmental Control, to support national emission standards for industry. Senator Muskie publicly opposed setting national emission standards and set out to prove their lack of

Table 1 National Air Pollution Policy Development

1. STATIONARY SOURCES, 1955–70		
MAJOR LEGISLATION	LENGTH OF PHASE	SUMMARY OF PHASE
Air Pollution Control Act of 1955	1955–63	Research and definition
Clean Air Act of 1963	1964–67	Encourage establishment of state-local-regional air pollution programs
Air Quality Act of 1967	1968–70	Demand establishment of state-local-regional air pollution programs

2. MOVING SOURCES, 1955–70		
Air Pollution Control Act of 1955		
The Schenck Act of 1960	1955–65	Research and definition
Clean Air Act of 1963		
Motor Vehicles Air Pollution Control Act of 1965	1966–67	Establishment of federal emission standards for motor vehicles
National Emissions Standards Act of 1967	1967–70	Federal regulatory pre-emption, with state assistance in implementation

workability in the most extensive congressional hearings ever conducted on air pollution. A subcommittee staff member explained:

> The Administration bill followed the National Conference on Air Pollution and it stressed national emission standards. Muskie warned them at the conference that he was not in favor of national emission standards, but they went ahead anyway with no attempt to consult us. Then they were taken aback when we objected. He held extensive hearings and we came down hard on the bill—trying to develop how national emission standards would improve air quality if they were set at minimum levels.

An NAPCA official discussed the problems NAPCA had in ratio-nalizing the standards before the Muskie subcommittee:

> Muskie was willing to have national emission standards if given a rationale that would support having them. And we worked desperately to provide that and I think the [record] for a couple of meetings will give the best evidence that we tried. Secretary Gardner was anxious that we try to have as much of that go as we could have go. So within the Administration there was a real goal to try and sell national emission standards. I remember we had about a week's time, a little less than a week's time, to try to get the last bits of information in to try and give a better rationalization. But you just can't do it.

Establishing national emission standards in 1967 would have been something more than an increment in national air pollution policy, and therefore would have required strong public support to counter-balance the lack of rationale. Public support was not available in 1967, however. As it was, Muskie successfully cut the provision from the bill and substituted authorization for a two-year study of the concept. In the Senate floor debate, he properly referred to the Air Quality Act of 1967 as "a logical expansion of the Clean Air Act of 1963."

Policy Characteristics

Table 1 shows classic incrementalism in policy development—though the policy progress for controlling moving sources was somewhat more definite than that for stationary sources. After a long period of research and definition, federal policy acted rather rapidly to pre-empt regulation of moving sources. Where state and local responsibil-ity was established for stationary sources, however, federal policy development was much more cautious and indefinite.

The Air Quality Act of 1967 sought to establish a federal-state-local network of control through elaborate and time-consuming stages. The procedures were variously described by critical respon-dents at all levels as "ponderous," "cumbersome," "a goddam mish-mash," "disastrous." One member of Congress reflected, however, that the confusion might have been beneficial—perhaps even inevitable. "As I look at it now, it probably was good to have it [ponderous] since we had to get the state and local units activated in this area and we needed to be very careful in doing that. We could not look as though the federal government were taking over completely in this area."

Air quality control regions had to be designated as a first step toward state action. By May 1969, the National Air Pollution Control Administration had plans for 57 such regions out of a projected total of 300 to 325 in urban communities. On December 8, 1969, Dr. Jesse L. Steinfeld, acting surgeon general, testified before the House Subcommittee on Public Health and Welfare on progress made. "Thus far [over two years after the passage of the 1967 Act], we have designated air quality control regions in 20 urban areas. In addition, . . . 37 other areas [have been identified] in which we expect to designate air quality control regions during the next several months."[7] Since so few regions had been established and so few of the other prerequisites to state action had been fulfilled, not one state had completed all requirements under the 1967 Act when the House Subcommittee on Public Health and Welfare began its hearings on legislation for 1970. Feeling no particular responsibility for the 1967 Act, which they had merely ratified, the subcommittee registered dismay with the lack of progress. Paul G. Rogers, in particular, was exasperated, asking over and over again: "What is holding it up?" He also demonstrated impatience with the lack of aggressiveness on the part of federal air pollution officials. Rogers was soon joined by other elected public officials in calling for dramatic change in federal air pollution policy.

PUBLIC SATISFYING-SPECULATIVE AUGMENTATION, 1970

By late 1969, it was virtually certain that "nibbling away at the problem," so characteristic of existing policy, would be an insufficient response to emerging public concern about the environment. Some-

---

[7]U.S., Congress, House, Subcommittee on Public Health and Welfare, Committee on Interstate and Foreign Commerce, *Hearings on Air Pollution Control and Solid Waste Recycling,* 91st Cong., 1st and 2d sess., 1969, 1970, 7.

thing more than the next increment in policy was necessary, despite limited federal capabilities for coping with air pollution problems. V. O. Key, Jr., observed that "public opinion does not emerge like a cyclone and push obstacles before it." And yet the magnitude of public expression and participation concerning the environment in 1969–70 was to have important policy effects in Washington. Without this demand, one would logically have expected further refinements of the 1967 Act (similar to those Senator Muskie, the congressional leader in air pollution, had introduced in December, 1969, and March, 1970). When this development of public expression occurred, we appeared to have a case in Lindblom's fourth quadrant—low understanding-large change. This situation evolves, according to Lindblom, with wars, revolutions, crises, and "grand opportunities." Presumably, the emergence of mass public interest in the environment would be the last.

Whereas majority building and incrementalism typify policy development under most circumstances, other concepts are necessary to describe and analyze action in the fourth quadrant. Lindblom concludes that "one would be hard put to formalize the methods appropriate to that quadrant." If we examine the appropriateness of two methods—"public satisfying," and "speculative augmentation"—we may find that a majority did not have to be fashioned. Rather, a public, however indistinct and ill-informed, had to be satisfied. Second, something more than an increment in policy was necessary if large change were the goal, regardless at this point of whether it would be reached or not. Still, knowledge and institutional capability were limited, as was technology. The term "speculative augmentation" is useful in meeting the analytic needs of this situation, and I now turn to describe and compare each set of characteristics under fourth-quadrant conditions.

Issue-area Characteristics

The growth in 1969–70 of public concern with the environment transcended the expected limits of multidimensional complexities and the diversity of special interests. The trend was demonstrated in public opinion polls, massive street demonstrations, the release of the Ralph Nader "Study Group Report on Air Pollution," and citizen participation at the local level. A Gallup poll taken in early May, 1970, provided comparative data on public attitudes concerning domestic issue-areas requiring government attention. "Reducing pollution of air and water" showed the most dramatic increase over a similar poll taken in 1965.

Table 2 Public Views on Major Domestic Problems

PROBLEM	MENTIONED AS ONE OF TOP THREE PROBLEMS REQUIRING ACTION		PERCENTAGE OF CHANGE	RANK IN 1965
	1965	1970		
1. Reducing crime	41%	56%	+15	2
2. Reducing pollution of air and water	17	53	+36	9
3. Improving public education	45	31	−14	1
4. Helping the poor	32	30	− 2	5
5. Conquering "killer" diseases	37	29	− 8	3
6. Improving housing, clearing slums	21	27	+ 6	7
7. Reducing racial discrimination	29	25	− 4	6
8. Reducing unemployment	35	25	−10	4
9. Improving highway safety	18	13	− 5	8
10. Beautifying America	3	5	+ 2	10

SOURCE: Gallup poll conducted May 2–3, in response to the question: "Which three of these national problems would you like to see the government devote most of its attention to in the next year or two?"

On April 22, 1970, a massive student-organized environmental "teach-in" occurred in major cities throughout the nation. E-Day, variously called "Earth Day," "Ecology Day," and "Environment Day," was counted a huge success. Thousands of middle-class suburbanites joined the students in this cause; there was full coverage by the mass media; and members of Congress cosponsored the event. Indeed, after months of campus turmoil, many people seemed relieved to have discovered an issue where they could join the students in constructive protest. Their union generated sufficient impact that not even the action in Cambodia—occurring during the same period—could totally submerge the environmental issue.

In May, 1970, shortly after E-Day, the Nader group report on air pollution, *Vanishing Air,* was released. The report was a scathing indictment of both industry and government. In the foreword, Nader observed: "[The] most significant conclusion is [our] analysis of the collapse of the federal air pollution effort starting with Senator Edmund Muskie and continuing to the pathetic abatement efforts and auto pollution policies of NAPCA."[8] The report received extensive news coverage, with special attention in editorials devoted to the Nader group's criticism of Senator Muskie. Since the three-year authorizations under the Air Quality Act of 1967 were expiring in 1970, the well-timed report would have an obvious impact in complementing other public pressures on national decision-makers.

At the local level, city councils and county commissioners found they had to pay more attention to environmental problems. For example, in Allegheny County, Pennsylvania, the Board of Health announced public hearings on the recommended air pollution code for September, 1969. In the past these hearings had been routine events, with little citizen participation. As one public official noted: "I had a public hearing in 1965 in Pittsburgh, and one in 1966. Even though they were well advertised . . . the hearing rooms on both days were filled but they were filled with people from industry . . . trying to tell us what we were trying to do was going to put them out of business." In 1969, however, "an army of people" attended the hearings.

The County's Air Pollution Advisory Committee after two years of work had finally produced a set of proposed rules and regulations which it felt would meet all Federal requirements.

Hundreds of residents turned out for a three-day public hearing on the new regulations and ripped them to shreds.

---

[8]John Esposito, *Vanishing Air* (New York: Grossman Publishers, Inc., 1970), vii–viii.

County officials were not prepared for the onslaught. As one noted: "When we first scheduled [the hearings] we arranged for a hall for one afternoon. We felt we would take care of all of them until the publicity came out in the paper that they were going to be held. And then the phone began to ring and requests kept pouring and pouring in."

Institutional Characteristics

This important shift in public support could not be expected to alter institutional characteristics in the short run. Such outside support is normally a source of power for an agency. NAPCA remained low in the HEW hierarchy, quite unprepared to manage or direct this potential source of power. Indeed, the agency actually had fewer employees in 1970 than in 1968! And though the House subcommittee took legislative initiative in 1970, its over-all capabilities had improved little. The Senate subcommittee remained the center of air pollution policy development in Congress. An NAPCA official compared the two in this way in 1970:

There is a world of difference between the two committees and these differences have increased. The differences are most notable at the staff level. The Muskie Subcommittee is staffed up to deal with this problem. . . . The House just passed amendments to the Act [the 1970 House bill]. They worked hard on them but their actions don't reflect a sophisticated look at the problem. They had testimony and they discussed it with us, and so forth, and of course they were all paying attention and working on the problem area, but they are not truly well informed. The Muskie Subcommittee has also conducted hearings. But the difference is in what they are doing with the material.

On the other hand, one could expect organizational changes to be made consonant with major policy shifts. As it happened, the National Environmental Policy Act of 1969 created a presidential Council on Environmental Quality (CEQ) to conduct studies and make policy recommendations to Congress. And President Nixon's Reorganization Plan No. 3, approved by Congress in September, 1970, combined the many federal pollution abatement programs (including NAPCA) into a newly created Environmental Protection Agency (EPA).

Decision-making Characteristics

It is rather in the decision-making and policy characteristics that public pressure may be expected to have more immediate effect. Public officials are sensitive to large-scale public expression on issues. Normally, of course, the message from the general public on issues is ambiguous: some vaguely for, some vaguely against, most indifferent. As Key observes, "Few public questions cross the threshold of attention of most people." However general were the instructions on E-Day (for example, "clear the air," "clean the water," "save the earth"), there was an unambiguous call for action. Though I lack definitive evidence on the point, it seems possible that a congressional majority was prepared to enact strong legislation in 1970—ready to support major changes in existing policy regardless of the limited intelligence and organizational capabilities of the federal air pollution policy system. Rather than having to find a coalition for policy, in 1970 air pollution policy-makers had to find a policy for a coalition.

Once public interest and concern were clearly established, air pollution policy proposals tended to escalate toward stronger and stronger regulations (irrespective of existing capabilities). The several factors which facilitated the escalation are summarized below with supporting evidence.

(1) Expansion of the number of participants in policy development without a proportionate increase in aggregate knowledge.

a. President Nixon spent a major portion of his "State of the Union" message on the environment—"a subject which, next to our desire for peace, may well become the major concern of the American people in the decade of the seventies."

b. The House Subcommittee on Public Health and Welfare, almost totally inactive in 1967, began hearings in 1969, and, in 1970 the House passed an air pollution bill before the Senate did.

c. A jurisdictional dispute over pollution matters was evident in the Senate, 1969–70, and a number of senators became actively involved in environmental policy development.

(2) Active competition among elected officials to produce and be credited with strong legislation.

    a. "With virtual wartime urgency," President Nixon sent extensive environmental proposals to Congress designed to "give the federal government an almost unprecedented leadership and power to act."

    b. The House committee held hearings first in 1970 and reported a bill in early June. "We decided to write the bill and not wait for the Senate bill," a committee member informed the author.

    c. Under pressure to produce strong legislation, the Muskie subcommittee finally reported a bill in September. It was immediately touted by the press as "the toughest air pollution clean-up bill ever."

(3) Constant monitoring of policy development by the media.

    a. Environmental programming and news coverage on television were increased.

    b. Newspaper coverage of legislative action concerning air pollution was more extensive than in 1967.

Why were there no correctives to escalation in 1970? Normally one would expect the regulated industries to resist escalating controls and the administrative agency to advise proceeding with caution. The effectiveness of these reactive pressures ordinarily explains the "tapering down" of majority building and the incremental results. In 1970, however, the regulated industries lost the advantage of access and expertise for the following reasons:

(1) Opposition to controls would be interpreted as favoring pollution.

(2) Their support was not necessary since a congressional majority appeared to precede policy development.

(3) Expert testimony is less relevant in an expansive process of escalating proposals.

(4) Regulated industries were not organized (or predisposed in regulatory policy matters) to offer alternatives and unsure, in any event, how to respond to the escalation.

For their part, NAPCA officials appeared satisfied to accept the next normal increment in policy. In describing early program formulation in the executive in 1969, one NAPCA executive recalled: "We were asked what new legislation did we want and our immediate reaction was 'for Christ's sake, go away!' We are trying to make the 1967 Act work. And_____said, 'Well look, we've got to have something new.' And so we had several discussions. We tried to identify what the deficiencies were."

Agency representatives appeared reluctant to accept new authority when testifying before the House subcommittee in early December, 1969, prior to the presidential message on the environment. The following colloquies—the first between Congressman Rogers and Dr. Jesse Steinfeld, acting surgeon general; the second between Rogers and Dr. John Middleton, NAPCA Commissioner—illustrate this reluctance.

MR. ROGERS. Do you see the problem is such that we should increase funding dramatically or not?

DR. STEINFELD. Well, words are hard to define. I would say that we agree with you and with the committee on the importance and on the urgency of the problem and on the fact that we must train more people and we must move faster, but in doing this we want to be sure that we marshall all of the available evidence.

MR. ROGERS. I understand that. What I am trying to get at is this: Are the figures in the bill, the funding in the bill, sufficient to allow the Department to move as it should, or is it insufficient?

DR. STEINFELD. In my interpretation, it would be sufficient to move ahead aggressively, even more aggressively than we have. Because there is a tuning-up period in any new program it takes longer to get started and less time as you move along.

MR. ROGERS. Are there any major changes that should be brought about in the legislation?

DR. STEINFELD. Major changes?

MR. ROGERS. Yes, sir.

DR. STEINFELD. I don't see any major ones, Mr. Rogers.[9]

---

[9]House Subcommittee *Hearings,* 91st Cong., 1st, 2d sess., 33.

This testimony was weighed by the subcommittee in light of the fact that no state had by that date completed the steps necessary to implement a federally-approved air pollution control program. Rogers frequently came back to the problem of resources.

MR. ROGERS. Do you have sufficient personnel to do this checking?

DR. MIDDLETON. (NAPCA Commissioner). We do the best we can.

MR. ROGERS. I know that. Do you have sufficient personnel? I am trying to help you, Dr. Middleton.

DR. MIDDLETON. I appreciate that.

MR. ROGERS. I am giving you direct questions where your bosses won't get on you. So, you can give me a direct answer.

DR. MIDDLETON. The answer is no. We don't have enough people.

MR. ROGERS. That is what I want to know. I would like to know how many you need. I would think you don't have enough people.[10]

This reluctance, itself explained in part by the insecurity and dependency of NAPCA, made it unlikely the agency could act as a check on policy development in 1970. As a result, the public-satisfying process of air pollution policy development in 1970 found decision-makers relying on a different set of cues from those they would have looked to for majority-building. In the latter, they look back to the nature of the problem and the store of knowledge for its solution and ahead to the trade-offs necessary for getting a majority. In public-satisfying, they look back to the public to determine what they *may* want and ahead to some of the complexities of applying a policy that appears to satisfy public wants. Policy-development based on the second set of cues obviously contains more risks in implementation than that based on the first set. More about those risks shortly.

Policy Characteristics

Though the House commerce committee and the president had taken the initiative in air pollution in 1970 and Senator Muskie had been

---

[10] *Ibid.*, 82.

strongly criticized in the Nader report, by late summer the Senate Subcommittee on Air and Water Pollution was again the central arena of policy development. The Senate subcommittee had completed its own hearings in mid-June and had before it the president's bill, the recently passed House bill, and two Muskie bills. The two Muskie bills can be treated most expeditiously here. Introduced before E-Day and the release of the Nader report, they were essentially refinements of existing law. In introducing the second bill, which dealt primarily with the regional network and the implementation plan procedure, Senator Muskie implied that Congress had, up to 1970, fulfilled its responsibility.

> Congress has passed laws to combat air pollution since the early 1960's, but the administration of the Federal programs has not matched the gravity of the problem. If our acknowledgement of the environmental crisis is to be more than rhetorical, those agencies charged with protecting and enhancing our environmental resources must show a greater sense of urgency, and Congress must strengthen their power to do so.[11]

It took the subcommittee three months after passage of the House bill to produce its version. Since both the president's proposal and the bill passed by the House were considered strong legislation, the subcommittee bill had to be stronger. It was. Table 3 shows the escalation provision-by-provision. Rather than get into the complex details of the legislation, I have judged the strength of the three versions in terms of authority granted and specified. The House bill was stronger than the administration proposal in seven of the eleven provisions. The Senate bill in turn was stronger than the House bill in seven of eleven and equal in strength in two others. The administration proposal was judged stronger than the House bill in just one provision and equal in strength to just one Senate provision.

This policy outcome (the Senate version eventually passed both houses with minor modifications) was clearly more than an increment in existing policy. I suggest the term "speculative augmentation"

---

[11]116 *Congressional Record* 5,966 (March 4, 1970).

Table 3 Escalation of Air Pollution Proposals, 1970

MAJOR PROVISIONS	ADMINISTRATION BILL	HOUSE-PASSED BILL	SENATE-PASSED BILL
1. Air quality standards	+[a]	+ +	+ +
2. Control regions	−	+ +	+
3. Implementation plans	+	+ +	+ + +
4. Stationary source emissions	+	+ +	+ + + +
5. Moving source emissions	+	+ +	+ + + +
6. Fuel standards	+ +	+	+ +
7. Aircraft emissions	−	+ +	+
8. Federal facilities	−	+	+
9. Money authorized	open	+	+ +
10. Judicial review	−	−	+
11. Citizen suits	−	−	+

[a] KEY: − No provision; + provision included; additional +'s indicate strength of provision relative to other bills.

summarizes the result—something more than an increment; something less perhaps than the far right on Lindblom's continuum of change. And given existing knowledge, technology, organization, and resources in federal air pollution control, the bold, new authority in the Clean Air Amendments of 1970 had to be based in large measure on *speculation* that capabilities would improve to meet the demands of the law.

Take, for example, the most drastic section of the bill passed by the Senate.

> Beginning with model year 1975 or after January 1, 1975, any new light duty vehicle or any new light duty vehicle engine . . . shall be required, for purposes of certification under this Act, to meet emission standards . . . which at a minimum, shall represent a 90 per centum reduction from allowable emissions for 1970, model year vehicles or engines.[12]

---

[12]U.S., Congress, Senate, Committee on Public Works, *National Air Quality Standards Act of 1970,* 91st Cong., 2d sess., S. Rept. 1196, 102. Muskie indicated in a press conference on June 9 that the subcommittee was seriously considering strict deadlines for automobiles.

Neither the administration nor the House-passed bills included any such deadlines. Both simply provided for improved motor vehicle testing and certification. That the technology was not presently available for meeting the 1975 standards in the Senate bill was indisputable. In fact, Senator Muskie pointed out in the floor debate that technology was rejected as a basis for decisions in this area. "The deadline is based not, I repeat, on economic and technological feasibility, but on consideration of public health."[13]

Though the press naturally selected the motor vehicle deadline for attention, those several sections dealing with stationary source pollution also speculatively augmented existing policy. The environmental protection agency administrator was authorized and directed to establish and enforce several sets of standards and direct the review and approval of complicated state implementation plans despite limited resources, an understaffed agency going through its fourth major reorganization in a decade and a restricted data-base for decisions.

In summary, air pollution policy development in 1970 contrasted sharply with earlier policy. The processes were not constrained, as expected, by confined scientific, organizational, and technological capabilities; nor was policy escalation checked by those economic interests to be regulated. As elected officials sought to satisfy general public interest, policy was augmented beyond normal increments. It remains to speculate about the broader effects of policy developed under these conditions.

POLICY IMPLEMENTATION—NOTES ON WHAT MAY COME

I have noted the probability of taking greater risks with speculative augmentation. Conditions supportive of the "leap forward" may be transitory. Public interest, in particular, may wane as policy moves to the less visible arena of application, and one may learn whether augmenting policy alone is enough to solve problems in an issue-area.

---

[13]This was in response to strong criticism from Sen. Robert Griffin (R-Mich.) for ignoring scientific knowledge and expertise in setting the deadline. 116 *Congressional Record* 32,906 (Sept. 21, 1970).

Given the significance of public support under conditions of satisfying the public, what might be the effects of its variation in policy implementation? I offer three possibilities.

(1) Active public pressure continues in the short run. Unsure of how long public support will last, enforcers are likely to capitalize on its thrust, and the probable lag in the effects of its decline, to improve procedural and organizational capabilities. The creation of CEQ and EPA can be expected to maintain public interest in environmental matters—at least among the mass media. In air pollution, EPA faced the complex task of maintaining a posture of strict enforcement, in line with the purposes of the Clean Air amendments, while reorganizing air pollution administration. Effectiveness during this period must be measured by the extent to which an agency increases its capabilities for applying policy after public interest declines. The decline in public pressure itself, however, will adversely affect the agency's future effectiveness.

Regulated groups may be expected to influence administrative rule-setting—primarily seeking to maintain flexibility for future enforcement and to insure that appeal procedures are included. They will also seek to influence public views so as to make certain that pressure is, indeed, short run. Additionally, they will do what they can to prevent major improvements in the enforcement capability of the agency.

(2) Active public pressure continues in the long run. Continuing public support for regulation means that elected officials will continue to monitor progress and provide the resources necessary for improving capabilities—that is, satisfy the public. Under these circumstances symbolic authority becomes very real and, in all likelihood, would be increasingly centered in the federal government. Effective enforcement in air pollution control will result in various economic and social effects—perhaps leading to broad-scale social planning.

Once regulating agencies come to possess real authority (as a consequence of increased capabilities), the regulated industries may be expected to pass on the costs and effects of regulation. Since their success may in turn affect priority setting, and thus reallocation of values, regulation may come to have major impact on society. Indeed, successful transfer of costs and effects of pollution control may result in "latent conflict emergence" among citizen groups. What seemed a simple matter of regulating industry comes to be a matter of conflict of values for individuals. Money payments are obviously involved when, for example, the auto industry does the research, design, engineering, and production necessary to meet the 1975 deadline for emissions. The consumer will bear most of these costs. But other results are also potentially involved in effective enforcement of air pollution controls that will not be borne by industry. Thus, an EPA with real authority (again defined in terms of capabilities) may come to regulate and/or influence individual choice in housing, transportation, entertainment, consumer goods—that is, life-style itself. Active public pressure in the long run, therefore, comes to expand greatly those to be regulated.

(3) Active public pressure wanes quickly. Under these circumstances, Murray Edelman, Charles E. Lindblom, and David B. Truman, among others, tell us to expect mutual role-taking and incremental adjustment. Edelman puts it most succinctly:

> The fervent display of public wrath, or enthusiasm, in the course of the initial legislative attack on forces seen as threatening "the little man" is a common American spectacle. It is about as predictable as the subsequent lapse of the same fervor.
>
> ... as far as the great bulk of law enforcement is concerned "rules" are established through mutual role-taking: by looking at the consequences of possible acts from the point of view of the tempted individual and from the point of view of the impact of his acts upon the untempted. The result is a set of unchallenged rules implicitly permitting evasions and explicitly fixing penalties. ... Out of their response to such mutual role-taking come the rules as actually acted out; the specification of the loopholes, penalties, and rewards that reflect an acceptable adjustment of these incompatible roles.[14]

Without public support, capabilities increase slowly. The regulators come to depend on the regulated. Following an initial period of tough talk, co-operative relationships develop—not unlike those typical at the local level in air pollution control in the 1960s. Enforcers no doubt will assume a public posture of active enforcement while seeking to develop mechanisms for accommodation with industrial interests.

---

[14]Murray Edelman, *The Symbolic Uses of Politics* (Urbana: University of Illinois Press, 1964), 23, 25.

Progress toward cleaner air will be measured and both sides will actually come to have a stake in the other's record of achievement—at least until the next phase of public fervor.

LEGITIMATION BEFORE FORMULATION: SOME BROADER IMPLICATIONS OF PUBLIC SATISFYING

Given the urgency of certain issues in modern society, the public-satisfying model has a number of attractive features. Public demand for action appears to meet one of the principal conditions for democracy. If the public is demonstrating preference among issues, in essence setting priorities, it is performing an important agenda-setting function and, as with the air pollution issue, perhaps demanding a monitoring of effects of the scientific revolution. If these judgments are consciously made, and therefore based on knowledge, then perhaps we are in John Dewey's terms approaching the "great community"—a community "organized as a democratically effective Public" —and are prepared to pay the costs and make the sacrifices noted in the second alternative above.

Dewey, however, sets high standards for his community. He places great stress on debate, discussion, social inquiry, and knowledge (to include "communication as well as understanding"). For him, ". . . genuinely public policy cannot be generated unless it be informed by knowledge, and this knowledge does not exist except when there is a systematic, thorough, and well-equipped search and record. Moreover, inquiry must be as nearly contemporaneous as possible. . . ."[15] This is not to say that such policy will be error-free. Policy decisions involve judgments, estimates, and opinions and "cannot escape the liability to error in judgment involved in all anticipation of probabilities." But the public bears a burden in Dewey's community, a burden of knowledge, the burden of awareness.

We take then our point of departure from the objective fact that human acts have consequences upon others, that some of these consequences are perceived, and that their perception leads to

---

[15]John Dewey, *The Public and Its Problems* (Denver: Alan Swallow, 1927, 1954), 179.

subsequent effort to control action so as to secure some consequences and avoid others ... the public consists of all those who are affected by the indirect consequences of transactions to such an extent that it is deemed necessary to have those consequences systematically cared for.[16]

It would presumably be satisfying for democrats to know that Dewey's conditions were met in the case of federal air pollution policy development. For example, "a democratically effective Public" consciously demanding greater attention to the environment in industrial applications of the scientific-technological revolution, would be evidence of a new, perhaps true, democracy. These conditions do not appear to have been met in this case, however. In fact, public interest and concern seemed only to reverse the typical sequence in policy development. Formulation ordinarily precedes legitimation. In 1970, legitimation—public and congressional approval of strong policy action—came first. Public demonstrations and opinion polls projected a clear message to decision-makers: "Do something dramatic about pollution." Denied the processes of filtering demands through those affected by regulation and of moderating policy choices in light of existing knowledge and capabilities, policy-makers were left to speculate as intelligently as they could, both about what would satisfy the public and whether the policy devised could in fact be enforced. If, as one suspects, the policy preferences of the general public were ephemeral (or not really "preferences" in the sense of conscious priorities), then the enforcers either have to build public support (in essence, "create" publics, in Dewey's terms) or make their accommodations with the regulated publics. For public policy, generated despite limitations of knowledge and organizational capability, stands very much alone when a public, once concerned about certain consequences, dissolves.

This case does then contribute to our wisdom about democratic politics in the "technotronic age." Mass expression of public concern can have an impact on policy development, despite the complexities and limitations of knowledge and organization. Major economic in-

---

[16] *Ibid.*, 12, 15–16.

terests were virtually without influence in the development of the Clean Air Amendments of 1970. But once policy is developed, it must be implemented to be effective. Until publics are organized in the longer run to assume the burdens Dewey speaks of, we cannot expect large change in policy to produce the intended large change in social life.

5. Policy Formulation in the Executive Branch: Central Legislative Clearance

Robert S. Gilmour

Central legislative clearance in the executive branch is widely regarded as one of the most powerful tools of the President. Under the aegis of the Office of Management and Budget (OMB, formerly the U. S. Bureau of the Budget) the hundreds of legislative proposals generated by federal departments, bureaus, and independent agencies are coordinated and reviewed to assess their acceptability as component parts of the presidential program.

Reprinted from *Public Administration Review* 31 (March–April 1971): 150–58. By permission.

Here, many observers would argue, the substance of the congressional agenda is determined. Richard E. Neustadt's constantly cited history of central clearance describes legislative clearance as "by far the oldest, best entrenched, most thoroughly institutionalized of the President's coordinative instruments—always excepting the budget itself. . . ."[1] Others have reaffirmed the view that the President's program is arrived at primarily by Budget Bureau, now OMB, review of proposals "welling up" from the agencies.[2]

While accepting the importance of centralized legislative advice within the executive branch, close students of presidential policy making have not always been enthusiastic about the results of this process. For example, Arthur Maass recorded his concern more than fifteen years ago about Executive Office decision making through a process of "piecemeal review, rejection, and modification of individual proposals flowing up from the administrative units. . . ."[3] More recently Norman Thomas and Harold Wolman have reported that even "Some participants in the policy process within the Executive Office of the President have contended . . . that this pattern has resulted in the adulteration of new ideas by internal bureaucratic considerations and clientele pressures exerted through the agencies."[4]

During the 1960s, observers focused special attention on the academic community, presidential commissions, task forces, and the White House staff as the ascending stars of legislative initiation.[5] One usually unstated but implicit conclusion is that these newer presiden-

---

[1]Richard E. Neustadt, "Presidency and Legislation: The Growth of Central Clearance," *American Political Science Review* 48 (September 1954): 642.

[2]See Michael D. Reagan, "Toward Improving Presidential Level Policy Planning," *Public Administration Review* 23 (March 1963): 177; Francis E. Rourke, *Bureaucracy, Politics and Public Policy* (Boston: Little, Brown and Co., 1969), p. 49.

[3]Arthur A. Maass, "In Accord with the Program of the President?" in *Public Policy,* C. J. Friedrich and J. K. Galbraith, eds., Vol. IV (Cambridge, Mass.: Harvard University Press, 1953), p. 79.

[4]Norman C. Thomas and Harold L. Wolman, "The Presidency and Policy Formulation: The Task Force Device, *Public Administration Review* 29 (September/October 1969): 459.

[5]See especially Adam Yarmolinsky, "Ideas into Programs," *The Public Interest,* no. 2 (Winter 1966): 70–79; Daniel Bell, "Government by Commission," *The Public Interest,* no. 3 (Spring 1966): 3–9; Nathan Glazer, "On Task Forcing," *The Public Interest,* no. 15 (Spring 1969): 40–45; and William D. Carey, "Presidential Staffing in the Sixties and Seventies," *Public Administration Review* 29 (September/October 1969): 450–458.

tial agents significantly augmented or supplanted traditional Budget Bureau powers over central clearance and presidential program development. Indeed, there is considerable evidence that important aspects of legislative clearance have been recentralized in the White House staff during the Kennedy and Johnson presidencies.

These evaluations aside, there has been surprisingly little examination of the legislative clearance process—systematic or otherwise—on which to base a firm judgment.

Our purpose here will be to consider how legislation initiated by the executive reaches the level of *central* clearance. What specific processes are involved and which actors figure most prominently at various stages in policy development? An attempt will be made, then, to re-examine the traditional conception of legislative proposals "welling up" from the bureaucracy for central clearance by the President's staff in the Executive Office.

Findings are based in part on interviews with career and political executives in eight of the eleven cabinet-rank departments and with officials in the Office of Management and Budget. Anonymity was offered all respondents, though some had no objection to being quoted or referred to as a source.

GROWTH OF LEGISLATIVE CLEARANCE

Development of presidential oversight of the legislative ideas and views of administrative agencies is usually associated with the Budget and Accounting Act of 1921, although no provision for central legislative clearance was contained in the act, and there is certainly no record that Congress intended to invest the executive with so powerful a tool in the legislative process. Ironically, it was the suggestion of a congressional committee chairman that, according to Richard Neustadt's sleuthing, "precipitated the first presidential effort to assert central control over agency views on proposed and pending legislation. . . ."[6] A second irony was that the initial proclamation establish-

---

[6]Neustadt, op. cit., pp. 643–644.

ing the Bureau of the Budget as a legislative clearinghouse was issued and vigorously implemented by the generally "Whiggish" administration of Calvin Coolidge. As an economy move, Coolidge insisted on Budget Bureau approval of all legislation proposed by executive agencies which committed the government to future expenditures. Budget Circular 49 required reports on pending fiscal legislation to be routed through the bureau for the addition of BOB advice before they were submitted to Congress.

For reasons quite apart from those of Coolidge, President Franklin D. Roosevelt enlarged the scope of legislative clearance substantially. Acting on Roosevelt's instructions in 1935, Budget Director Daniel Bell required all agency proposals for legislation and advice on legislation pending to clear the Budget Bureau "for consideration by the President," before submission to Congress. Agency proposals subsequently sent to Congress were to include a statement that the "proposed legislation was or was not in accord with the President's program."

There is little question that the Budget Bureau took its expanded clearance role with utmost seriousness. Yet Budget apparently remained little more than a clearinghouse for sporadic, though numerous, agency proposals and reports on pending bills throughout the Roosevelt administration. Neustadt credits "The custom of compiling formal agency programs as a preliminary stage in presidential program making" to "White House requirements imposed . . . in the four years after World War II."[7]

When the Republicans returned to power in 1953, the annual Budget call for departmental and agency programs initiated during the Truman administration was continued without interruption. During mid-summer of 1953, President Eisenhower joined the Budget Bureau's call for legislative proposals in a personal letter "bearing signs of his own dictation" addressed to each cabinet officer. Neustadt notes that the cumulative response was "astonishing" to those members of the White House staff who either assumed or believed that

---

[7]Richard E. Neustadt, "Presidency and Legislation: Planning the President's Program," *American Political Science Review* 49 (December 1955): 1001.

Congress was the rightful place for legislative initiation. "For here were departmental declarations of intent to sponsor literally hundreds of measures great and small, *most of which the President was being asked to make his own by personal endorsement in a message.*"[8]

In the present study, respondents whose experience extended to the Eisenhower period agreed that the Budget Bureau exercised extremely close supervision over executive channels for legislative proposals. One suggested that it took the combination of CEA Chairman Arthur Burns and Secretary of the Treasury George Humphrey to end-play the bureau in getting legislative proposals to the President. Similarly, others indicated it was easier to risk an end-run to Congress, skirting BOB authority.

During the 1960s, the Budget Bureau's veritable monopoly over executive branch legislation built up in the Eisenhower administration appears to have eroded seriously. Nearly all "career" respondents having the perspective of relatively long tenure offered much the same view as one thirty-year veteran: "Since the Kennedy administration, the role of the White House in legislative clearance has been multiplied many times. White House staff members can operate at the highest level, hammering out programs directly with the secretary. Sometimes during the Johnson administration there was even direct communication between the White House and agency heads to develop legislative proposals."

Despite apparent changes in the relative importance of central clearance by the OMB, institutional procedures for agency submission of proposals and reports continue to operate much as they did in the Bureau of the Budget for more than twenty years. An examination of those procedures and processes should thus precede an evaluation of recent trends.

BUREAUCRATIC INITIATION

In the public mind, line bureaucrats appear to have been eclipsed as legislative innovators by presidential task forces and other outsiders

---

[8]Ibid., pp. 986–987.

to the traditional process. Nonetheless, in the business of elevating ideas as serious proposals and issues, bureaus remain well situated and prolific. To cite but one illustration, the Department of Housing and Urban Development alone proposes approximately three hundred separate bills in the space of a single legislative year, most of which are initiated by the HUD bureaucracy. Although the great bulk of these proposals are "minor amendments" or bills of "middling importance," taken collectively they can hardly be ignored as the definers of larger policy.

Legislative drafting is a continuing activity in the agencies, but most bills are generated in a hurry-up response to the annual call for legislation. Budget Circular A-19 prompts agency action with the note that "annually proposed legislative programs for the forthcoming session of Congress . . . are to be used . . . in assisting the President in the preparation of his legislative program, annual and special messages, and the annual budget."

Not surprisingly, agency-initiated bills must run the gamut of clearance channels—in the sponsoring bureau and in the departmental hierarchy above—before the process is in any way centralized by the Office of Management and Budget. Each agency has its own routing procedure for legislative proposals, yet these will normally include critical reviews by finance officers, the agency planning units, and by line divisions of the agency which have a direct interest, depending upon the substance of each proposal. Typically, centralized responsibility for the coordination of agency bills is vested in a small staff such as the U. S. Forest Service Division of Legislative Liaison and Reporting. At a later stage, and with a fair assurance of departmental support, such bills are likely to be rendered as formal drafts by the agency's legislative counsel.

ASCENDING THE HIERARCHY

Assistant secretaries and their deputies in charge of designated line bureaus normally encourage their agencies—even the field offices—to send up ideas for legislative improvement. Successful efforts of this sort have the effect of maximizing supervisory control over agency submissions, making it possible for political executives to winnow out those proposals that they believe merit departmental support. The assistant secretaries also perform an important role as mediators in ironing out the inevitable differences among bureaus' plans for legislative enactment. And once they have formally approved an agency bill —offered by a bureau immediately subordinate—they may find themselves cast as negotiators with their departmental counterparts.

The legislative counsel (assistant or associate general counsel) of a department has strong potential influence over final clearance outcomes. He is characteristically not only a routing agent, but is also expected to offer advice on the language and general desirability of each proposal. Actual influence of this position varies greatly among departments canvassed. In departments such as Commerce and Treasury, which do not generate large numbers of bills, small legislative divisions occupy most of their time with the preparation of reports on bills pending in Congress, and principally serve an "editorial function" during the clearance process. In the action departments of the 1960s, legislative attorneys have played a much more vital role. Drafting of HEW bills, for example, has been centralized in the Division of Legislation. Clearance powers of the legislative counsel are even greater in Housing and Urban Development. Preparation of HUD's "omnibus package" of legislation involves both the collection of agency proposals and the sifting of ideas recommended by HUD's architectural, construction, housing, and mortgaging clientele groups. Associate General Counsel Hilbert Fefferman recalled, "We drafted major bills on model cities, rent supplements, FHA Title 10's 'new communities,' the College Housing Act, the Housing for the Elderly Act, and a good many others."

The general counsel in most departments is not only immediately superior to his legislative attorneys and, as one respondent described him, "the final arbiter for legal language," but he is also responsible for coordinating and compiling proposals and bills originating in the agencies. Some departments additionally rely on a program review committee for this purpose, but in any case the general counsel has substantial influence over the final shape of the department's legislative package. As an appointed official, however, and quite possibly a departmental newcomer, the general counsel can hardly help but place heavy reliance on the legislative counsel and other "career" subordinates.

In addition to the general counsel's office, other staff divisions of a department, especially the finance and planning divisions, may be consulted as a part of normal clearance procedure. Indeed, the OMB formally requires that an agency ". . . shall include in its letter transmitting proposed legislation or in its report on pending legislation its best estimate of the appropriations . . . which will be needed to carry out its responsibilities under the legislation." Budget officers are necessarily consulted when proposed legislation authorizes new departmental expenditures. Drafts may also be routed to departmental program planning officers, but this consultation appears often to be the exception rather than the rule.

Most departments have at least a pro forma routing of otherwise approved proposals across the desks of the secretary and his most immediate subordinates. It is understood that the secretary may intervene at any point during the process as an initiator, advocate, or veto agent, but the typical bill will not receive the secretary's or even the undersecretary's personal attention. In effect, clearance of most departmentally-generated legislative ideas takes place in the staff offices manned by career bureaucrats. "Political" oversight is largely exercised by the assistant secretaries and the general counsels. Of course the secretary and other high officials are likely to become deeply involved in clearance when this process takes the form of policy planning to develop major departmental or presidential program thrusts.

Most respondents indicated that the secretary also performs the roles of mediator and arbiter. One strategically placed observer in HEW remarked that the "settlement of disputes between assistant secretaries, career officials, or both is about the only way he can gain any real measure of control in this circus." Another, in HUD, recalled, "When Robert Weaver was secretary during the Johnson administration, he and undersecretary Robert Wood held relatively frequent meetings to settle conflicts between assistant secretaries." If those differences were not "bargained out," then it was said that the secretary or the undersecretary "made the decision."

INTERDEPARTMENTAL CLEARANCE

Before reaching the Office of Management and Budget, there is often an interdepartmental phase in the clearance process that some consider to be as important as final OMB review. One respondent in Transportation explained, "Where there's a substantial outside interest in legislation that we're drafting, we generally clear it with other agencies before going to Management and Budget." Another in Justice held, "Usually you get things worked out without the necessity of OMB negotiations."

Apparently, the points of contact between departments vary with legislative complexity and with the relative importance attached to bills by their initiators, but most are made at the operating level—one agency to another. Liaison between departments on the few major, controversial bills is likely to take place at a higher level. As a legislative attorney in Transportation put it, "Of course, if the problem were significant enough, it would go to the secretarial level."

Consultation and coordination of agency and departmental positions is not in the least secretive or inappropriate. OMB guidelines actually encourage each agency:

> ... to consult with other agencies concerned in order that all relevant interests and points of view may be considered and accommodated, where appropriate, in the formulation of the agency's position. Such consultation is particularly important in cases of overlapping interests, and intensive efforts should be made to reach interagency agreement before proposed legislation or reports are transmitted. ...

The Office goes further to suggest that "Interagency committees and other arrangements for joint consultation may often be useful in reaching a common understanding."

In view of Management and Budget's limited staff—twelve professionals—in its Division of Legislative Reference and the considerable technical complexity of many federal programs, OMB's formal encouragement of interdepartmental efforts to accommodate overlapping interests may be understood as a matter of practical necessity. Nonetheless, it's surprising that interdepartmental liaison in legislative policy making has drawn so little attention.

OMB CLEARANCE

Legislative proposals cleared in the departments and sent forward to Management and Budget in response to the annual call may be seized upon for translation to presidential prose and rushed to the drafting boards, or they may be shuffled to the files of good ideas in repose.

In either case, formal clearance awaits the preparation of a draft bill submitted by the sponsoring department. These are typically sent separately, following the initial proposals by weeks or months.

When each draft arrives, OMB's Division of Legislative Reference assesses its general compatibility with the President's announced program and with current budgetary projections. In making these judgments, heavy reliance is placed on presidential messages, consultation with White House staff members, and perhaps direct communication between the director and the President. "On the less important matters," as one assistant director admitted, "we rely primarily on the compromises that can be negotiated out among the departments and their respective agencies, these negotiations beginning within the general context of the President's objectives as he has stated them. In effect, a good portion of the President's program consists of the compromises that are struck here." Drafts deemed generally to be "in the right ballpark" are sent to the relevant line agencies for comments and deferred internally to the appropriate OMB program division where interagency negotiations over particular provisions will be held.

In dealing with each legislative proposal, Management and Budget has several alternatives. First, the Office may approve, stating with authority that the bill is "in accord with the program of the President," or appraising the bill "consistent with the objectives of the administration," or noting feebly that there is "no objection from the standpoint of the administration's program." Taking this option, OMB obviously offers varying degrees of support from strong backing to lukewarm tolerance. All the same, it here assumes a passive role which usually hinges on prior interdepartmental agreements, and it may be just those agreements that assure clearance at the lowest level of acceptance.

Secondly, Management and Budget may negotiate changes in a bill with the agencies immediately concerned to adjust differences. This course of action is much more commonly adopted, both as a means of resolving interdepartmental conflict and sometimes as a delaying tactic until a definite presidential position can be developed and enunciated. To reach agreement on points disputed in each bill, Legislative Reference may elect to act as a mediator or referee during formal meetings involving participants from departments and their agencies ranging from the assistant secretarial level downward. "The main task" of OMB, as one assistant director described it, "is that of persuading agencies to get together on proposed legislation, unless we hold strong independent views of our own. We suggest compromises and try to operate on a persuasive basis, but we stick to our guns in bargaining for the president's program."

On some occasions the OMB's efforts to "persuade" have been more direct, and the Office, as the Budget Bureau before it, takes the part of overt supervisor for legislative activities and pronouncements of line agencies. When negotiations were held over the Land and Water Conservation Fund in the early 1960s, for example, the Army Corps of Engineers and the Bureau of Reclamation (Interior Department) made known repeatedly their desire to be excluded from the fund's provisions. One member of the OMB's staff recalled, "It was necessary for us to persuade the Corps and the Bureau of Reclamation to refrain from taking an official position against their inclusion under the new conservation law." A close observer in another agency remarked, "From where we sat, that 'persuasion' looked a good deal more like a firm command." However, respondents more often criticized Management and Budget's indecisiveness and apparent inability to "take a stand."

Performance of the Office's supervisory role may also take the form of its final alternative in the clearance process, an outright block of legislation under review causing permanent rejection or at least temporary delay. It is not at all uncommon for OMB to return an agency-sponsored bill indicating that it would not be in accord with the president's program. In the past this advice has occasionally been moderated with a notation that the offending bill would not be in accord "at this time" or "at least at this time."[9]

Despite a firm prohibition against agency submission to Congress of bills which are held to be in conflict with the presidential program, it is well known that agencies frequently "get around" the confines of clearance procedures. This is accomplished through informal and nonofficial channels, most notably in the legislative drafting and information services agencies provide congressional committees and individual congressmen. Additionally, as one budget officer expressed it:

---

[9]Carl R. Sapp, "Executive Assistance in the Legislative Process," *Public Administration Review* 6 (Winter 1946): 16.

If an agency is dissatisfied with the outcome of our negotiations, it can quite easily arrange—and they often do—to have a congressman question them at the hearings in order to bring out that our office has made them water down the bill it wanted. Certainly the people I deal with play that game, but there are disadvantages as well as advantages involved.

By implication the prime disadvantage of this latter tactic, and apparently one that is well understood by the agencies, is the notion that OMB has a "long memory" for bureaus that repeatedly employ it. An agency must therefore weigh short-term tactical gains of a successful "end run" against longer-range objectives which may be jeopardized by opposition from Management and Budget in the future.

Continuing contact between OMB and line bureaus for general management, fiscal, and legislative matters is primarily maintained by the budget examiner assigned to each agency. The examiners have also become Budget and Management's chief mediators for interdepartmental disputes centering on their agencies' programs. Stalemate of interagency negotiations will, of course, receive the attention of an OMB division chief, an assistant director, or perhaps even the director himself.

Traditionally, decisions of the director "on behalf of the President" were understood to be final, or nearly so. After a contested ruling by the director, an agency or department head was, in a formal sense, "always free to appeal to the President." But the success of this gambit was unlikely, and the logic of presidential denial in such cases seemed quite convincing. Former Budget Director Kermit Gordon has argued:

If the President reverses his Budget director fairly frequently, the latter's usefulness to the President will be gravely impaired if not destroyed, for it will have become evident that he has failed in his effort to tune in on the President's wave length, and his desk will become only a temporary resting place for problems on the way to the President.[10]

---

[10]Kermit Gordon, "Reflections on Spending," in *Public Policy,* J. D. Montgomery and A. Smithies, eds., Vol. XV (Cambridge, Mass.: Harvard University Press, 1966), p. 59.

Nonetheless, there is mounting evidence that the pattern has changed. From the standpoint of increased influence, the White House staff appears to have been the prime beneficiary.

WHITE HOUSE INTERVENTION

Perhaps the best illustration is that of a young OMB examiner who explained to the writer, "I'll come to work and learn that 'There was a meeting at the White House last night, and it's all settled.' The bill I've been negotiating for weeks has been pulled up from the Office by the White House staff." It is quickly learned that this is not an isolated instance. High-level Management and Budget officers have had a role in these White House sessions, but OMB no longer has the monopoly claim on clearance decisions held by the Bureau of the Budget in the 1950s. Most of us were keenly aware of the strong legislative initiatives taken by the president and White House staff during the '60s, yet few students of administration noticed that the White House staff has directly intervened in central legislative clearance.

This change has been perceived by departmental and agency administrators throughout the executive branch. The opinion is widespread that the White House has taken over from Management and Budget on legislative matters of "any real importance." Said one respondent, "During the past ten years, especially, meetings have been called by the White House staff to hash out legislative agreements where the Department of Agriculture has been involved." The same point was made by others. In Transportation: "It is my experience that White House meetings to discuss our legislation have been called only after clearance by the secretary. These meetings usually mean, then, that there is disagreement between our department and another." In HEW: "During the last five years there have been a great many meetings called by the White House to discuss our legislative items. The Nixon administration hasn't changed that trend." A budget officer in Legislative Reference argues that the Nixon staff "has, if anything, been even more active in clearance than Johnson's or Kennedy's. The fact of the matter is that there are now many more men in the White House for this kind of work. They are better organized, and they have definite legislative and program assignments."

With this change there has apparently been a greater willingness on the parts of departmental officials to challenge the Budget director. As one respondent put it, "There has got to be a way to go over the OMB on a regular basis without going directly to the President. There is. That's the White House staff. Ted Sorensen and Joe Califano, in the Kennedy and Johnson administrations respectively, were constantly available to mediate and arbitrate between the secretary of a department and the director of the Budget." In the Department of Transportation a respondent allowed "that the Office of Management and Budget still calls negotiations to iron out agreements on legislation, but once conflict over a bill escalates to the point that the director becomes involved, the OMB is no longer in a position to act as a mediator. This is when the disagreement between parties is likely to be carried over to the White House." A Justice Department attorney in the early Nixon administration stated flatly, "[Budget Director] Mayo doesn't overrule [Attorney General] Mitchell unless Mayo represents the President." Observations of this sort were volunteered in every department interviewed, and they were intended to apply to all three administrations of the '60s.

For Presidents Kennedy and Johnson, who wished to achieve a high level of legislative accomplishment, reliance on traditional initiatory and clearance procedures was understood to be inadequate. Neither President found that the bureaucracy could supply the ideas and advice needed for a major legislative program. William Carey reports, for example, that President Johnson "spent the better part of a year badgering the Budget director to assign 'five of the best men you have' to drag advance information out of the agencies about impending decisions and actions so that he could pre-empt them and issue personal directives to carry them out, but the Budget Bureau never came anywhere near satisfying him because its own radar system was not tuned finely enough."[11]

The answer to intelligence difficulties supplied by the Kennedy and Johnson administrations was, in part, the establishment of congressional liaison offices operating closely with the secretary of each cabi-

---

[11]Carey, op. cit., p. 453.

net-rank department. It was reasoned that this machinery would highlight major policy questions and assist the President and the secretaries in dealing effectively with Congress. According to Russell Pipe's description:

> The Johnson administration's legislative program has included many proposals affecting more than one department. Liaison officers collaborate on such legislation to see that maximum effort is expended to promote the legislation. Omnibus bills require joint liaison ventures. In addition, personal friendships, political debts, and a kind of collegial relationship growing out of shared legislative skills bring liaison officers together to work on measures requiring all-out drives for passage. Thus, a network of liaison interaction has been created.[12]

At the White House Joseph Califano's office became "a command post for directing the Great Society campaign, an operational center within the White House itself, the locus for marathon coffee-consuming sessions dedicated to knocking heads together and untangling jurisdictional and philosophical squabbles."[13] Respondents in the departments indicated repeatedly that Califano was the presidential assistant who constantly "initiated negotiations," "called us in" for conferences, and "ironed out conflicts" among the agencies.

The Nixon administration counterpart to Califano is presidential assistant John Ehrlichman, who has also become executive director of the newly established Domestic Council staff. The "Ehrlichman Operation" is considerably larger than any of its predecessors and, according to some informants, even more vigorous. The Domestic Council—functionally the cabinet without Defense and State Department components—was set in motion by President Nixon's Reorganization Plan No. 2 of 1970, and it is intended to provide an "institutionally staffed group charged with advising the president on the total range of domestic policy." As yet Ehrlichman's staff shows

---

[12]Russell B. Pipe, "Congressional Liaison: The Executive Branch Consolidates Its Relations with Congress," *Public Administration Review* 26 (March 1966): 20.

[13]Carey, op. cit., p. 454.

no signs of becoming a career unit like the supporting staff of the National Security Council, but that is apparently what originators of the concept in the President's Advisory Council on Executive Organization have in mind for the future. With or without a careerist orientation, the Domestic Council staff under Ehrlichman has institutionalized the process of White House clearance for controversial or high-priority legislation beyond Management and Budget's Division of Legislative Reference.

The White House deadline is an additional structural device that has made an impact over the past decade and has had the effect of short-circuiting interdepartmental negotiations. A career attorney in Commerce commented, "It's not at all uncommon for legislative clearance to be greatly abbreviated because of short-fuse deadlines set by the White House, Management and Budget, or both." His counterpart in another department viewed this development as "unfortunate because it means that legislative outputs are uncoordinated and often drafted in a slipshod fashion."

Still others interpreted these deadlines as a means for agencies to avoid the rigors of interdepartmental bargaining. In HEW an experienced observer noted that deadlines have "more than once facilitated a shortcut in the clearance process." He went on to suggest:

> As a department strategy for approval of its bills, specific departments have dragged their feet until the eleventh hour. Thus when the draft went in from the line departments to the OMB there was virtually no time for Budget clearance, much less for a thoughtful and coherent response from other concerned departments. In the face of a firm White House deadline, the initiating department's proposal would earn the official blessing of the President as a reward for tardiness.

A respondent in Agriculture said, "Sometimes I think agencies wait until the deadline is upon them on purpose—so they won't have to consult and coordinate with other departments." Others added that deadlines imposed by the White House have been just as firm during the first year and a half of the Nixon administration as they were under Johnson.

CONCLUSION

Of the approximately sixteen thousand bills annually processed by the Office of Management and Budget, probably 80 to 90 percent do come "welling up" from the agencies to be cleared in the ascending hierarchy of career bureaucrats and political overseers in the line departments and finally to be negotiated by OMB and given a grade in the President's program. Treatment of the remaining bills, those singled out for special attention by the White House, provides the most striking change in central clearance during the past decade. All three Presidents of the '60s have short-circuited normal clearance channels to put a personal stamp on high-priority legislation. On crucial new programs, the White House has imposed strict deadlines for policy development, rushing Management and Budget coordination and allowing more discretion to individual departments. When OMB clearance negotiations have dragged or stalemated, the White House has not hesitated to intervene, dealing directly with departmental program managers. Indeed, this new process appears to have been institutionalized in the Domestic Council staff. At the same time, with the encouragement of the Budget Bureau and its successor, the Office of Management and Budget, line bureaucrats may have become their own best negotiators and mediators for clearance. The result, it appears, is a substantial challenge to OMB for authority for central clearance from above and below.

6. The Presidency and Policy Formulation: The Use of Task Forces

Norman C. Thomas
Harold L. Wolman

Every modern President since Franklin D. Roosevelt has made important contributions to the presidency. This article concerns an innovation in the process of formulating presidential legislative programs in domestic policy areas—the systematic use of White House task forces. After an initial venture by John F. Kennedy, the task force device was extensively used by President Lyndon B. Johnson; it seems likely to be continued in

Reprinted from *Public Administration Review* 29 (September–October 1969): 459–71. By permission.

some form by Richard M. Nixon. Use of the task forces, although hardly revolutionary, is a departure from past practices that may have some important consequences for national domestic policy making. We will examine the early use of the task forces, focusing on the policy areas of education and housing. Our findings are based in part on interviews with participants in the policy process in those areas.

Students of American government are familiar with the general pattern of presidential policy formulation, including the method of developing the President's legislative program that became routinized in the Truman and Eisenhower Administrations. Until recently, the legislative program was formulated almost exclusively on the basis of proposals prepared by the departments and agencies and submitted to the President through the Bureau of the Budget. The Bureau and the White House staff analyzed these proposals, and from their analysis and subsequent presidential choices, the legislative program emerged. The departments and agencies carried most of the burden of policy innovation, drawing on their own experience and expertise and the inputs from their clientele groups for new ideas.

Most political scientists have paid little attention to the operational consequences of this pattern of dependence of the President, the White House staff, and the Bureau of the Budget on the agencies for ideas and information. Some participants in the policy process within the Executive Office of the President have contended, however, that this pattern has resulted in the adulteration of new ideas by internal bureaucratic considerations and clientele pressures exerted through the agencies. There has been, it is said, a tendency to repeat proposals until they eventually are adopted or until the rationale for them has long disappeared. Agency-oriented proposals have tended to be un-imaginative, remedial, and incremental rather than broadly innova-tive. Phillip S. Hughes of the Bureau of the Budget summarized this point of view:

. . . The routine way to develop a legislative program has been to ask the departments to generate proposals. Each agency sends its ideas through channels, which means that the ideas are limited by the imagination of the old-line agencies. They tend to be repetitive—the same proposals year after year. When the ideas of the different agencies reach the department level, all kinds of objections are raised, especially objections that new notions may somehow infringe on the rights of some other agency in the department. By the time a legislative proposal from a department reaches the President, it's a pretty well-compromised product.

THE KENNEDY EXPERIMENT

A partial switch to new sources of legislative proposals occurred at the beginning of the Kennedy Administration. Upon leading his party to victory after eight years of Republican rule, John F. Kennedy needed outside help in establishing a legislative program. Shortly after his election, Kennedy commissioned 29 task forces of leading Democrats and experts in various areas of foreign and domestic policy; 24 of them had reported back to him by inauguration. The task force reports served to collate for the new Administration some of the nation's best thinking on the critical problems confronting it. While most of Kennedy's legislative proposals were scaled down from the broad scope of the task force recommendations, the thrust and direction of the reports survived. Subsequent publication of the reports provided a ready reference for policy proposals for individuals and groups inside and outside of the government.

Although the preinaugural task forces were an important innovation, Kennedy did not repeat their use in the original form. He did experiment with other variations of the task force, however. The preinaugural task forces composed largely of outside experts gave way to intragovernmental groups which Kennedy used to deal with foreign policy crises and domestic problems on an ad hoc basis. Of course, many members of the original task forces by now were in the government.

DEVELOPMENTS UNDER JOHNSON

Soon after President Johnson assumed office, he faced the need to develop a legislative program which could be identified as "his own." There apparently was a feeling within the White House and in the Bureau of the Budget that such a program was not likely to be developed from proposals submitted by the departments and agencies.

The need for outside advice and suggestions was especially critical in an Administration which had retained the basic values and goals and most of the key personnel of its predecessor.

Early in 1964 a number of President Johnson's close advisers, including Budget Director Kermit Gordon, Presidential Assistants Bill Moyers and Richard Goodwin, and Chairman Walter Heller of the Council of Economic Advisers—all of whom were familiar with the preinaugural Kennedy task forces—suggested a series of task forces to study specific policy areas. The President adopted the suggestion. In order to avoid some pitfalls encountered in the Kennedy operation, e.g., charges of over-representation of intellectuals and a consequent lack of realism in proposals which forced the Administration to defend the reports even before they had become the basis for action, it was decided that the Johnson task forces would operate under a cloak of secrecy. The members agreed not to reveal their assignments to the press or to professional associates and not to disclose the substance of their deliberations or reports. The Administration promised to reciprocate.

The 1964 experience with task force operations was deemed successful and was refined and developed in the following years. As we have observed, policy planning prior to the Johnson Administration was primarily a function of the departments and agencies with review by the White House staff and the Bureau of the Budget. President Johnson brought that function more effectively under his control through the integration of the task force operation with legislative submissions and budget review and the creation of a small policy-planning staff under one of his key assistants. Under the direction of Special Assistant Joseph A. Califano, the White House staff assumed the paramount role in setting the framework for legislative and administrative policy making. A career official in the Bureau of the Budget observed that "At the stage of developing the presidential legislative program, the task force reports play a more significant role than any documents or proposals emanating from the agencies." "The task forces presented us with meaty propositions to which we could react," recalled a former Budget Bureau official, "not the nuts and bolts stuff which we usually got from the agencies."

The impact of the departments and agencies in the development of the presidential legislative program may still have been considerable, but it tended to come more through the participation of their policy-level personnel in White House meetings where task force reports were evaluated. The agencies also proposed a substantial amount of technical legislation which corrected defects and filled gaps in existing statutes, but many of the most important substantive contributions came from elsewhere. The agencies made major contributions to public policy in the course of drafting bills and implementing programs, but their participation in the formulative stages was somewhat reduced during the Johnson Administration. Perhaps the distinction which should be made is that task forces and key presidential advisers operated at a much more general level than all but a few top-ranking agency personnel. Department and agency personnel took what were often vague task force ideas and fashioned specific legislative proposals from them. As an HEW official explained, "We had to come up with the conception of the idea in legislation, not task force rhetoric."

JOHNSON PATTERN EMERGES

The processes of policy formulation in the Executive Office of the President varied widely in the period from 1964 through 1968, but a general pattern appears to have emerged in the cycle of the task force operation as it developed under Califano and his staff. Each year in late spring, Califano and his assistants visited a number of major university centers throughout the country in search of ideas for new programs. At the same time, the White House canvassed the Administration for new ideas. Various officials who were regarded as "idea men" were invited to submit proposals on any subject directly to the White House, by-passing normal bureaucratic channels and departmental and agency hierarchies. For example, according to a White House staff member, former Secretary of Defense McNamara submitted over 50 proposals on various domestic problems in one year.

Califano's assistants prepared one-page descriptions of all the ideas received. These "write-ups" included a "proposal" section which briefly explained the idea, a description of the problem and its relationship to ongoing programs, and a recommendation for action. Next, these papers were categorized and a high-level group within the institutionalized presidency reviewed them. In 1967 this group included Califano, Budget Director Charles Schultze, his deputy Phillip

S. Hughes, Chairman Gardner Ackley of the Council of Economic Advisers, Special Counsel to the President Harry McPherson, and Califano's staff. This group also reviewed the reports of previous task forces, presidential commissions, and other advisory bodies which were filed during the course of the previous year. Following the review, Califano and his assistants compiled a loose-leaf book in which the remaining ideas were grouped by substantive policy areas. The screening group then reconvened for a second examination after which it sent the book to the President with a cover letter indicating the areas which it felt required further study. The President and Califano then reviewed the proposals and decided in each case whether to abandon the idea, study it further, or mark it for additional study if time and staff were available.

OUTSIDE AND INSIDE GROUPS

Further development of the ideas which were not abandoned occurred through referral to individual consultants or formal advisory councils, study by departments and agencies, or examination by task forces. The assignment of a task force signified that the President and his top advisers regarded the problem as one of considerable significance. Although task forces did not routinely operate in all of the Great Society areas, they did function fairly frequently. In 1967 a total of 50 separate task forces were operating in various domestic policy areas. The scope and purpose of the task force assignment determined whether its members would be drawn from outside or inside the government, or from both.

Outside task forces were primarily used to secure new ideas for policy. According to participants on various task forces in education and housing, they received broad directives which accorded them maximum freedom to come forth with ideas. "The President," observed a high-ranking presidential staff member, "wants their judgment on substance—not political feasibility."

There was some adjustment in the functions of outside task forces after 1964. In the words of one participant, the 1964 task forces were "happenings." President Johnson used them as ad hoc devices to develop proposals which almost immediately became part of his legislative program. By 1966 the task forces were a normal and rather elaborate aspect of the operations of the presidency. The President and his staff took steps to institutionalize the task force activity by integrating it with the highly structured and formal budget review process. The task forces also began to be used to seek long-range views of major policy areas and problems as well as to develop immediate legislative proposals.

As compared to outside task forces, inside, or interagency task forces functioned more to coordinate agency approaches and seek interagency agreement in areas of dispute. Inside task forces also served agencies as vehicles for broad review of the reports of outside task forces. An important function of the interagency task forces was to conduct a detailed "pricing out" of new proposals. Members of inside task forces usually included representatives of the Bureau of the Budget and Califano's staff, as well as agency heads or departmental assistant secretaries.

PUBLIC COMMISSIONS

Task forces did not displace that older and more familiar advisory mechanism, the public study commission, which also served as an outside source of policy advice in the Johnson period. President Johnson appointed a number of public commissions including the Kaiser Committee on urban housing, the Heineman Commission on income maintenance, the Crime Commission, and the Kerner Commission on civil disorders. One such body, the Douglas Commission on housing, was actually authorized by Congress.

Public commissions can, as cynics have suggested, give the illusion that something is being done about a problem. Establishing a commission is a safe response—it suggests action but is unlikely to stir the real political opposition which would emerge if substantive action were attempted. The impact of the report of a public commission is likely to be through its educational effect on public opinion rather than by direct translation into the Administration's policy proposals. Occasionally, however, when the President has complete confidence in the commission chairman and stays in close contact with him, the report may have a direct impact on Administration policy. This was the case with the Kaiser Committee in 1967–68.

By establishing representative commissions and then exposing their deliberations and their reports to public attention, it is sometimes possible for the Administration to develop support for policies it would like to advance. One problem with the use of commissions is that reports which are innovative tend to be controversial and potentially embarrassing to the White House, which may have difficulty in either embracing or backing away from the recommendations. The Administration's awkward response to the report of the Kerner Commission (President's Commission on Civil Disorders) in March 1968 and the subsequent criticism it received from both friends and critics of the report, illustrates the point. Public commissions do not often serve as sources of important information or new ideas. According to one respondent, "the basic ideas in the Kerner report came to us at least two years ago in various task force reports." In the Johnson Administration, task force reports were more likely to receive intensive scrutiny at the White House than the reports of public commissions.

AFTER THE REPORTS

When the task forces completed their reports, they submitted them to the President and deposited them with the Bureau of the Budget. Usually, outside task forces reported during the fall. The Bureau of the Budget and the relevant departments and agencies (if the latter were consulted) forwarded their comments directly to the White House.

Following the initial evaluation, the White House staff, under Califano's direction, took the lead in winnowing down task force proposals. If it appeared that an outside task force report should be followed by an interagency task force, that decision was made by Califano, the Budget Director, the Chairman of the Council of Economic Advisers, and the appropriate department and agency heads. Otherwise, in a series of White House meetings, the department and agency heads and their top assistants, representatives of the Bureau of the Budget's examining divisions, representatives of the Council of Economic Advisers, and members of Califano's staff examined all task force reports. The participants received continuous direction from the President as to his priorities. After much discussion and bargaining, they developed a proposed legislative program which was presented to the President for final decisions.

TYPICAL SEQUENCE

The process of developing presidential legislative programs in domestic policy areas established under the Johnson Administration occurred in a more or less orderly time sequence. The pattern is described in Figure 1.

TASK FORCE OPERATIONS

A better picture of the Johnson task force operation can be obtained by detailed examination of some of those which operated in the areas of education and housing. The major task forces and public commissions in these areas from 1964 through mid-1968 included:

In education:
    1964 Gardner* Task Force
    1966 Early Childhood Task Force
    1967 Friday Task Force
    1967 Interagency Task Force
    * By popular convention, outside task forces and public commissions are usually referred to by the name of the chairman.
And, in housing:
    1964 Wood Task Force
    1965 Wood Task Force
    1966 Ylvisaker Task Force
    1967 Interagency Task Force
    1967–68 Kaiser Committee

MEMBERSHIP SELECTION

The President and his top policy advisers usually selected the members of outside task forces. The selection process operated quite informally. The White House staff, the Bureau of the Budget, the Council of Economic Advisers in the case of housing, and the Office of Science and Technology in the case of education, and in some cases the concerned department or agency, suggested prospective members. The White House staff took the lead in screening the initial nomina-

Figure 1 Sequence of Events in Preparing the Legislative Program: The Johnson Administration

IDEA GATHERING: VISITS TO UNIVERSITIES; CONTRACTS WITH OUTSIDE EXPERTS AND "IDEA MEN" IN GOVERNMENT	INTERNAL DISCUSSIONS OF IDEAS GATHERED	APPOINTMENT OF OUTSIDE TASK FORCES	RECEIPT AND REVIEW OF TASK FORCE REPORTS	WHITE HOUSE MEETINGS	PREPARATION OF MESSAGES
			AGENCY SUBMISSIONS	FINAL PRESIDENTIAL DECISIONS ON THE PROGRAM	INTRODUCTION OF BILLS
April/May/June	July	August	Sept/Oct/Nov	December	Jan/Feb/Mar

tions. Then the President approved the final choices, sometimes adding names and deleting others.

The criteria employed in selecting members tended to vary with the mission of the task force. Many of our respondents emphasized the importance of independence of viewpoint. In language resembling Neustadt's in *Presidential Power,* a White House staff member commented that "the President has to have advice from someone who knows the right answers and who has no political axe to grind." However, persons supposedly holding radical points of view were not likely to be included. "The names were selected on the basis of a kind of common sense soundness," recalled one participant in the selections. "We would not have picked a Michael Harrington, for example. We looked for people who had written with perspective and reasonable freshness and who haven't been in the government for several years."

The composition of outside task forces was not as carefully balanced as membership of public commissions tends to be (see Table 1).

Table 1 Representation on Outside Task Forces

	EDUCATION					
	STATE AND LOCAL OFFICIALS	COLLEGE ADMINIS-TRATORS	COLLEGE PROFES-SORS	BUSINESS	FOUNDA-TION OFFICIALS	OTHER
1964	3	3	2	2	2	1
1967	2	6	3	0	1	1

	HOUSING						
	STATE AND LOCAL OFFI-CIALS	COLLEGE ADMINIS-TRATORS AND PROFESSORS	BUSINESS	LABOR	CIVIL RIGHTS GROUPS	INTEREST GROUPS IN HOUSING	OTHER
1964	1	6	0	0	0	1	3
1965	2	2	1	1	1	0	2
1967	2	5	0	1	1	0	1
1967*	1	1	10	3	1	2	0

* Kaiser Committee.

However, since the President wanted politically saleable policies, representativeness became a factor in selecting members, especially when the objective was to come up quickly with new legislative proposals. If a task force report was unanimous, a supporting coalition representing most of the major elements in American society would already have been constructed.

Occasionally federal officials served on predominantly outside task forces. In 1964, Commissioner of Education Francis Keppel was an ex officio member of the Gardner task force; in 1965 Budget Director Kermit Gordon and Senator Abraham Ribicoff served on the housing task force. In 1967 Secretary Gardner, Commissioner Howe, and a few other HEW officials sat with the Friday task force on a number of occasions.

One striking thing about the outside task forces is the extent to which academically based persons were overrepresented in their memberships. This is particularly apparent when the housing task forces are compared with the Kaiser Committee.

In selecting task forces a conscious attempt was made to avoid overrepresentation of established clientele groups such as the National Association of Housing and Redevelopment Officials, the National Education Association, and the American Council on Education, which customarily worked closely with the departments and agencies in developing policy. As the agency role in initiating policy began to decline as a consequence of the task force operation, the access of the clientele groups to the central policy makers also began to fall. These groups responded by criticizing the task forces. A representative of a higher education association said, "The task forces represent the worst form of intellectual and educational elitism. They are based on the implicit assumption that the education associations are incapable of any sort of creative or innovative thought."

Representative task forces and public commissions may have the added benefit, for the Administration, of co-opting relatively powerful but essentially conservative elements of society for social problem solving. As a key presidential adviser volunteered:

> We try to bring some of these elements in, in effect, to co-opt them. We rub their noses in the problem and bring them along with the

solutions. Hell, some of them have never seen slums before. We take them to the ghettos and they are amazed that such things exist. It's surprising how radical some of them become.

PROCEDURES AND STAFFING

The operating procedures of the task forces in education and housing followed a similar pattern. Generally, there were one to three initial meetings at which the members, in the course of reacting to one or two broad position papers, ranged over the entire subject. During these sessions the groups identified areas for future study and commissioned additional position papers. The papers provided the basis for discussions at subsequent sessions. After a few more meetings, either the staff or a task force member, usually the chairman, prepared drafts of various sections of a proposed report. Further discussions focused on these drafts, and the task forces began to move toward consensus on recommendations and reports.

The task forces do not appear to have used formal votes to reach decisions; the usual mode of decision was to bargain back and forth until agreement was reached. When members raised strong objections, efforts were made to satisfy them. According to one participant, the prevailing decisional norm was one of acquiescence—"If the rest of you agree, then I won't make a fuss." In some cases, however, members refused to yield, as when Whitney Young of the Urban League opposed shifting community action programs from the Office of Economic Opportunity to HUD in 1965 because the Negro community was suspicious of HUD. As this example suggests, the members do represent their institutional affiliations during task force or commission deliberations. Indeed, a staff member of one task force commented, "The members not only actually do speak in terms of the interests of that sector of society from which they are appointed, but in many cases, they perceive their role on the task force as doing exactly that."

The secrecy of the task force operation was one of its most important characteristics. One task force staff member told us:

Our task force was a CIA-type operation. I felt very odd about it. We were not sure about what should be said and what shouldn't be said.

There was no name on our door for the task force. The task force staff director simply had his own name on the door. Papers were put under lock and key every evening.

These remarks were not atypical of comments by people who were intimately involved. In the eyes of the President and his staff, secrecy was crucial for the task force operation. Without secrecy, they felt, the task forces would have become merely a series of public commissions and study groups, subject to all the problems of that form of advisory organization. Secrecy enabled the President to ignore proposals which he considered impossible to carry out. Recommendations could be adopted or rejected without having to spend energy and political resources defending the choices that were made. The range of options was not only maximized, it was kept open longer and at very little political cost. The secrecy of the reports prevented opposition to task force proposals from developing until a much later stage in the policy process.

One of the principal differences among task forces is in the role played by the staff. There seems almost unanimous agreement that a competent staff is essential to a successful task force operation. The Johnson groups were variously staffed with personnel from the Executive Office of the President, from the agencies, or from outside government. The Bureau of the Budget had primary responsibility for staffing the three education task forces and the 1964 housing task forces. Starting in 1965, housing task forces operated with professional staffs responsible to the White House. This was apparently a consequence of a feeling in the White House that financial conservatism in the staff of the 1964 housing task force had been responsible for a cautious and somewhat unimaginative report. In contrast, the Budget Bureau officials who served as staff directors for the education task forces tended to prod them to be more venturesome.

The White House assigned a staff member to act as liaison to every task force. The Bureau of the Budget also maintained liaison with the task forces, primarily to advise them on related federal programs. When a Budget Bureau official served as a staff director, he automatically provided this liaison. Budget Bureau liaison men assumed an especially important role in the operations of outside task forces. This occurred in 1967 when the task forces were asked to make projections at alternative budgetary levels, thus assigning priorities to their proposals.

DEPARTMENTAL ROLES

The departments and agencies—HUD and its predecessor, the Housing and Home Finance Agency, and HEW and USOE—played an ambiguous role in the outside task forces we have examined. Since the manifest intent in using outside task forces was to bypass the departments and agencies as major instruments of policy formulation, their officials tended to distrust task forces and to minimize their significance. Thus, a HUD official disdainfully observed, "I think the task forces have done an editing job that hasn't been done elsewhere and little more." An HEW executive remarked that "The reports are kept so secret that they don't really pollinate anything."

In interagency task forces, however, the key department was likely to dominate the proceedings. One participant in the work of the 1967 housing interagency task force remarked, "Interagency task forces often reflect the lead agency's legislative program. Last fall HUD did all the staff work and [Secretary] Weaver chaired. The report would have been about the same had it simply come out of HUD without the participation of other agencies."

In education, the situation was somewhat different. Francis Keppel participated actively in the Gardner task force which largely approved his ideas. Since he was the head of the agency, no one down the line in the U.S. Office of Education could officially react negatively to the report. Some USOE officials, however, informally opposed the Elementary and Secondary Education Act and the main recommendations of the task force. A former Budget Bureau official remarked that "the old-line OE bureaucrats tried to sabotage the Gardner Task Force report." HEW and USOE officials continued, however, to sit with subsequent task forces and Commissioner Howe was the key figure in the work of the 1967 interagency task force.

The evaluation of the reports of outside task forces was a flexible and somewhat unstructured process. After being sent to the President and deposited with the Budget Bureau's Office of Legislative Reference, the reports went to the Bureau's examining divisions, other units in the Executive Office, and the agencies for comment. The role of the agencies in evaluation was minor, however, compared with that of the Bureau of the Budget and the White House staff. Significantly, the same personnel from the Bureau and the White House who served on task force staffs and sat with them as liaison men were usually involved in evaluating the reports.

This dual role of the Bureau and the White House staff meant that the reports had an Executive Office bias which was not openly acknowledged. One departmental official charged that "there is an incestuous relationship between the task forces on the one hand and the Budget Bureau and the White House on the other." (Presumably the reports are the offspring of the incestuous unions!) The Bureau was aware of the duality of its role and the problems inherent in it. "I leaned over backward to be fair, but I did feel like I was meeting myself coming back," one of its officials said. "We are involved at the Bureau with task forces as participants and as critics. We have to be a force for sifting out the most workable proposals." But the dual role was perplexing and frustrating for those outside the Executive Office who were affected by its actions.

When an outside task force report was found to be of little immediate value, the White House sometimes commissioned an interagency task force to develop legislative proposals. This apparently happened in 1967 when the Friday and Ylvisaker reports were followed by the creation of interagency task forces in education and housing, both of which had a major impact on the development of 1968 legislation in those areas.

AGENCY REACTIONS

We have already observed that the reaction of many department and agency officials to the outside task forces was substantially negative. The principal objection was to the secrecy about both the existence of the task forces and the substance of their reports. While most officials recognized the rationale for secrecy, they felt that it had consequences adverse to their interests. According to a USOE program official:

> The task force reports are textual exegeses used by those who have access to them. It is assumed in the higher echelons that the task force position is correct. The problem for us is that our performance is

evaluated in terms of the objectives set in the reports, but we do not have adequate access to them.

There is little question that the independent expert advice and suggestions obtained from the task forces proved highly valuable to the Johnson Administration. But the Administration also recognized, apparently, that there are limits to the degree to which the President can and should insulate himself from agency influence in policy formulation. The expanded use after 1964 of interagency task forces as vehicles for legislative program development represented an effort to involve the agencies more effective in Executive Office policy development, to ease agency resentment of the use of outside task forces, and to promote interagency cooperation in complex policy areas like housing and education. This form of participation enabled the Administration to secure agency support and commitment to its proposals without accepting agency domination of their substance.

IMPACT ON POLICY

It is, of course, impossible to measure directly the impact of task force reports on public policy. Our research suggests, however, that in many cases the basic concepts of President Johnson's legislative program were in large part shaped by task force recommendations. It does not appear to be mere coincidence that a sizeable number of task force proposals ultimately became part of the Administration's program and were enacted, with amendments, by Congress. Specifically, the rent supplement program authorized by Congress in 1965 was the major recommendation of the 1964 Wood task force, and the model cities program enacted in 1966 was the major proposal of the 1965 Wood task force. One of the major innovative programs authorized in the Elementary and Secondary Education Act of 1965, Title III, clearly originated with the 1964 Gardner task force. Most of the recommendations of the 1966 Early Childhood task force were adopted, although at lower funding levels than the task force recommended.

Not all task force reports, however, became part of the President's legislative program. For example, only a few recommendations of the 1967 Friday task force, principally the Networks for Knowledge and the Partnership for Learning and Earning proposals, appeared in

President Johnson's 1968 education message or the Administration's 1968 education bills. The muted impact of the Friday task force report can be explained in part by its focus on long-range rather than immediate problems and in part by the political and budgetary constraints imposed by the Vietnam war. The 1966 Ylvisaker task force also had little direct impact on policy because its recommendations were considered "too radical" and because its predecessors had been quite productive in terms of legislative accomplishments. As one White House staff member remarked:

> The Ylvisaker report had little policy impact, partly because it was the third in a row and the first two had set policy. Actually it served as a basis for the Kerner Commission report in that it changed the framework from urbanism to racism. But I admit, that observation is mostly hindsight. We didn't see the report as terribly important when it came in.

Task force reports can have a major impact on administrative actions as well as on the President's legislative program. For example, the 1966 Early Childhood task force recommended changes in federal welfare regulations which were subsequently adopted by the agencies involved. In addition, the possibility of task force recommendations becoming Administration policy is enhanced if a key task force participant becomes a member of the Administration. This, of course, occurred in the case of John Gardner, who became Secretary of HEW, and Robert Wood, who served as Undersecretary of HUD. As one agency official observed:

> Because they wrote the reports they are more likely to take up the cudgels for the task force proposals than someone else would be. What they can't get through legislation, they are likely to push for through administrative changes.

NIXON TASK FORCES

During the campaign of 1968 both Vice President Humphrey and Richard Nixon appointed a variety of expert advisory groups which apparently were intended partly as window dressing, partly as sources of policy statements and speech material, and partly as first steps toward preparation of a program in the event of victory. In late October Nixon headquarters announced plans to establish approximately 30 task forces, some of which were already in existence, to report on various aspects of domestic policy before inauguration. The personnel and the topics for these groups, and their relation to various campaign advisers, was not clarified until November 21, when Mr. Nixon announced the chairmen and assignments of 10 major task forces in the domestic area. These groups had been organized by Professor Paul W. McCracken, economist of the University of Michigan, soon to be designated Chairman of the Council of Economic Advisers. Other task forces were formed in the ensuing weeks, so that by late December there were, by different counts, 18, 19, or 21 task forces in existence and beginning to return reports to the President-elect.

Recommendations of the Nixon outside task forces were not made public, and at present it is impossible to say precisely how influential they were. The fact that most of the chairmen of the 10 task forces announced in November were subsequently appointed to high positions in the Administration is evidence that their products were taken seriously. Clearly, however, the rapid and relatively direct conversion of task force recommendations into presidential legislative proposals which occurred at the outset of the Kennedy Administration was not repeated this time. Mr. Nixon proceeded quite cautiously with Congress and by late spring had made only a few specific legislative proposals. Apparently the Nixon task force reports in most cases served as starting points for more extended studies and policy reviews conducted by presidential staff and new appointees in the relevant departments. In some areas interagency task forces were established to reexamine and carry forward the work of the earlier outside groups, thus repeating the later Johnson pattern. Presumably at least some of the work of the outside task forces was reflected in the legislative proposals that began to move to the Hill in greater numbers in the summer of 1969. It remains to be seen whether President Nixon makes use of task forces in subsequent years when he must prepare a legislative program under more normal circumstances.

APPRAISAL AND PROSPECTS

Through the employment of secret White House task forces, the Johnson Administration expanded a device pioneered by Kennedy and fashioned from it a substantially altered pattern of policy formulation and legislative program development. The extensive, though selective, use of groups of outside experts to identify problems and issues and generate new ideas and approaches, coupled with the frequent use of interagency task forces to temper the recommendations of the outsiders with pragmatic considerations, were the basic changes. Through them the Administration sought to expand the process of policy formulation beyond traditional reliance on the bureaucracy to develop most new policy proposals.

While manifesting distinctly identifiable patterns, the operations of the task forces were highly flexible and adaptable to presidential requirements. There are signs, however, that the flexibility and adaptability of the task forces, at least in housing and education, had begun to decline as their operations became increasingly systematized; they were tending to become elaborate instruments of incremental adjustment rather than catalytic agents of change. A leadership technique designed to produce policy innovation worked so well initially that overuse may have rendered it counterproductive. After all, the scope for creative policy leadership is limited by circumstantial factors, and even the most effective techniques can work successfully only part of the time.

It also appears that although the task forces were an important *procedural* innovation, the substantive innovations resulting from them may have been less than their advocates in the Johnson Administration have claimed. As a Budget Bureau official acknowledged, "they tended to pull together existing things instead of coming up with new ideas." A staff member of a housing task force agreed: "We didn't really come up with any innovations, nor were we particularly creative." The task forces which had the greatest immediate impact on legislation recommended programs which could more appropriately be characterized as political rather than intellectual breakthroughs.

To the extent that task forces were made representative through their membership, tendencies toward innovation may have been mitigated. This appears likely since consensus was the fundamental decision-making rule and final agreement tended to represent compromise rather than creative thinking. As one official in the Executive Office admitted, "It is true that with so many interests involved the result is, in some sense, the lowest common denominator."

However, the fact that task forces may not have been quite as inventive as their proponents claimed does not mean that essentially the same courses of action would have been followed without them. The ideas which they promoted may not have been entirely new, but they were not yet embodied in presidential policies, nor, in most cases, were they supported by the bureaucracy. Without outside task forces it is not likely that the supplementary educational centers and regional education laboratories or the rent supplements and model cities programs would have been pushed by the Administration and authorized by Congress at the time and in the form that they were. But more important than the immediate legislative consequences are the long-range effects of the task force process. They provide a means of maintaining a steady input of ideas new to the thought processes of high-level policy makers. The consequences of this phenomenon cannot be measured, but its significance is manifest.

On balance, we believe that the task force operation was a significant contribution to presidential policy leadership. Many Johnson Administration officials who served in the Executive Office of the President view the task force operation as a major institutional contribution. That President Nixon commissioned a series of preinaugural task forces supports this view. But whether the on-going use of task forces will survive depends on future Presidents, their personalities, their attitudes toward the necessity for policy innovation, and the extent to which they employ secrecy and surprise as elements of their leadership styles.

Future Presidents are likely to utilize those features of the task force operation which they find compatible with their own styles and appropriate to their policy objectives. An innovation-minded President would find secret outside task forces to be most useful for purposes of broad policy planning. In this context, he could employ them to identify problems, sharpen issues, and suggest alternative solutions. These task forces might develop some new ideas independently, but more importantly they would collate and bring to the attention of the

President and other top policy makers innovative and creative thinking done elsewhere. However, the President could not expect such groups regularly to develop the specifics of proposed legislation. He could more appropriately assign that function to interagency task forces working in conjunction with policy planners in the departments and agencies. The President would also find that outside task forces are more suitable than public commissions for reaching out and acquiring fresh ideas and approaches. They do not tend to be as concerned with the balancing of societal interests as commissions, by their very nature, must be. Correspondingly, however, commissions are more appropriate for developing a consensus behind a set of policy recommendations.

In determining whether to employ outside task forces, the President must assess the costs and gains associated with their use. In addition to being a promising means of assembling new ideas, outside task forces will afford him a maximum range of options which can be kept open over a long period of time with a minimum of energy required to defend his choices. The principal costs are the resentments engendered in the bureaucracy and among powerful clientele groups. These costs can be reduced somewhat by balancing interests in selecting task force members, thus rendering them more like public commissions, and by reliance on interagency task forces to review outside task force recommendations and to take the lead in developing specific legislative proposals. To the extent that the President takes these countermeasures, however, he risks losing some of the potential gains from the use of outside task forces. Unfortunately, our information is not sufficient and our measuring instruments lack the precision to permit a more definitive assessment of such costs and gains. Whatever the goals of future Presidents, it is highly likely that they will examine carefully the uses of presidential task forces and that some elements of the task force operation will become permanently institutionalized.

part three POLICY ADOPTION

A policy decision involves action by some public official or body to approve or reject an alternative for affecting a public problem. In democratic political systems, the task of making policy decisions tends to be most closely identified with the legislature, but in addition to the enactment of legislation, it may involve such actions as the issuance of an administrative rule or directive or the promulgation of a judicial decree. While many private individuals and groups may participate in or seek to influence the making of policy decisions, formal authority for them rests with public officials such as legislators or administrators. Once adopted by an official or body possessing the requisite constitutional or legal authority and following accepted procedures, a policy will probably be regarded as legitimate, that is, as proper or appropriate and as binding on those affected by it.

Decision-making can be viewed and analyzed as either a collective or an individual process. When studied as a collective process, attention is given to the ways in which majorities are built or approval is gained for the adoption of particular policy alternatives.

When decision-making is considered as an individual action, the focus is often on the criteria used by a person in making a choice among alternatives. A congressman confronted with the task of how to vote on a given issue or an administrative official in a decision-making situation may be subject to a variety of influencing factors. These may include personal values, organizational values, policy preference, partisan affiliation, constituency interests, public opinion, and deference to the judgment of others. In the selection on "Congressional Voting Decisions," Professor Reiselbach discusses a variety of factors which empirical research indicates may affect the voting decisions of congressmen. He does not indicate, however, the relative weights of these factors in shaping voting decisions.

Administrative agencies and officials are often delegated or permitted to exercise considerable decision-making authority. Administrative decision-making, as Wade's treatment of General Hershey and selective service policy suggests, is often less visible and open to public scrutiny than legislative decision-making. Moreover, Wade indicates some of the factors which may operate to cause an official to make an arbitrary and improper policy decision, as Hershey did on the induction of draft protestors.

The enactment of major legislation by Congress requires the formation of a numerical majority, or what is more accurate, a series of numerical majorities because of the dispersion of power between the two houses, among standing committees and subcommittees, and so on. These majorities, given the lack of strong disciplined political parties, are most commonly created by negotiation, bargaining, and compromise. The selections by Marmor on the enactment of medicare legislation in 1965 and by Barton on the passage of agricultural price support legislation by the House of Representatives in 1973 provide ample illustration of the bargaining and majority-building processes in Congress. The Marmor article further demonstrates a point made in the introduction to the preceding part, namely, that the formulation and adoption processes often in practice become blended. Although Marmor argues that the outcome of the 1964 elections guaranteed the adoption of medical care for the aged legislation, this should not be taken to mean that there were no limitations on what could be gotten through Congress, and particularly the House. Much negotiation and bargaining went into the development of the legislation finally enacted.

In all, the material in this part should provide the reader with insight into policy decision-making as both an individual and a collective process.

7. Congressional Voting Decisions

Leroy N. Rieselbach

When debate ends, the main point of congressional decision, the calling of the roll, is reached. In the House of Representatives, this means that the Committee of the Whole—in which the lower chamber carries on most of its deliberations, including preliminary action on amendments, under relaxed quorum requirements—rises and the House reverts to

Reprinted from Leroy N. Rieselbach, *Congressional Politics* (New York: McGraw-Hill, 1973), pp. 267–79. Copyright © 1973 by the McGraw-Hill Book Company and used with their permission.

its regular quorum rule.[1] Here, on the floor, the ultimate policy choice is made; here the bill is accepted or rejected; here the nature of the system's output is specified. Put another way, when the roll is called, the coalitions for and against the bill are identified. While it is often the case that the outcome is known in advance, only when the members of Congress state their "ayes" and "nays" do their positions become a matter of public record. Roll calls do not, however, necessarily represent the personal convictions of the legislators. Votes may reflect party or constituency appeals rather than individual lawmakers' assessment of the issues at hand; the congressman may feel the need to support a position which his own judgment may suggest is incorrect because he wants to support his party or because he fears electoral reprisals if he fails to back the view popular in his constituency.[2]

Interpersonal relationships among legislators influence vote decisions. The norms of each chamber, especially those of apprenticeship, specialization, and reciprocity, enhance the stature of the experts of the standing committees. These men frequently decide early in the policy-making process and others, the nonspecialists, look to them, especially if they share the same party affiliation, for advice, much of which may be accepted uncritically. One senator reports "I try . . . to read the report on a bill before voting on it, but I must admit that I have voted on many hundreds of bills solely on the basis of what other senators told me about them." Other legislators may look to their personal staffs or to the committee staff for cues about how to vote.

---

[1]Voting in the Committee of the Whole is by voice, standing, and teller votes, which often go unrecorded. In 1970 the Reorganization Act permitted twenty House members to demand a recorded teller vote. While relatively noncontroversial items may be shouted through by voice vote, once the House is in regular session rather than sitting as the Committee of the Whole, virtually all major issues are resolved by roll call voting.

[2]In the unsuccessful 1970 battle to confirm the nomination of Judge G. Harrold Carswell to the Supreme Court, a number of Southern Senators seem to have supported the nominee despite reservations about him because they needed to support a candidate from their region. Reported *Time* magazine: "Even many Southerners felt insulted that Nixon had chosen Carswell to represent them. 'I'm voting for the guy,' said one Southern Democratic Senator, 'but it's great to see the Republicans stewing in their own juice. They made this bed.' " Quoted in Bloomington (Ind.) *Sunday Herald-Times*, Apr. 19, 1970, p. 11.

Some will promise to vote one way if their ballots will be decisive but will go their own way if the contest is already settled.[3] These sorts of decisions reflect the division of labor in Congress: the experts in one area give advice on that topic and must get counsel on most, if not all, other matters.

INDIVIDUAL VOTES

Nonetheless, examination of the factors which seem related to the vote choices of individual members of Congress may achieve considerable insight into congressional alignments. On most, but not all, issues party affiliation remains "more influential than other pressures on Congress." Legislators' votes also may reflect other factors—their own social backgrounds (e.g., their training and experiences prior to service in the legislature), their political situations within the legislative system, and the kinds of constituencies they represent. Which elements within each of these categories are most important will vary from issue to issue and from one time period to another. Such shifting patterns of coalition formation are exactly what we would expect to find in a representative assembly characterized by multiple centers of influence and decision making through negotiation and compromise.

The political party provides a central point of reference for many members. Other things being equal (which they seldom are), lawmakers prefer to vote with their parties, especially if their side occupies the White House. We have also pointed out, however, that congressional norms condone defection when constituency interests or individual conscience dictate voting against the party position. Thus, partisanship remains an important but not inviolable basis for intralegislative conflict; on many questions each of the contending coalitions has its base in one of the two parties and each seeks to hold its

---

[3]In the Carswell fight, Sen. Winston Prouty (R., Vt.) appears to have promised the Republican leadership to vote for confirmation if his vote was needed; since the battle was lost by the time his name was called, he opposed the nominee. Ripley (1967, p. 74) reports that the Speaker of the House can often count on as many as ten of the "pocket votes" if he needs them.

partisans in line while adding enough defectors from the most vulnerable members of the opposition to offset any losses from its own ranks which may nonetheless occur.

Table 1 indicates the limited nature of party competition and loyalty in recent years. Column 2 suggests that between one-third and one-half of the roll calls are party votes on which majorities of the two parties oppose one another; on the remaining votes—at least one-half and sometimes as many as two-thirds—the divisions are along other than party lines.[4] Note that the two most recent Congresses showed a diminution of partisan conflict; by 1967 the relatively high interparty polarization that marked the surge of new social legislation passed during the Kennedy-Johnson administration of the mid-1960s had receded substantially. And in the Ninety-first Congress, where a Republican President confronted a Congress controlled by the Democrats, party lines were blurred still further. Where the parties did oppose one another, each could count on the loyalty of about two out of three of its members. In the Ninety-first Congress, for instance, the average senator voted with the majority of his party on about six of every ten roll calls.[5] These data reveal the incomplete character of party unity; lawmakers vote with their parties more often than not, but defection is common and widespread.

The minority party, lacking control of the Presidency, has been found to be less cohesive than the majority (or President's) party. As previously discussed, the Chief Executive frequently intervenes in the

---

[4]Using a more restrictive definition of a party vote—when 90 percent of one party votes against 90 percent of the other—Turner (1951, p. 24) found that only 17.1 percent of all rolls during the 1921–1948 era could be so classified. Schneier's (1970) revision of Turner reveals a reduction in the number of party votes, defined by Turner's restrictive criterion, in recent years. The percentage of roll calls on which 90 percent of one party opposed a similar proportion of the other varied from 8.0 (1959) to 1.3 (1966). Similarly Shannon's (1968) study of the Eighty-sixth and Eighty-seventh Congresses found that 5.1 percent of the roll calls were strict party-line votes.

[5]These averages mask wide individual variations. In the Ninety-first Congress, for example, Sen. William Proxmire (D., Wis.) and two Republicans—Sens. Roman Hruska (Neb.) and Clifford Hansen (Wyo.)—led their respective parties, voting *with* the majority of their colleagues 86 and 89 percent of the time, respectively, on party votes. On the other hand, Sens. Spessard Holland (D., Fla.) and Clifford Case (R., N.J.) voted *against* majorities of their own parties on 63 and 69 percent, respectively, of the party roll calls. See *Congressional Quarterly Weekly Report,* Jan. 29, 1971, pp. 237–241.

Table 1 Party Voting in Congress, 1963–1970

CONGRESS	ROLL CALLS	PARTY VOTES (%)	DEMOCRATIC UNITY (%)	REPUBLICAN UNITY (%)
91st (1969–1970)				
Senate	663	35	58	59
House	443	29	59	61
90th (1967–1968)				
Senate	596	33	57	60
House	478	36	63	70
89th (1965–1966)				
Senate	483	46	60	65
House	394	47	67	69
88th (1963–1964)				
Senate	534	41	64	66
House	232	52	71	72

NOTE: Party votes refers to the percentage of all chamber roll calls on which a majority of voting Democrats opposed a majority of voting Republicans. Party unity indicates the percentage of the time the average member voted with the majority of his party on party votes.

SOURCE: *Congressional Quarterly Weekly Reports,* Jan. 29, 1971, pp. 237–241; December 29, 1967, pp. 2662-2666; Oct. 30, 1964, pp. 2588-2592.

legislative process on behalf of those bills central to his program. On such occasions, as the data in Table 2 indicate, and particularly with respect to domestic policy matters, his party gives him considerably more support than does the opposition. For instance, in the Ninety-first Congress, President Nixon won support from the average Republican senator and representative 60 and 63 percent of the time, respectively; he won the votes of the typical Democrat in the Senate 42 percent of the time, while the average Democrat in the lower chamber cast 50 percent of his votes in keeping with the President's preferences. In the prior Congress, Lyndon Johnson received greater support from House and Senate Democrats than from the Republican contigents in either house.

On some issues, especially in the foreign affairs domain, party differences are less clear-cut. In the Ninety-first Congress, for example, House Democrats viewed Mr. Nixon's foreign policy proposals more favorably than did the House Republicans (Table 2). In general,

Table 2 Presidential Support, by Parties; Selected Congresses

CONGRESS	PRESIDENT	DOMESTIC POLICY		FOREIGN POLICY	
		DEMOCRATIC SUPPORT (%)	REPUBLICAN SUPPORT (%)	DEMOCRATIC SUPPORT (%)	REPUBLICAN SUPPORT (%)
91st (1969–1970)	Nixon (R)				
Senate		42	60	63	74
House		50	63	59	54
90th (1967–1968)	Johnson (D)				
Senate		53	47	59	57
House		67	49	66	44
87th (1961–1962)	Kennedy (D)				
Senate		63	36	68	45
House		73	37	76	45
86th (1959–1960)	Eisenhower (R)				
Senate		34	69	55	69
House		38	66	60	60

NOTE: The figures in the table refer to the average percentage of roll call votes by members of each party cast in agreement with the stated position of the President on each type of issue.

SOURCE: *Congressional Quarterly Weekly Report*, Jan. 29, 1971, pp. 218–231; Oct. 26, 1962, pp. 2035–2046; *Congressional Quarterly Almanac*, vol 16 (1960), pp. 106–116, and vol. 15 (1959), pp. 108–124.

however, issues on which the administration stakes its prestige; matters of economic policy, including measures dealing with the tax structure, welfare programs, and the regulation of industry; and votes on organizational and procedural matters internal to the legislative system tend to array the two parties against one another. Other issues which tend to evoke controversy along partisan lines include reciprocal trade, conservation, and farm policies. Froman has suggested one reason for such differences: the two parties have their bases in different types of constituencies. Democrats in Congress tend to represent districts with fewer owner-occupied dwelling units (i.e., more homes occupied by renters), greater concentrations of urban population, more nonwhite residents, and greater population density. These kinds of districts have "liberal" populations which tend to elect "liberal" Democrats. In the same vein, those representatives chosen in atypical districts (i.e., Democrats from Republican-type areas) are most likely to bolt their party and vote with the opposition.[6]

There may, moreover, be differences between the two parties which account for greater loyalty among Democrats. More than their Republican counterparts, the Democrats seem to display a greater flexibility, a greater willingness to accommodate other interests within their own party. Specifically, Democrats whose constituencies seem to demand particular policies can count on the voting support of their colleagues whose districts have no real stake in the decision. Republicans, by contrast, who feel the need for specific programs, are often left to stand alone by their "disinterested" fellow partisans, who seem to prefer to vote a conservative, economizing position rather than to support a colleague. That is, mutual support, perhaps a concomitant of the specialization and reciprocity norms, lead Democrats to back one another's proposals while Republicans are more prone to divide along ideological lines rather than to "logroll" within the party ranks.

---

[6]A number of examples come immediately to mind: the large number of Southern Democrats representing rural, low-density areas who vote frequently with the conservative Republicans; and Republican senators—for instance, Javits (N.Y.) and Case (N.J.) —whose states are urban, industrial, and densely populated, and whose voting records resemble those of Northern Democrats more closely than the records of many of their fellow Republicans. For comparable data on the House, see Shannon, 1968, chap. 7.

The time dimension also affects the impact of party on congressional voting. As time passes, the partisan perspective on particular issues may alter; events occur which may cast particular policies in a new light. The example of the shift in Republican votes to enact civil rights legislation has already been cited. In foreign affairs, once a Republican occupied the White House, GOP support for the foreign aid program dramatically increased while Democratic backing for the aid principle declined sharply. In the same vein, changes in the social, economic, and political climate in the Southern United States eroded the votes of Democrats from that region for the lowering of tariffs through reciprocal trade agreements. Some issues, such as social security, become noncontroversial as the years go by and the party which initially opposed them comes to support them with a fervor almost equal to that of the original proponents of the idea.[7]

In short, while party seems to influence the votes of individual congressmen to a greater extent than other factors, it is by no means always decisive. Many other features of the legislative system compete with party for lawmakers' attention; in such role-conflict situations, party loyalty wins out often but not inevitably. We may predict, for instance, that the stronger the attachment to party, that is, the more powerful the orientation toward playing a loyalist role, the greater the likelihood that a member of Congress will vote the party line. Similarly, the more a legislator feels the need to act on behalf of "the people" (as a tribune or inventor) the less need he will feel to back his party when party and conviction conflict; conversely, ritualists and brokers, once the formalities have been observed, should be more apt to align themselves with their partisan leaders and experts.

When members defect from party position, as they often do, their votes may reflect a variety of contending forces. For one thing, their personal experiences, their political socialization, may leave them

---

[7]The disavowal of presidential candidate Barry Goldwater's proposals to make social security voluntary and to sell the Tennessee Valley Authority to private enterprise by numerous Republicans testifies to such a change in partisan outlook. Goldwater's views, which would have struck a responsive chord in the 1940s, were no longer acceptable in the mid-1960s.

with values and beliefs which lead them to vote a more conservative (or liberal) position than their fellow partisans. The data in Table 3 indicate that where one is born and raised seems to have a lasting impact on legislative voting. Those whose homes were in small-town, rural America seem to have developed a more parochial, provincial outlook on issues of public policy; at least, they tend to vote a more conservative position than their legislative colleagues from larger, metropolitan areas. Note also that place of birth makes a difference no matter what region the lawmaker represents, regardless of his party affiliation, and quite apart from whether he is chosen in a rural or urban congressional district.

Other studies reveal a similar effect for additional social-background attributes. Andrain found younger senators; those with occupational experience in law, journalism, and teaching; and those of Catholic, Episcopalian, and Presbyterian religious affiliation more favorable toward civil rights legislation than senators with contrasting personal attributes. In foreign affairs, Catholics appear more inclined to vote for foreign aid bills than non-Catholics and representatives with business backgrounds are more supportive of the aid program than those with other occupational experience. What a man was before he became a politician, thus, may influence how he acts once in elective office.

In addition, the legislator's position in Congress may influence his vote decision. Committee service, and the consequent exposure to committee norms, may inculcate specific values which find expression when the roll is called. Thus, the Senate Foreign Relations Committee members tend to back internationalist foreign policy proposals and programs. In the House, Foreign Affairs committeemen favor foreign aid legislation to a greater degree than do nonmembers; Armed Services panelists take a dimmer view of reciprocal trade than do those serving on other committees. Identification with, or a strong, positive orientation toward, the committee to which he is assigned may thus lead the lawmaker to espouse a position characteristic of many members of the committee; integrated committees may give cues which carry weight with their members.

More difficult to assess is the effect of a second political factor, the nature of electoral competition with the congressman's state or district. By one view, a hard-fought contest, where the winner gains his

Table 3 Size of Birthplace, Constituency Type, and Support for the Conservative Coalition

SIZE OF BIRTHPLACE	NORTHERN DEMOCRATS		SOUTHERN DEMOCRATS		REPUBLICANS	
	METRO-POLITAN	NONMETRO-POLITAN	METRO-POLITAN	NONMETRO-POLITAN	METRO-POLITAN	NONMETRO-POLITAN
Rural, small town (under 10,000)	14.7 (23)	24.4 (32)	60.0 (23)	67.3 (46)	69.8 (28)	73.4 (73)
Urban (10,000 and over)	7.6 (62)	9.8 (24)	47.9 (15)	53.1 (14)	56.6 (25)	68.7 (59)

NOTE: The cell entry is the mean percentage of support for the conservative coalition for each category of congressman. The number of cases is given in parenthesis.

SOURCE: Rieselbach, 1970.

victory with less than 55 percent of the vote,[8] serves to depress the representative's spirit of adventure. That is, when his margin is narrow, the winner is less likely to take an extreme position and more likely to be cautious, for if he is indiscreet, alienation of even a small group from his electoral coalition may cost him his seat. Conversely, this line of reasoning predicts that those from safe seats, where electoral competition seldom if ever poses a severe threat, will feel freer to disregard constituents' or party wishes and to vote as they see fit without fear of reprisals at the polls. Some data support these contentions: MacRae found that Republicans from marginal areas were more sensitive to constituency characteristics than those from safe districts, that is, their votes tended to reflect the demographic attributes of the electorate. No such relationship existed for Democrats. Froman found that those from competitive seats and those whose districts were atypical of their parties were more likely to eschew extreme voting positions than their party colleagues from safe, typical districts.

Huntington has produced contrary evidence. He argues that the closer the election contest, the greater the tendency for the candidates to take dissimilar stands, as each seeks to mobilize his own partisans rather than to entice the "middle-of-the-road" voters. This leads Democrats to assume a "liberal" stance while Republicans adopt a "conservative" line. Miller produced evidence in support of this view: congressmen representing safe districts are more sensitive to constituent opinion than those from more competitive areas. Thus, while it is uncertain what the precise effect of a legislator's electoral situation is on his voting behavior, there is support for the notion that constituency conditions may induce caution and defection from extreme party positions. Moreover, we would predict that such tendencies would be more pronounced among those congressmen who assume a district-oriented focus of representation and those who adopt a dele-

---

[8]Conventionally, seats where the winner amasses more than 60 percent of the vote are classified as "safe"; those where he wins with from 55 to 60 percent as "intermediate"; and those where his victory is secured with less than 55 percent as "marginal" or "competitive." For a suggestion that such a classificatory scheme oversimplifies reality, that what is "safe" in one state or for one office may, in fact, be "competitive" in another state or for a different office, see Schlesinger (1960).

gate orientation toward their constituents. Nationally oriented law-makers and trustees should be more likely to vote against constituent interests and for party, even if their electoral situations are marginal.

This discussion suggests a third category of relevant forces for interpreting congressional voting. The representative's response when the clerk calls the roll may reflect the nature of his district as well as his orientation toward the district's residents. Substantial quantities of research reveal relationships between constituency characteristics and congressional roll call behavior. Such relationships are most visible in situations or on issues when party pulls are reduced or nonexistent; in such circumstances the representative falls back on his knowledge of the "folks back home" as a guide in casting his vote. In other instances, there will be direct role conflict between the wishes of the party leaders and the legislator's perception of constituent interests; here he may choose to support the latter at the expense of the former.

Among the most visible of these constituency factors is region: there are clear differences within each party among the members from particular sections of the nation. On the Democratic side of the aisle, in both the House and the Senate, the differences between Northerners and Southerners are well known. Northern Democrats tend to be more liberal than their colleagues from below the Mason-Dixon line on numerous issues. Civil rights is, of course, primary among these topics, but similar regional differences have been found on social-welfare topics, agricultural policy, and foreign policy issues, including foreign trade and foreign aid.[9] On each of these items, the Southerners hewed to a more conservative line, resisting efforts to enlarge the scope of federal government activity and to increase the size of federal expenditures in these areas.

The Republicans have been split along regional lines as well, though the cleavage has been much less clear-cut than the division among the Democrats. Most often, the intra-Republican conflict has

---

[9]In gross terms, *Congressional Quarterly* reports that over the past dozen years the percentage of roll call votes in Congress which saw a majority of voting Southern Democrats in opposition to a majority of voting Northern Democrats varied from 40 (1960) to 21 (1962). The 1960–1970 average was 31 percent. See *Congressional Quarterly Weekly Report,* Jan. 29, 1971, p. 254.

seen Eastern senators and representatives break away from the larger, dominant Midwestern wing of the party to vote a more liberal line on civil rights and to support a more internationalist foreign policy. This coastal-interior split is less clearly seen because during most of the contemporary era, the Republicans have been the minority party and, as such, less cohesive than the majority; this greater fluidity of voting alignment may obscure the operation of regional forces.

Other constituency factors seem important as well. The urban-rural division is also reflected in roll call voting. Urban congressmen have been found to differ from the representatives of rural areas on a number of measures including prohibition, farm programs, civil rights, foreign aid, foreign trade, and immigration. Urban legislators seem more willing in all these domains to see the government become actively involved in dealing with social and economic issues, that is, they take a more liberal, in the conventional sense of that term, view of what policy decisions are required. Similarly, lawmakers from high socioeconomic status districts and those whose constituents are well educated have been discovered to be supportive of foreign aid bills; so have the representatives of constituencies containing substantial proportions of German, Irish, and other immigrant stock. In short, especially when party pressure is reduced, congressmen's votes reflect the demographic features—the region, economic and educational character, urban or rural nature, ethnic composition, and the like—of their constituencies.

There are numerous reasons why a member of Congress can be expected to pay heed to his perceptions—however accurate or inaccurate they may be—of his district, its inhabitants, and their desires. For one thing, if his goal is to remain in office—and reelection is a paramount consideration for a vast majority of national legislators—then he must seek to retain the support of his constituents. Next, he may share the basic outlook of the district electorate; he may be a farmer elected in an agricultural area or a union leader chosen in a blue-collar, working-class district, and as such he may "know" without direct communication from the district what its inhabitants desire. Finally, the lawmaker may adopt a district-oriented focus, a trustee style, or both as his guiding premises. To the extent that any or all of these considerations operate, it is not surprising that on some occasions the congressman will "vote his district" rather than his party or his committee.

Lastly, we may note that an individual legislator's personality, ideology, or even his idiosyncracies may influence his response when the roll is called. Admittedly, information on such matters is hard to obtain; the standard data sources on social-background or constituency attributes do not help much with regard to such personal factors. Yet there is fragmentary evidence on the point. Two studies compared the voting records of holdover legislators (incumbents) in successive Congresses with the performances of new men—of the same party and representing the same districts—in the same Congresses and found the former to be more consistent than the latter. Put another way, when a new man comes to Congress—even though he is of the same party and from the same constituency as his predecessor—his votes will differ from those of the man whom he has succeeded to an extent not seen in the votes of the man who wins reelection. It appears, then, that the new man, though his objective circumstances resemble markedly those of the previous incumbent, brings to Congress something of himself—personal characteristics, beliefs, values—quite apart from party and constituency features, which influences his response to the issues on which he must vote.

The individual voting choice, thus, appears as a complex act, influenced by the congressman's party affiliation, his prelegislative experiences, his political situation of the moment, the nature of the constituency he represents, and his own particular set of personal attributes. Out of this welter of often conflicting forces he must make his choices; he will decide—perhaps unconsciously, perhaps with full awareness—on an orientation toward his party, his committee, his district, his politics, his conscience; and from these orientations and the resolution of conflicts among them will emerge his vote decision. Where these forces largely push in the same direction—e.g., where party, committee, and constituency all seem to favor the same course of action—his choice will be easy; where there are sharp differences among those to whom he pays heed, the legislator's choice will be difficult, his behavior less predictable, and his vote often at odds with the desires of his party leaders, committee colleagues, or constituency interests.

Much of this complexity can be seen in Table 3 which relates party, background characteristics (place of birth), and constituency features (region and metropolitanism) to representatives' support for the Southern Democratic-Republican conservative coalition. Each of these factors contributes to the voting records. Party contributes most —the differences across the rows of the table between Northern Democrats, on one hand, and the Southern Democrats and the Republicans, on the other, are the largest—but the other elements are important as well. Support for the coalition is minimized among Northern Democrats born in larger cities and representing metropolitan areas and is maximized among Southern Democrats and Republican representatives born in small towns and elected in nonmetropolitan districts. Thus, while party loyalty—the loyalist orientation—is strong, conflicting pulls from social-background experiences and constituency produce deviations from strict adherence to the party line. We should also remember that the interplay of these forces varies from issue to issue with the passage of time; party cleavages dominate some issues at some periods of time, while on other matters or in other eras, lines of division in Congress reflect constituency or other forces.

VOTING PATTERNS

The discussion to this point has focused on the forces moving individual lawmakers to vote with or against their political parties, to act as party loyalists or as mavericks. Much effort has gone into the attempt to specify these forces, but this should not be permitted to obscure the fact that legislative outcomes reflect the sum total of individual votes; policy decisions are made by majorities constructed from the votes of single representatives. Thus, a few words are in order about the patterns which these individual votes form. We have already noted possible lines of cleavage other than party which may characterize congressional conflict. One of these is the regional factor. On some issues like foreign aid, at least during the 1950s and early 1960s, clear-cut sectional alignments are visible. Coastal lawmakers of both parties were, in this era, the chief proponents of the aid program; interior legislators were notable among the opponents of the aid principle. Moreover, civil rights divisions commonly fall along a North-South line.

Similarly, we have pointed out the possibility that when party is divided or inactive, votes may reflect an urban-rural division, or, more precisely, may indicate conflict between metropolitan and less densely settled areas. Turner, for instance, has found that while the city-farm dimension is less powerful than party or regional pressures as an explanation of congressional voting, nonetheless such a cleavage did appear on roughly one-fifth of all the roll calls examined, and was independent of other forces impinging on the lawmakers from city and country. Similarly, MacRae discovered that urban representatives were, in the Eighty-first Congress, more liberal on welfare legislation than their colleagues from more rural parts of the country. This is not surprising given the tendency of such measures to benefit big-city populations. Finally, urban lawmakers have, within both parties, been more supportive of foreign aid and reciprocal trade bills than have farm-district congressmen.

The most well noted and probably most frequent nonpartisan cleavage in Congress is the so-called conservative coalition which unites Southern Democrats and Republicans in opposition to the liberal proposals most effectively backed in the national legislature by Northern, most often Democratic, interests. Table 4 presents a picture of the coalition's strength. The coalition, it can be seen, appears on anywhere from one-tenth to nearly 30 percent of the roll calls in a given Congress; it comes into existence somewhat more often in the Senate than in the House, perhaps because it is sustained by the "inner club" in the upper chamber. When the Southern Democratic-Republican alignment occurs, it has a mixed but generally strong record of success: its victories occurred, in the past decade, on about six of every ten roll calls on which the alliance was consummated. Thus, when party loyalty breaks down it is frequently because the Southern Democrats choose to make common cause with the Republicans rather than with their Northern brethren.

The coalition does not appear randomly, nor are its victories spread evenly across the variety of issues which Congress considers. Rather the conservative alliance emerges more on some matters than on others. In 1969, for example, the coalition was activated most

Table 4 The Conservative Coalition in Congress, 1963–1970

	COALITION ROLL CALLS	COALITION VICTORIES (%)	SOUTHERN DEMOCRATIC SUPPORT (%)	REPUBLICAN SUPPORT (%)	NORTHERN DEMOCRATIC SUPPORT (%)
91st (1969–1970)					
Senate	27	65	62	60	18
House	20	71	66	65	17
90th (1967–1968)					
Senate	21	68	62	61	21
House	22	67	65	70	13
89th (1965–1966)					
Senate	27	46	62	60	19
House	22	28	65	74	13
88th (1963–1964)					
Senate	18	46	68	63	17
House	12	67	64	69	12

NOTE: Coalition roll calls refer to the percentage of all roll call votes on which a majority of voting Southern Democrats and a majority of voting Republicans combine to oppose the voting majority of Northern Democrats. Coalition victories are the percent of coalition roll calls on which the coalition wins. The support figures are the percent of the time the average legislator in each party-regional category votes with the coalition on coalition roll calls.

SOURCE: *Congressional Quarterly Weekly Reports*, Jan. 29, 1971, pp. 242–247; Nov. 1, 1968, pp. 2983–2990; Dec. 29, 1967, pp. 2649–2661; and Nov. 27, 1964, pp. 2741–2750.

frequently in the Senate on taxation and spending matters, where it won twenty of twenty-seven contests including a minimizing of the reduction of the oil-depletion allowance granted to the oil industry.[10] The coalition was often visible on foreign affairs and defense matters; the most notable of its ten victories (in fifteen contests) was its successful struggle to carry President Nixon's antiballistic missile program through the Senate. As might be expected, the coalition is also active in the civil rights field; in 1969, it won all four of the Senate battles which it waged. Thus, in recent years, the conservative coalition has achieved considerable results in pushing a "hard line" in foreign relations and in imposing restrictions on the scope of federal government activities in the areas of social welfare and civil rights.

Despite its accomplishments, however, the coalition is no more cohesive than the political parties. As the right-hand columns of Table 4 indicate, the average Republican and Southern Democrat supports the coalition on about two-thirds of the coalition roll calls; the average Northern Democrat casts one vote in five with the conservative alliance. These figures, as might be expected, mask wide differences among individual lawmakers. For example, in the Ninety-first Congress such Southern Democratic senators as Fred Harris (Okla.), Ralph Yarborough (Tex.), Jennings Randolph (W.Va.), and J. William Fulbright (Ark.) opposed the coalition on more than half of the coalition votes; some Republicans—notably Clifford Case (N.J.), Jacob Javits (N.Y.), Richard Schweiker (Pa.), and Edward Brooke (Mass.)—cast more than 60 percent of their votes in opposition to the coalition. Conversely, some Northern Democrats—such as Alan Bible (Nev.), Clinton Anderson (N. Mex.), and Gale McGee (Wyo.)— support the coalition more than twice as frequently as the average for their Northern colleagues. Coalition lines, thus, are no more solid than those of the parties; as an informal alliance, it has even fewer means than the parties to ensure the backing of its "members." The conservative coalition remains, nonetheless, the most potent of the nonpartisan alignments in Congress.

---

[10]The data for 1969 are from *Congressional Quarterly Weekly Report,* Jan. 16, 1970, pp. 158–165. They do not differ appreciably from data for earlier years available in appropriate numbers of the *Congressional Quarterly.*

In general, when lines of division do not coincide with partisan cleavages, there appears a configuration which approximates a "liberal-conservative" split. The liberal cause draws its heaviest support from Northern Democrats, buttressed by some Republicans from the urban areas, particularly the Eastern metropolitan centers in New York, New Jersey, and Pennsylvania. Southerners of both parties, many representing rural districts, together with the bulk of the Republicans vote most often for conservative policy alternatives. Put in other terms, it appears, by inference at least, that Eastern, urban Republicans on the one hand, and Southern rural Democrats on the other, are the legislators most apt to be impelled—by ideology or constituency pressures—to defect from their respective parties and to vote with the opposition. When such forces operate, the conservative coalition replaces the party alignment as the organizing feature of congressional roll-call voting. There remain, of course, a substantial number of votes so lacking in controversy that they are essentially bipartisan in character.[11] Even here, those who are in the minority may be moved by their orientations toward lawmaking (tribune or inventor) or constituency (district focus or trustee style) to bolt the more commonly held position.

---

[11]Roughly two-thirds of all roll calls—68 percent in the Ninety-first Congress, 63 percent in the Ninetieth Congress, and 54 percent in the Eighty-ninth Congress—are bipartisan in character, according to the *Congressional Quarterly* definition. Roll calls are so classified when voting majorities of the two parties adopt the same position. See *Congressional Quarterly Weekly Report,* Jan. 29, 1971, pp. 248–252; and Dec. 29, 1967, pp. 2643–2647.

8. Coalition-Building in the United States House of Representatives: Agricultural Legislation in 1973

Weldon V. Barton

INTRODUCTION

In a late evening session of July 19, 1973, after five days of floor debate on the farm bill, the Committee of the Whole House "rose" and Speaker Carl Albert (D., Okla.) took the chair. Although normally at this point in the legislative process only pro forma votes remain before clearance of the bill by the House of

Paper delivered at the 1974 Annual Meeting of the American Political Science Association, Palmer House, Chicago, Illinois, August 29-September 2, 1974. Reprinted, with deletions, by permission of the author.

Representatives, in this case the House plunged back into the intractable, basic issues that had marked the debate of the previous days.

"Mr. Speaker," Louisiana Congressman Joe Waggonner's voice rose above the incessant buzzing of voices within the House chamber,

> there is more confusion than we can solve here in the next moment or two, but the committee chairman handling the bill, and the minority leader, and both sides are under the impression that on the separate vote cotton is still out of the bill. We need a decision as to whether or not cotton is in the bill, Mr. Speaker.
>
> THE SPEAKER. Of course, the parliamentary situation is that the amendment on which the first vote was taken was to strike the cotton section from the bill. That amendment was rejected.

Agriculture Committee Chairman Robert Poage (D., Tex.) and Minority Leader Gerald Ford (R., Mich.) were not alone in their confusion. The *Congressional Quarterly Weekly Report* captioned its story on the farm bill (which finally passed 226–182 later that night) "In Spite of Itself, the House Passes a Farm Bill," and Representative John Anderson (R., Ill.), chairman of the House Republican Conference, called it the wildest night he had seen on the House floor during his thirteen years in Washington.

The present paper focuses upon House consideration of the Agriculture and Consumer Protection Act of 1973, and is designed to serve essentially two purposes: (1) to improve our understanding of the coalition-building process that surrounded House action on the farm bill, and in particular to shed light upon the persistence (stability) of the structure of coalition behavior through which the bill passed the House, and (2) to contribute to existing theoretical knowledge of coalition behavior in the policy-making process.

Because theorizing about coalitions remains quite tentative, this paper does not impose any narrow analytical framework upon the data. Instead, the author has attempted throughout the paper to keep the bits and pieces of existing theory constantly in mind, and wherever appropriate to apply and extend such fragments of theory.

CONTEXT OF COALITION-BUILDING ON FARM LEGISLATION

Since the mid-1960's, the federal farm price support programs for the three most significant commodities in terms of size of budgetary outlays (feed grains, wheat, and cotton) have been enacted in a single "package" bill incorporating all three commodities. As Table 1 shows, each commodity sector has had a significant *individual* stake (measured in federal payments) in decisions to coalesce for their mutual political advantage.

A "packaged" extension of the feed grains, wheat, and cotton programs was enacted in 1965, 1970, and 1973; the 1973 Act has a four-year duration, through 1977. The fact that there has been a "package" ("coalition") farm bill each time indicates that, on balance, the respective commodity sectors perceived that they had more to gain than to lose from intra-agriculture (intercommodity) coalition. Since production of the three commodities tends to be geographically sectionalized (feed grains—middle "corn belt" states; wheat—Great Plains and Pacific Northwest; cotton—South and Southwest), a "package" bill can elicit votes from rural House districts across the nation.

Table 1 Government Payments to Farmers Under Feed Grains, Wheat, and Upland Cotton Programs for Selected Crop Years (In millions of dollars)

PROGRAM	1965	1969	1970	1972
Feed Grains	$1,391	$1,643	$1,510	$1,865
Wheat	525	858	891	859
Upland Cotton	773*	828	918	809
Total	2,689	3,329	3,319	3,533

* Data are for 1966, since the 1965 cotton program is not comparable to subsequent years.

SOURCES: Charles Schultze *et al., Setting National Priorities; the 1972 Budget* (Wash.: Brookings Institution, 1971), p. 300; U.S. Department of Agriculture, *ASCS Commodity Fact Sheets,* April, 1974 (wheat and feed grains) and November, 1974 (upland cotton).

However, a majority (winning) coalition in the House of Representatives requires more than the total votes from predominantly rural districts, and (as Table 2 shows) the proportion of required urban and suburban votes has increased significantly each time the farm bill has been renewed. Rural districts comprised 83 percent of an absolute majority in the House in 1966; the percentage dropped to 71 by 1969, and to 60 by 1973.

In view of the fact that an increasing number of nonrural votes is essential for a majority coalition on agricultural policy, and because certain farm commodity sectors are more ideologically (or otherwise) compatible with labor and other potential urban-suburban allies, the feed grains-wheat-cotton alliance (or any other combination of commodity sectors) cannot be taken as a "given" of agricultural policy coalitions. Instead, coalition-building must be a dynamic process that slices through the farm commodity sectors. The agricultural policy leadership must make strategic decisions on whether, overall, more favorable votes would be gained than lost by attempting to commit any specific group (whether a farm commodity group or a nonfarm group) to the agricultural policy coalition.

As the percentage of rural districts in the House has declined in recent years relative to metropolitan districts, a feed grains-wheat-labor alliance has tended to emerge as the most stable cluster of interests for farm policy-making. E. W. Kelley has theorized that

Table 2 Trends in Urban-Suburban-Rural Characteristics of House Districts, 1966–1973*

CHARACTERISTIC	1966	1968	1973	CHANGE, 1966–73
Urban	106	110	102	−4
Suburban	92	104	131	+39
Rural	181	155	130	−51
Mixed	56	66	72	+16

* The criteria for categorization of the districts are: 50 percent or more of population in standard metropolitan statistical area (SMSA) central city ("urban"); 50 percent or more of population outside central city but within SMSA ("suburban"); 50 percent or more of population outside SMSA ("rural"); less than 50 percent of population in any of three above categories ("mixed").

SOURCE: *Congressional Quarterly Weekly Report,* April 6, 1974, p. 878.

"continuous coalitions always involve those of more similar preferences, or in the political world, those of more similar ideologies." Organized labor is ideologically compatible with wheat and feed grain farmers, in that the image of producers in those sectors tends to be that of the "small, family farmer," of the farmer in knee-patched overalls of the Herblock cartoons whose economic status is perceived more as a laborer than as an entrepreneur. Labor supports a panoply of legislation on which rural-farm support is desired: trade, occupational health and safety, food stamps, minimum wage, etc.

The minimum-wage legislation is particularly amenable as a basis for farm-labor alliances. Although the Fair Labor Standards Act is "permanent" in the sense that it has no absolute termination date, inflation erodes the relative purchasing power of specific minimum-wage levels so that—similar to the farm price support programs—the minimum-wage legislation must be "extended" periodically. A logical strategy for labor, therefore, has been to juxtapose the scheduling of minimum-wage and farm bills in the Congress, to promote a distributive (log rolling) approach to the two spheres of policy, and to trade votes with rural representatives in an effort to maximize the payoff to both farmers and workers.

The emergence of labor as a potential farm coalition partner has rendered the participation of cotton more marginal. Cotton tends to have a "plantation" rather than a "small, family farm" image. The concentration of federal price support payments in a smaller number of cotton farms than is the case in feed grains or wheat makes the "payment limitation" issue more salient in regard to cotton, so that the leadership of a wheat-feed grains coalition must balance the costs (in terms of lost urban votes) against the benefits (in terms of gained cotton-area votes) in deciding whether to structure a coalition to include or exclude cotton.

Furthermore, the "permanent" price support programs enacted prior to 1965, and which would become operative if the post-1965 price support statutes with fixed (limited) time durations expired, are, in the short run at least, more favorable to cotton than to feed grains or wheat. Cotton, therefore, is a less dependable coalition partner for labor and other farm commodity sectors. The threat of abandoning a coalition—and thereby forcing reversion to the "permanent," pre-1965 programs after defeat of the legislation to extend the limited-duration programs—is a more viable option for cotton than for feed grains or wheat. That option tends to be perceived by the leadership within the cotton sector as a "painful last resort," however; the leadership has been willing to suffer substantial costs to maintain cotton in the feed grains-wheat-cotton "package" of programs.

THE LABOR PERSPECTIVE: 1973

At the outset, we should acknowledge that it is somewhat superficial to draw a distinction between "organized labor" (in this case, the AFL-CIO and UAW, the two groups most active on farm legislation) and Democrats in the House. COPE, the political affiliate of the AFL-CIO, gave 83 members of the House a 100 percent rating for their votes in 1973; whereas 26 of the 28 representatives who received a zero rating from COPE in 1973 were Republicans. Based upon consistency of voting patterns, it would be as reasonable to speak in terms of a "democrat-farm," as a "labor-farm," coalition.

Theorists have argued that more is required for a coalition situation than similarity of voting, since that may result from factors other than coalition activity. The crucial distinction, it is argued, is that "a coalition's members must be in some sort of communication with one another." That is drawing a fine line of distinction, especially since a high degree of ideological compatibility among allies can in some cases reduce the necessity for explicit communication virtually to zero. Nevertheless, in 1973 at least, leaders who are identified more with organized labor than with the Democratic Party were conspicuous in scheduling minimum-wage legislation so as to facilitate alliances with farm interests, and in shaping strategies of coalition behavior.

The general strategy of labor in 1973 was to schedule legislation to increase minimum-wage levels to come onto the House floor ahead of legislation to extend the Agricultural Act of 1970 beyond its end-of-1973 expiration date, so that rural representatives could vote for minimum wages in exchange for urban (labor) votes subsequently on the farm bill.

The minimum-wage bill passed the House June 6, 1973, by a vote of 287–130. The crucial vote, on which labor had actively sought the support of representatives from rural and farm districts, was on a substitute measure offered earlier by Representative John Erlenborn (R., Ill.), which among other provisions would have established a "subminimum" wage for students and persons under eighteen years of age. (In 1972, rural votes had provided the margin of victory for a similar Erlenborn substitute to minimum-wage legislation, which prevented final congressional approval of the bill.) Immediately preceding the vote on the Erlenborn substitute, Representative Burt Talcott (R., Calif.) sought to amend the Erlenborn motion to accelerate the increases in the minimum wage for farm workers. The Talcott amendment was rejected 186–232; the Erlenborn substitute was then rejected 199–218.

Since Erlenborn was the key vote on which labor was bargaining for rural votes, one would expect those rural representatives who might be labeled as "reliable traders" to shift from an antilabor position on Talcott (where they presumably voted their constituency interest) to a prolabor position on Erlenborn. (The two motions are not completely comparable, since Talcott would have raised the minimum wage of farm workers at a faster rate than Erlenborn, but the Erlenborn "package" which included the youth subminimum probably was perceived almost as unfavorably by rural representatives in terms of their constituency interests as was Talcott.) Therefore, an analysis of the number of rural representatives who shifted from antilabor to prolabor between Talcott and Erlenborn affords a rough indicator of the predisposition of rural representatives on the minimum-wage issue.

The House Republicans shifted by only one net vote (36–148 on Talcott; 149–37 on Erlenborn), so that no significant trading by Republicans is apparent. Some 31–33 Democratic votes shifted (150–84; 50–181), however, which suggests that substantial vote trading might have occurred among the Democrats.

Table 3 indicates that fifteen Northern Democrats and sixteen Southern Democrats switched to labor's position on Erlenborn after voting against labor on Talcott. Three additional Southern Democrats who voted against labor on Talcott apparently "took a walk" on Erlenborn. Moreover, the "traders" tended to represent rural districts. Ten of the fifteen Northern Democratic "traders" were from districts with more rural than either urban or suburban constituents (four from districts with 60 percent rural; six additional from districts with a rural plurality). Among the Southern Democrats, twelve of the sixteen "traders," and one of the three who "took a walk," were from districts with more rural than either urban or suburban constituents (eight from districts with 60 percent rural; four additional from districts with a rural plurality).

Table 3 Shifts by Selected Categories of House Democrats from Antilabor to Prolabor Position on Talcott and Erlenborn Amendments

CATEGORY	PROLABOR**		ANTILABOR**	
	TALCOTT (AYE VOTE)	ERLENBORN (NAY VOTE)	TALCOTT (NAY VOTE)	ERLENBORN (AYE VOTE)
All Northern Dems.	135	150	18	3
All Southern Dems.	15	31	66	47
Northern, Rural Dems.	13	17	4	0
N = 17 (38)*	(25)	(35)	(13)	(3)
Southern, Rural Dems.	1	9	27	19
N = 30 (43)*	(2)	(14)	(39)	(26)

* Democrats are categorized as "rural" according to two criteria: (1) the numbers *outside of parentheses* are based upon a definition of "rural" identical to that in Table 2, above, except that in this case 60 percent (rather than 50 percent) of the population outside of SMSA was required for a rural classification; (2) the number *within parentheses* are based upon a definition of a rural district as one where a *plurality* of the population resides outside of SMSA—that is, where a greater percentage of the population resides outside of SMSA than resides either within the central city of a SMSA ("urban") or within a SMSA but outside the central city (suburban").

** A "prolabor" vote is a vote for Talcott and against Erlenborn; an "antilabor" vote is the converse.

SOURCE: The data on percentage of population that is urban, suburban, or rural in each congressional district is from *Congressional Districts in the 1970's* (Wash.: Congressional Quarterly Service, 1973). Individual members of the House are designated as either "urban", "suburban," "rural," or "mixed" according to the 60 percent criterion (as described below) in *Congressional Quarterly Weekly Report,* April 3, 1974, pp. 5–6. The record votes on Talcott and Erlenborn motions are in *Congressional Quarterly Weekly Report,* June 9, 1973, pp. 1468-1469.

As noted above in this paper, production of cotton tends to be concentrated in the South of the United States; whereas feed grains and wheat for cash sale (i.e., the production that qualifies for federal payments) tends to be concentrated in other sections outside the South. Consequently, the voting behavior of the Southern rural and Northern rural Democrats on Talcott and Erlenborn serves as a rough indicator of the contributions of cotton and feed grains-wheat, respectively, to labor's favorable outcome on the minimum-wage legislation in the House. Since the result on Erlenborn could have been changed by a switch of ten votes, it might be inferred that cotton and feed grains-wheat *individually* "delivered" the margin of victory to labor. Conversely, each tended to hold a veto power. This would mean that labor was somewhat indebted to both cotton and feed grains-wheat, and would be sensitive to both of them in coalition behavior on the farm bill, wherever the positions of cotton and the grain commodities diverged.

LEADERS IN THE FARM POLICY COALITION: 1973

The leadership of the farm policy coalition in 1973 performed two critical functions: (1) it developed and adapted the "grand strategy" that set the basic parameters of the coalition situation and, in effect, determined which interests were "invited" to coalesce; (2) it carried the brunt of the explicit communications that were essential for execution of coalition strategy.

The following is an enumeration of the key leaders in the 1973 farm policy coalition situation within the House, and a brief indication of the primary function of each:

Robert Poage (D., Tex.), chairman of Agriculture Committee: central decision-maker on the parameters and strategies of coalition behavior.

Thomas Foley (D., Wash.), chairman of key Agriculture Subcommittee on Livestock and Grains: communications link between Poage and organized labor; floor broker with urban representatives; floor handler of food stamps and other sensitive issues.

Robert Bergland (D., Minn.), member of Agriculture Committee: communications link between Poage and general farm groups (National Farmers Union, National Farmers Organization); floor handler of several sensitive issues.

Phillip Burton (D., Calif.), immediate past chairman of Democratic Study Group: floor broker to expedite distributive (log rolling) politics among rural and urban (especially labor) representatives.

Bernie Sisk (D., Calif.), chairman of the Agriculture Subcommittee on Cotton: floor handler for cotton interests.

Jamie Whitten (D., Miss.), Joe Waggonner (D., La.), George Mahon (D., Tex.), "back-stage" bargainers for cotton interests.

Gerald Ford (R., Mich.), Minority Floor Leader: handler of administration's position on the floor.

THE SOUTHERN DEMOCRATS: COHESION FOR COTTON

Coalition behavior on the 1973 farm bill must be understood in terms of the substantial degree of cohesion evidenced by the Southern Democrats on issues where the interest of cotton was clearly definable. . . . the Southern Democrats manifested a high degree of unity on all . . . record votes where cotton's interest was clear, both in absolute terms and relative to the other major party voting segments. The Southern Democrats delivered an average (mean) of 57 *net* votes to their side of the issue on each of these votes. . . . A switch of 23 votes on either the recommittal motion or on final passage would have changed the outcome in the House of the farm bill.

A number of factors are relevant to an explanation of the high cohesion of Southern Democrats on cotton issues, including the extraordinary number of senior Democrats in the South (Whitten, Mahon, Mills, Poage, etc.) and their persuasion over their regional colleagues on issues generally. Moreover, on the cotton issue in particular, it is relevant that the agricultural economy of the South tends still to revolve around cotton producers, textile mills, and related aspects of cotton production, which extend the influence of cotton on Southern Democrats generally.

THE HOUSE FLOOR PROCESS

We will now trace the coalition-building process in the House on the farm bill during the six-weeks period between June 6, when the House passed the minimum-wage bill, and July 19, when the farm bill was passed. We have attempted to include those events that were significantly related to coalition behavior, and to integrate explanation and interpretation into the descriptive account of events.

June 7–8. Poage asked the chairmen of Agriculture Subcommittees, to whom sections of the farm bill as approved by the Senate Agriculture and Forestry Committee had been referred, to complete their work by the following Wednesday (June 13), so that the farm bill might be brought to the House floor by July 1. Poage's strategy was to limit the time span between floor action on the minimum-wage and farm bills, in order to facilitate vote trading between the two issues.

June 14. Poage opened full Committee mark-up on the farm bill with a motion to close the mark-up sessions to the public. The motion was approved 12–11, and about 150 farmers, farm lobbyists, and reporters were cleared from the room. Poage apparently perceived that an executive session would afford more discretion within the Committee to avoid the sensitive issue of prohibiting food stamps to striking workers and in order to reduce payment benefits to farmers (budgetary outlays) sufficient to enlist Republican support of the bill on the floor.

The Committee approved a bill with price support payments 10 percent below the Senate-passed bill, and with a revised version of the "escalator" provision (which was designed to increase automatically federal payment levels to compensate for increases in farm production costs), whereby federal payments would be discounted in the amount of any productivity increases in agriculture. Furthermore, Poage was able to prevent any decision within the Committee to prohibit food stamps to striking workers.

July 9–10 (Monday-Tuesday morning). Poage met with House Speaker Albert, Minority Floor Leader Ford, and others, and agreed to a floor strategy along the following lines: Bergland would offer an amendment to limit price support payments to any one producer to $20,000, but allowing continuation of sale or lease of acreage allotments. (Allotment transfers among persons has afforded a "loophole" to cotton producers with which to minimize the adverse impact of a payment limitation.) The "traders" among the cotton representatives were expected to vote for the Bergland motion, the passage of which was designed to forestall passage of a $20,000 limitation with prohibition of allotment transfers to be offered subsequently by Paul Findley (R., Ill.). Ford agreed to urge Republicans to support Bergland and to oppose Findley.

Poage expected that the AFL-CIO either would oppose Findley provided that the Bergland motion was approved, or at least (from Poage's perspective) would remain inactive on the Findley motion. However, he apparently expected such behavior by labor to flow rather "automatically" from the rural support for the minimum wage; there was little explicit communication linkage between Poage and the AFL-CIO in specific regard to the Findley motion.

The parameters for a winning coalition, as developed under Poage's leadership at that point, went something like this: (1) protect the interests of cotton and pick up some 65–70 votes among Southern Democrats; (2) ameliorate partisan pressures on the Republicans (primarily by the concessions made in Committee, as noted above), so that some 80–90 Republicans disposed in the absence of party pressure to go along with farm bills could do so; (3) secure the votes of perhaps 70–75 Northern Democrats, who due to ideological identification with the "family farmer" tend to support farm legislation—provided that prohibition of food stamps to strikers or another such issue intertwined with the farm bill does not engender the active opposition of organized labor. The above strategy therefore might produce 215–235 favorable votes, probably enough to win in the Committee of the Whole.

Presumably outside of Poage's involvement, Sisk, in an effort to strengthen the Republican's resolve in support of cotton interests, made a side deal with Secretary of Agriculture Earl Butz that he (Sisk) would offer an amendment to strike the escalator provision from the bill in return for Administration efforts to defeat the Findley payment limitation.

July 10 (Tuesday afternoon). The House passed the Bergland payment limitation 319–89, but then also passed Findley 246–163. The coalition strategy failed at this point because only 59 Republicans followed Ford in opposition to Findley, and because only 35 Northern Democrats opposed Findley despite a plea on the floor by Burton to his "urban and suburban colleagues" to support Bergland and oppose Findley.

Why did these votes fall short? For one thing, the AFL-CIO did not, as Poage anticipated, oppose or "sit out" the Findley amendment. Instead, labor gave at least halfhearted support to Findley. Later, in a meeting with Poage, a spokesman for the AFL-CIO blamed a communication breakdown for labor's behavior on Findley.

A more basic factor behind the inability of both Ford and labor leaders to deliver a larger number of votes was the "mood" of the House on the payment limitation issue, particularly with respect to cotton. That mood might be described as "hard-line reformist," in the sense that Republicans and Northern Democrats who generally might be called "reliable traders" yielded to the climate of reform that pervaded the House on the cotton payments issue. (The House on June 15 had attached a similar Findley amendment, including a loophole-closing clause, onto the agricultural appropriations bill.) The AFL-CIO perceived that the "hard-line reformist" mood of the House would carry Findley regardless of their lobbying activities, and did not want to impair the reputation of organized labor as an influential force with Poage and other political actors with whom labor deals on a continuing basis. As Richard Neustadt has emphasized, a political actor's "professional reputation" for influence among those with whom he interacts is the crucial factor in bargaining situations. Labor perceived that its own longer-range power stakes were best served by going along with the tide in this instance.

July 11 (Wednesday). After the House also passed a Conte (R., Mass.) amendment to delete funds for cotton promotion programs, the Agriculture Committee leadership devised a motion to attempt to hold cotton in the coalition. Introduced by Foley, the amendment would have extended price support loans to "nonparticipant" producers. It was designed to allow cotton farmers to remain outside the production restrictions imposed upon "participants" in the federal payments program for cotton and still qualify for federally-guaranteed prices in the "nonrecourse loan" section of the bill. However, the reformist mood against cotton continued to prevail; the House rejected the Foley amendment 160–247.

July 12 (Thursday). To this point, the other Southern cotton leaders in the House had communicated on the House floor mostly through Poage (and Sisk), but now Jamie Whitten surfaced with a thinly veiled threat that cotton was prepared to kill the bill and revert back to the "permanent" farm legislation in 1974. Whitten, chairman of the Appropriations Subcommittee on Agriculture, informed the

House: "it is my personal opinion, that under the existing law we would be much better off and the Treasury would be much better off." He read into the *Congressional Record* a "Summary of Statutory Provisions Effective on Expiration of Agricultural Act of 1970" for members of the House to examine over the weekend. Poage then moved that the Committee of the Whole "do now rise," and pulled the farm bill off the floor until the following Monday.

It should be noted that, on Wednesday, the House had rejected the Sisk amendment to delete the payments escalator 174–239, and also defeated 186–220 a Michel (R., Ill.) amendment to phase out federal payments over three years. Neither of these votes focused predominantly upon cotton, and on both of them the House supported the farm bill as it had been reported by the Agriculture Committee. A winning majority for the Committee bill was achieved in both cases with a bloc of Southern Democratic votes as anticipated in the strategy with which Poage and the coalition leadership had approached the House floor. The important deviation from that strategy was that the Republicans contributed fewer votes to the Committee position on Sisk and Michel (48 and 35 votes, respectively), and the Northern Democrats contributed more (123 and 120). The voting pattern on these two motions manifested the kind of feed grains-wheat-labor alliance already discussed, and it suggested a revised coalition strategy that could perhaps succeed on the House floor: forego attempts to neutralize the Republican leadership, and concentrate upon maximizing favorable votes among the more "trader-oriented" Northern Democrats while attempting to hold the Southern Democrats.

July 13 (Friday morning). Such a shift in strategy would have required a more explicit coalition with organized labor, however, and instead Poage sought to rebuild a winning coalition along bipartisan lines.

Poage had always worked "at a distance" in relation to organized labor, and had preferred to make explicitly communicated deals with the Republican leadership. On Friday morning, Poage met with Speaker Albert, Minority Leader Ford, Agriculture Secretary Earl Butz and Assistant Secretary Carroll Brunthaver, Foley, and Bergland. The Republicans at the meeting took the position that, as conditions for administration support, the escalator clause must be removed, the price support payments further reduced, and the duration of the bill cut from four to two years. No deal was made. "The price the administration was asking was too high," Bergland later revealed. When the meeting adjourned, Bergland asked Poage if he would meet with the representatives of labor and two farm groups, the National Farmers Union (NFU) and National Farmers Organization (NFO). "He wanted to very badly," Bergland said later. However, Poage dispatched Bergland and Foley to conduct a "dry run" (i.e., without Poage) in Bergland's office with labor and the farm groups, to feel out potential points of tension or agreement.

July 13 (Friday afternoon). After a midday, preliminary meeting, Poage met with representatives of the AFL-CIO, UAW, NFU, and NFO. Foley and Bergland also were present. Although the agreements were generally tacit rather than clearly explicated, the following "understandings" on strategy resulted from the meeting: (1) The House, with Agriculture Committee leadership, would likely resolve an issue involving the Occupational Safety and Health Act (OSHA) with an amendment to the farm bill to labor's liking; (2) labor was prepared to support final passage of the bill even if the House amended the bill to prohibit food stamps to striking workers, with the understanding that the Senate-House conference would probably "take care" of that issue in labor's favor; (3) labor agreed to accept a prospective conference decision to re-open the allotment transfer loophole on the payment limitation.

That strategy, which embodied mostly Poage's initiatives, was designed to produce a winning coalition by holding the Southern Democrats, and by achieving the necessary support of organized labor (and the votes of urban-suburban Democrats) to overcome Republican opposition sufficiently to pass the bill. However, labor remained uneasy about the prospect of supporting any bill that prohibited food stamps to workers on strike, and the cotton leadership was concerned that given the Findley amendment the conferees would have insufficient discretion to reimpose the payment limitation loophole in conference. Consequently, labor and the cotton leadership made a side deal over the weekend, whereby AFL-CIO would support removal of the cotton section from the bill, in return for a promise that the Southern Democrats would help to defeat an amendment to deny food stamps to workers on strike.

July 16 (Monday). During the first thirty minutes of debate after the House returned to the farm bill, Whitten and Appropriations Committee Chairman George Mahon (D., Tex.) conveyed to Bergland (through Poage and Speaker Albert) that they would like him to sponsor an amendment to delete the cotton section. The House approved the Bergland amendment to delete cotton 207–190. The House also approved 221–177 a Bergland motion to alleviate labor's problem with OSHA, indicating that a winning coalition perhaps had been put together. (Further consideration of the farm bill was postponed for two days, while the House took up other, previously scheduled bills.)

July 19 (Thursday). However, before the vote on final passage of the farm bill was taken during a late-night session July 19, every "rational" coalition strategy had disintegrated and the House was plunged into the state of bedlam noted at the beginning of this paper. It would be irrelevant, in a paper on coalition behavior, to fill in all of the perplexing details of that day and night. Suffice it to say that the House voted to prohibit food stamps to striking workers. Also, through a confusing array of votes in the Committee of the Whole and after the Committee rose, the House managed (at least in the House Parliamentarian's judgment) to reinstate the cotton section in the bill.

In the introductory section of this paper, we quoted Joe Waggonner (D., La.), to illustrate the chaotic situation on the House floor. But Waggonner, a shrewd interpreter of the House, also pointed the way for order to be restored from the chaos:

> Mr. Chairman, this country needs a farm bill. . . . Now, it has come time to be practical or impractical. If the Members want a farm bill, regardless of what their opinions are on cotton, regardless of what their opinions are on food stamps, . . . let us send this bill to conference and let us write a farm bill.

In effect, Waggonner was saying to the members of the House: Cotton has a veto power. It appears that no farm bill package is forthcoming that both protects the essential interests of cotton and satisfies enough representatives in addition to the Southern Democrats to provide a legislative majority. In other words, no winning coalition can be put together on the farm bill, given the mood of the House and the rules of procedure that are applicable. Yet, the disposition of the House is that the "country needs a farm bill." The rational way to proceed, therefore (particularly in view of the exhausted condition of many members), is to defer to the conference committee, where in executive session the conference can "write a farm bill." Since the conference report will not be open to amendment, the House, faced with the choice between the conference version and no bill at all, likely will approve the conference version.

Waggonner's scenario succeeded. The House passed the bill 226–182. The conference reopened the loophole in the payment limitation and (through a parliamentary maneuver) also omitted the ban on food stamps for striking workers from the conference version subsequently approved by the House August 3.

PERSISTENCE OF FARM POLICY COALITION

From the perspective of a specific area of policy such as agriculture, a key consideration is the stability of the policy-making coalition, and thus the probability that the structure (or structures) of coalition will persist in the future. Will the "politics of agriculture" be essentially the same in 1977 (when the Agricultural Act is scheduled for renewal) as it was in 1973? If not, how will it differ? These are basically theoretical questions, because a response to them requires an understanding of the factors relevant to the perpetuation or termination of a "continuous" coalition.

In a sense, one might conclude that the process through which the 1973 farm bill passed the House manifested no continuous coalition at all, but was based instead on episodic coalitions "of the moment" which formed and dissolved on a one-shot basis. Indeed, the chaos preceding final passage could be viewed as the failure of coalition-building efforts, and eventual passage might be considered an accident, devoid of "rational" coalition behavior.

However, we developed the thesis above that a feed grains-wheat-labor complex is, for reasons that were indicated (including ideological compatibility), a rather promising cluster of interests for a continuous farm policy coalition. We also noted above that, in the cases of the Sisk and Michel votes on the farm bill where cotton was not the dominant commodity at issue, a voting pattern indicative of such a coalition was evidenced.

Table 4 shows the voting pattern of the major party segments on the four key recorded votes on the 1973 farm bill where the interest of cotton in particular was subordinate to the interest of the feed grains-wheat-cotton package: the Sisk motion to delete the escalator clause for all three commodities, the Michel motion to phase out federal payments for all three commodities over three years, the Teague (R., Calif.) motion to recommit the bill with instructions to delete the escalator, and the vote on final passage. (The vote on final passage of the 1974 sugar bill, also shown, is discussed below.)

Table 5 Voting Patterns on Selected Motions, 1973 Farm and 1974 Sugar Bills

MOTION	TOTAL VOTE	ALL REPS.	NORTHERN DEMS.	SOUTHERN DEMS.
Delete payment escalator for all 3 commodities	174–239	136–48	27–123	11–68
Phase out payments	186–220	146–35	30–120	10–65
Recommit bill, with instructions	182–225	135–45	35–115	12–65
Final passage, 1973 farm bill	226–182	87–94	74–77	65–11
Final passage, 1974 sugar bill	175–209	47–121	72–70	56–18

SOURCE: *Congressional Quarterly Weekly Report,* July 14, 1973, pp. 1912–1913; July 21, 1973, pp. 2021–2022; June 8, 1974, pp. 1522–1523.

The winning margin of the farm policy coalition on all four 1973 farm bill votes was rather similar; the total vote margin on recommittal and final passage is identical except that one more member voted on final passage than on recommittal. The first three farm bill votes (not including final passage) evidenced a high degree of interparty cleavage, with an average (mean) of 82 percent of the Democrats voting in favor of farm price supports and 77 percent of the Republicans opposing price supports. The behavior of the Northern Democrats on these three votes indicates that the kind of farm-labor alliance noted above was operating—whereby a bloc of "trader-oriented" Northern Democrats, sufficient to provide the victory margin, voted for price support payments. A potentially continuous farm-labor coalition, in view of the ideological compatibility noted above, was operative.

How stable is that coalition? Is it likely to persist, in spite of the confusion that surrounded final passage of the 1973 farm bill, and guide agricultural politics in 1977 and beyond?

Some clue to the coalition's stability is afforded by the change in voting pattern on final passage of the 1973 bill. In contrast to the rather similar vote breakdown among the Republicans and Northern Democrats on the first three votes in Table 4, on final passage, compared to the immediately preceding vote on recommittal, 41 Republicans and Northern Democrats exchanged positions. While the total vote margin on recommittal and final passage was almost identical, the substantial degree of cohesion within the Republican Party and among the Northern Democrats dissolved almost entirely on final passage.

The different breakdown on final passage resulted because the party leadership (including the labor leadership in regard to the Democrats) tended to "release" the members on the final vote, so that they might vote according to their perceived constituency interests. The [Voting] data indicate that, when party "pressure" was removed, the Northern Democrats divided more along rural-metropolitan lines. A total of 29 Northern Democrats from urban and suburban districts shifted from a pro- to an anti-farm bill position—more than the number of net changes (23) required to alter the result on final passage and on two of the other three votes on the 1973 bill shown in Table 4.

The significance of the above shifts in voting patterns, in terms of the persistence (stability) of a farm-labor coalition, might be clarified by treating agricultural policy within categories developed by Theodore Lowi. He has distinguished between "distributive" policies, whereby resources are allocated according to "log rolling" politics among private groups, and "redistributive" policies, whereby resources are taken from some groups and allocated to others. In those terms, it might be said that the Republican Party and Administration on the farm bill practiced "redistributive" politics, which was designed to take financial resources (i.e., federal payments) from farmers and allocate such resources to taxpayers. The Democrats, reflecting the farm-labor coalition, tended to practice "distributive" (log rolling) politics on the minimum-wage–farm bill package, in an effort to maximize the allocation of financial resources (wage levels, federal payments) to farmers and workers.

On the 1973 farm bill, when the Republican Party and Administration applied "pressure" on Republicans to support the redistributive position (remove escalator, phase out payments), it was stymied by the votes "delivered" by the "trader-oriented" Northern Democrats who supported the farm-labor coalition. Conversely, when the Republican leadership removed that pressure, so that greater support by Republicans for the farm bill reduced the need for the "traders" among Northern Democrats to stay with the coalition, the constituency (consumer, taxpayer) interests of many Northern Democrats motivated them to switch and vote along redistributive lines.

On June 5, 1974, the House rejected the price support bill for sugar, by vote of 175–209. A breakdown of the vote on sugar (see Table 4) suggests that viable farm price support policy is dependent upon the farm-labor coalition. On sugar, 72 percent of Republicans held in opposition to the bill. However, Northern Democrats voted essentially the same as they did on final passage of the 1973 farm bill (i.e., with their constituencies rather than with the coalition). The bill failed to secure a majority.

We cannot realistically infer that participation of labor in the policy coalition was the crucial factor that varied between the two bills, and that determined the result at the margin. The fact that an intercommodity coalition existed within agriculture on the 1973 farm bill, and that feed grains-wheat-cotton production is more dispersed than sugar production among regions and congressional districts, attracted Republican votes to the 1973 bill on final passage. (Note, however, that the Southern Democrats voted rather solidly for both bills, and that sugar beets production occurs in the Midwest and West.) Furthermore, an episodic (ad hoc) farm-labor alliance developed on final passage of the sugar bill; after floor amendments were attached to the bill to improve the wages of workers in the sugar sector, the AFL-CIO gave halfhearted support to the bill on final passage. Obviously, other variables also intervened.

Nevertheless, it is significant that labor support for the sugar bill on final passage was not based upon any enduring, ideological compatibility between labor and sugar producers. The image of sugar producers (especially cane sugar) is similar to cotton rather than to feed grains-wheat; sugar producers are perceived more as "corporate entrepreneurs" than as "family farmers." The leaders associated with the farm-labor coalition (Burton, Foley, etc.), who carried the burden of communication with urban Northern Democrats on the 1973 bill, were subdued or absent on the sugar bill. Poage, whose committee handled both bills, was virtually alone as a floor leader on sugar.

If we assume that the structure of the agricultural economic sector (and especially the feed grains-wheat subsectors) will continue to change only incrementally from the dispersed, independent-farmer pattern, the "family farmer" image will also tend to persist. To the extent that it does, it will probably continue the ideological compatibility that appears necessary for the bloc of urban, Northern Democrats to "trade" on farm and labor legislation. Whether that will be *sufficient* for viable agricultural policy, in view of the panoply of intervening variables, is problematic.

Even if basic change in the agricultural sector is incremental over the longer run, political and economic change since 1973 has unsettled the coalition situation in the short run. Congress in the 1973 Act made the innovative decision of eliminating "guaranteed" price support payments divorced from the prevailing level of market prices, so that federal price support payments for feed grains, wheat, and cotton vary inversely with commodity market prices. In 1974, total payments (and budgetary outlays) probably will be negligible, because market prices are above the "target" prices in the 1973 Act. To the extent that the current supply-demand and market price situation persists, the context of agricultural policy-making (and coalition-building) is substantially altered.

9. Selective Service and Draft Protestors: A "One Man" Policy Decision

Larry L. Wade

GENERAL HERSHEY AND HIS PROPOSED INDUCTION OF DRAFT PROTESTORS

The policy incident discussed below involves a statement sent on October 26, 1967, to the nation's 4,087 local draft boards. The statement was issued by General Lewis B. Hershey, national director of the Selective Service System. In the wake of student protests

Reprinted from Larry L. Wade, *The Elements of Public Policy* (Columbus, Ohio: Charles E. Merrill, 1972), pp. 113–22. Copyright © 1972 by the Charles E. Merrill Publishing Company and used with their permission.

against the draft during 1967, Hershey suggested that local boards review the draft status of anyone who (1) interfered with military recruiting on campus, (2) invaded a selective service office, or (3) burned or mutilated a draft card. Hershey recommended that, if such persons were draft eligible (classified I-A), they be inducted immediately. He further suggested that if the protestors held a draft deferment, such as a student's II-S, their deferment be revoked by the local board and the registrant inducted into military service as soon as possible. Hershey suggested that all of the above decisions be made by administrative action at the local board level. The net result of this particular bureaucratic policy decision was failure in the sense that the decision produced a response quite contrary to the effect desired by General Hershey. Draft protest was not curbed, but was in fact spurred to greater heights in the face of Hershey's recommendation. It appears that the failure of the policy was due to the violation by Hershey of certain features of a widely-held democratic myth, together with other reasons discussed below.

Since policy can and does often reflect the personality of the individuals formulating it, it is relevant to this study to include the following observations concerning General Hershey.

Hershey was the first and, until late 1969, when he was asked to resign by President Nixon, only head of the twenty-nine-year-old Selective Service System. He was appointed by President Roosevelt in 1940 to head a draft system that had been established as an emergency measure prior to World War II. In 1969 Hershey was 76 years old and the nation's oldest military officer on active duty. Throughout his tenure as Selective Service Director, the general staunchly opposed any radical change in the system, and public policy with respect to conscription had remained, with relatively minor exceptions, unchanged since it was developed in 1940. *Time* magazine called Hershey a "nineteenth century man unread in constitutional law, but totally dedicated to what used to be called Americanism." The general's opinions about the draft and draftees had remained rather constant over the years. During the Korean War, he had said that he felt "six out of ten draft rejects were faking disability on their induction physicals." In an interview in 1960, Hershey made the following comments about draft protestors: "I'm afraid this talk of objecting to the draft is some more of our softness—our desire to do no work, to shirk our responsibility as citizens. We want everything as painless as possible, everything with comfort and ease." When asked in 1967 how he felt about the president's proposal to abolish local draft boards, Hershey replied, "such action would violate most everything we have gained in democracy."

Although references such as these provide no adequate basis for a full assessment of Hershey's personality or political philosophy, they do suggest that important relationships exist between personality and public policy. In Hershey's case it is not unreasonable to believe that his personal sense of patriotism had much to do with his formulation of a policy calling for the induction of protestors. The fact that an important official in the executive branch could recommend actions that could so easily be construed as a threat to constitutional rights of speech, assembly, and petition poses interesting questions concerning personality, bureaucracy, and policy formation.

The Selective Service Act deals with all aspects of the draft. The law establishes the rules for the registration, induction, and discharge of all draft-age men. The law also outlines what it is that constitutes violation of the draft act, as well as the penalties applicable to such violations.

The president has legal responsibility for administering the draft. He appoints the director of the Selective Service who reports directly to him. As with many routinely functioning bureaucracies, Hershey had administered the system with little or no presidential involvement, at least up until the time of the incident in question. He had already survived five presidents and was, at the time of his famous letter, serving under a sixth. He was, indeed, a well-entrenched bureaucrat with whom presidents, Congress, and the courts found it inconvenient, or unnecessary, to intervene in the conduct of his office.

Under the Selective Service Act, the president has the power to determine the guidelines for induction, as shown by the wording of the law, which reads, in part: "The selection of persons for training and service . . . shall be made in an impartial manner under such rules as the President may prescribe. . . ." So while Hershey was the appointed head of the Selective Service, he held no *legal* authority of his own to establish induction priorities. Such authority rests with the president, acting by executive order, or with Congress, acting through the statutory amendment process. But with few exceptions, presidents had for all practical purposes delegated the responsibility for developing induction guidelines to General Hershey. This is important to remember when assessing Hershey's October, 1967, letter: he had for many years been the effective promulgator of induction standards.

Another aspect of the law which should be made clear concerns the theoretical legal autonomy of local draft boards. This autonomy lies with the manner in which local boards implement presidential guidelines for induction. Ostensibly, the president establishes age limits, registration procedures, methods of classification, rules for deferments, and so forth. Local boards interpret these guidelines to fit their own peculiar community needs. National Selective Service headquarters is supposed to furnish local boards with the quotas to be filled, and local boards in turn are to furnish the individuals according to previously established presidential rules. There is to be no governmental pressure concerning whether or not particular individuals are inducted. The head of the Selective Service is expected to *monitor* local board activities to insure compliance with presidential directive, but he is not supposed to *dictate* to the boards.

In reality, however, Hershey exercised a good deal of control over local boards, stemming less from legal authority than from the ideological or normative bureaucratic leadership he was in a position to provide. This moral suasion served to reduce sharply the autonomy of local boards. Norman S. Poole, assistant secretary of Defense for Manpower under President Johnson, said in 1965 that Hershey "strongly influences" local boards. When asked if the boards were autonomous, Poole replied, "They are autonomous *under* General Hershey." Continued Poole, "It is important to note that word *under.*"

The Act also outlines the legal punishments applicable to draft law violators. None of these penalties includes induction or reclassification as proposed by Hershey. And what must also be noted is that such activities as draft card burning were not in themselves violations of the law in 1967. It was not until 1968 that Congress amended the law to make draft card burning a specific crime under the statute. So while there was little explicit legal backing for Hershey's attempt to induct draft protestors, the realities of his past influence in administering the system may well have led him to attempt to make such induction a matter of operative public policy.

The Selective Service is an agency that deals with a well-defined segment of the population, i.e., males aged 18 to 35. Its decisions, however, impinge upon, and invoke reaction from, a far greater segment of society, e.g., inductees' families, employers, peace groups, patriotic organizations. Consequently, the Selective Service System places demands upon, and seeks the support of, a substantial proportion of the entire population.

The initial public action taken by Hershey against draft protestors occurred in January, 1966. Several students in Ann Arbor, Michigan, were arrested for a sit-in at the local draft board. The young men were later found guilty of violating a civil ordinance and were fined. Subsequently, General Hershey suggested that their cases be reviewed by their local boards for possible action. This was done, and some of the students were reclassified as I-A. A similar episode occurred in New York in late 1966, when four pacifists burned their draft cards on the steps of a federal court building. Although at that time there existed no laws against such conduct, Hershey suggested that the pacifists be relieved of their deferments by their draft boards and inducted immediately. Similar events continued over the next year in many places.

Several members of Congress questioned the legality of Hershey's actions in the above cases. Emanuel Celler (Dem.–N.Y.), chairman of the House Judiciary Committee, sent Hershey a letter asking him to clarify his position with respect to the induction of protestors. In his reply, Hershey reaffirmed his stance on the question. He said, in answer to Celler, that, "It has always been my view that any young man who violates the Selective Service Act should be given an opportunity to enter the armed forces rather than being prosecuted for his violation of the law." As the volume of protests against the war and the draft had grown in 1967, Hershey had translated his established personal views into a form of official Selective Service policy. The factors that led him to issue the policy statement cannot be known with certainty; perhaps Hershey himself is the only person who knows exactly why he did it. In any case, Hershey issued a statement on October 26, 1967, calling for local boards to immediately reclassify and induct anyone who burned his draft card, interfered with campus recruitment, or staged a sit-in at a local board.

This was a policy decision arrived at by one man, a man not subject to election; a policy that was never subjected to a vote of any type; a policy that was instigated before any public discussion was solicited; and a policy that was, as later shown, illegal in light of existing law. It was also a policy that failed. Before considering possible reasons for its failure, let us consider some examples of public reaction to the statement.

The reaction to Hershey making official what he had previously kept personal was immediate, and, as far as can be documented, overwhelmingly negative.

Although Hershey claimed that he had cleared the matter with the White House prior to issuing the directive, a White House statement in the wake of the controversy claimed otherwise. The statement, presumably issued with presidential approval, although never publicly attributed to President Johnson, said, "The draft should not be used as a means of punishing dissent." Regardless of whether prior White House approval had been sought or not, the White House thus moved quickly to dissociate itself from the statement. Representative John Moss (Dem.–Calif.) threatened to call Hershey before the House Armed Services Committee unless the order was rescinded. In keeping with his earlier objections to Hershey's tactics, Representative Celler condemned the Selective Service Director for his "flagrant disregard for the law" and said the draft "should not be used by Hershey as an instrument to punish or compel adherence to any political belief." The Justice Department's first reaction to the Hershey decision was a statement saying that the order would be difficult to uphold on constitutional grounds. The *New York Times,* in a December editorial, called the proposal "controversial."

Hershey's stand in the face of this controversy was a reaffirmation of his position. In a December *Washington Post* interview, the director claimed that "deferments were a privilege, and if a person violated the rules, he lost his deferment." In the same interview Hershey stated that a "student's school record does not form the entire basis for such deferments, but that obeyance of United States law also enters into the picture." He further contended that, "Decisions on the legality of a student's activities can be determined by the administrative action of local boards." *U.S. News and World Report* quoted Hershey as saying, "It is obvious that any action violating the military Selective Service act or related processes cannot be in the national interest." In these statements Hershey seemed clearly to reject the need for judge, jury, and trial in determining innocence and guilt. Joseph A. Califano, then special aide to President Johnson, issued an opinion contrary to Hershey's when he said, "Draft boards do not have the legal right to judge individual conduct."

The culmination of administration opposition to Hershey came on December 9, at a joint news conference attended by Hershey and Attorney General Ramsey Clark. At this conference Hershey insisted that the Selective Service system had the right to induct protestors who, in the opinion of local boards, had violated the Selective Service Act. Attorney General Clark dissented, saying that the Justice Department had not laid down any specific rules for handling protestors. Reaction from the general public to Hershey's induction edict is difficult if not impossible to assess.

The year drew to a close with General Hershey and much of the government still at odds. Direct public controversy between the administration and Hershey ended at the close of 1967. Whatever ingovernmental fighting continued beyond this point can only be a matter for speculation.

In order to explain Hershey's failure, it is necessary to first establish it. The record shows that the Justice Department, under presidential sanction, reaffirmed in early 1968 its stand that the draft could not be used as a means of punishing dissent. General Hershey, on the other hand, staunchly refused to countermand his order of October 26 and continued to insist that local boards had the right to induct protestors. But the administration's disapproval of such action was apparently enough to dissuade local boards from implementing Hershey's statement, since no further cases of protestors being inducted were reported. Congress did move to amend the draft law to include draft card burning as an illegal act, but the punishments for draft law offenders remained what they had been, that is, fines and imprisonment following due process, and not induction.

In August of 1969, the Supreme Court added the final defeat to the controversial directive when it overturned the induction of a New York pacifist on a 1967 draft card burning charge. Hershey's action was repudiated therefore by the administration, the Court, and most of the press. These were the obvious results of Hershey's policy directive.

There were many contributing factors to the failure of Hershey's effort at policy making and some, of course, played a larger role than others. Several suggestions on this subject are advanced below, some of which undoubtedly made a significant contribution to failure, and some which possibly had no effect on the outcomes at all. The reader may want to add to, or criticize, these speculative explanations in terms of whether or not they contribute to an understanding of this, and perhaps other, unilateral, bureaucratically-based failures at policy making.

The first, and seemingly most obvious, cause of failure consisted in the fact that Hershey's induction directive was technically illegal in light of existing law. Induction and reclassification were not outlined as penalties in the statute, and neither were draft card burning nor recruitment interference specified as crimes. As was pointed out however, Hershey had long supported induction as an alternative to prosecution for draft offenders, and such a philosophy had not been explicitly rejected by prior administrations and courts. The Johnson administration, however, was under fire for its involvement in the Southeast Asian war at the time of the incident, and some segments of the public had grown more sensitive to the rights and limits of dissent. Hershey's policy attempt might have succeeded in calmer times (although such times might not have produced the dissent which occasioned the directive). But since issues involving freedom of dissent were in serious contention at the time, and since significant public opposition to the draft had been mobilized, the policy was doomed. It was not only the technical illegality of the policy that defeated it, but as well, the larger political context within which the law had to be administered.

Hershey may have misread or underestimated both the level of general opposition to the war and the specific opposition to the draft, opposition which could be organized around what appeared to be an autocratic, unilateral, and vindictive public policy. His actions appeared to many as violating all semblance of democratic policy making, and the order itself raised a threat to constitutional protections of free speech. In answer to his critics, Hershey contended that innocence and guilt could be determined by local boards, that trials were not necessary, and that draft deferments were mere privileges. These statements immediately raised questions about the democratic myth of due process, which turns on questions of jury trial, legal representation, presumed innocence, and similar factors. If dissent had not been a public issue at the time, the policy might have succeeded. But once issues involving freedom of speech and due process were publicly brought to bear on the General, he was lost. Because of implied threats to free speech, the Johnson administration could not hope publicly to support Hershey in his policy, even though it may have been sympathetic to his efforts. When criticism was launched against the policy, Hershey found himself isolated from effective political support. Had he sought official government support before issuing the order, he might have weathered the crisis and retained some measure of credibility. But he was caught outside of an effective coalition and had to absorb singly all criticism raised against him, including that raised by the administration he was supposed to have represented. The same was true of congressional opinion. With no prior official support, Hershey was not later in a position to gain approval for his actions once such democratic ideals as free speech were brought into play.

It is possible also that General Hershey's successes of twenty-five or so years, during which he had received congressional, judicial, and presidential support for his administration of the draft system, had lulled him into a false sense of security. Perhaps he believed that he had more allies than later results proved him to have and that his membership in a coalition that had sustained him in the past would hold firm as well in the controversy at hand. It is quite true that some coalitions in American politics are remarkably stable, but it is also the case that their durability requires continual testing and that some of the less basic ones can be transitory indeed. Precisely why Hershey failed actively to enlist prior support for his policy is hard to say. But the unchallenged power he had exercised in the past may well have had something to do with it. When all or most parties to the dominant ruling coalition in America choose to ignore democratic values, then a public challenge to the coalition is extraordinarily difficult to mount. But if some elements of the coalition seek to invoke a democratic value such as free speech, perhaps in order to defend its public action on other questions or issues, then the myth is likely to prevail. The Johnson administration, hard pressed to maintain a semblance of public support for an intensely unpopular war, was hesitant to provide its critics with still further issues upon which to base a challenge to the very legitimacy of the government.

Another factor that may have contributed to Hershey's failure was his personality. He was far from being a warm and engaging public personality and, in the face of criticism, was unable to respond in a manner that might have earned him significant public support. His curt and harsh reactions to his critics only added to his already adverse public image, one that had been created by the initial publicity on the incident. The vindictive nature of the original directive was borne out in subsequent public statements made by the General. Large portions of the public expect bureaucrats to conform to a set of expectations which turn on disinterestedness, neutrality in the face of controversy, even-handedness. It was not, apparently, in General Hershey's nature to play such a role. He was a man of staunch and decided opinions which he was frank to reveal and defend. He was an overt partisan in a social role that required an emphasis upon the reconciliation of contentious values. Hershey was a bureaucrat whose age and personality were liabilities in a position as sensitive as his became in a time of severe crisis. The democratic myths were invoked, and Hershey failed to assess correctly his position within these new realities. Adverse publicity presented him as an insensitive bureaucrat who was attempting to curb free speech, and he was insufficiently flexible in his policy stance to counter such charges.

An important question to be asked now concerns the implications of this particular case for other unilaterally-developed public policies. Quite obviously, a good deal of such policy is made daily so it is useful to note at the outset that this method of policy making can be successful. But in order for such policy to succeed, it must conform to certain unwritten rules.

The public has limited access to most processes of policy making, even less to policy which originates within the public bureaucracy, and less still to the type of "one-man" policy outlined in this case. For the most part, indeed, various publics and elites are willing, often anxious, to allow bureaucrats to exercise their expertise with relatively little interference. As long as the requirements of bureaucratic or "invisible" policy making are tolerable, and no crises arise, the public is content. But when a bureaucrat is brought to public attention for initiating an unpopular policy, as was Hershey, he must be prepared to defend himself if he is to survive as a public man. If he has been careful to monitor the state of the coalitions of which he invariably is a part, or if he can move quickly to mobilize important sources of political power, he may weather the crisis. On the other hand, if he has wandered too far from the central myths of his society and forgotten the dangers of political isolation, a crisis can mean personal disaster and failure for the policy.

Most bureaucrats in a position to shape policy in the manner of Hershey have influence over a narrow and specialized segment of society. Such individuals can make important policy decisions without public debate as long as they avoid precipitating a public crisis. Publicity of any type, but particularly adverse publicity, can be a threat to nonvoting, bureaucratically-based policy. And once the attention of significant political elements is drawn to the fact that bureaucrats have in some important way violated the game of democracy, trouble arises.

Success in these sorts of policy decisions, then, lies in dealing with a narrow, technical segment of society which understands the realities of the bureaucrat's job in light of existing democratic myths. Exposure to the public should be avoided by the prudent self-interested bureaucrat whenever possible and, above all, proof of public approval and support for a proposed policy must be kept ready at all times. The community may allow itself to be deceived about its access to public policy as long as it is to some extent content with the government. But should public discontent be generated by an adverse policy, or by a policy which can be made to seem undemocratic, then sections of the public are quick to invoke the myths of democracy and to demand justification for the bureaucrat's actions.

10 Congress Adopts Medicare: The Politics of Legislative Certainty

Theodore R. Marmor

THE IMPACT OF THE ELECTION OF 1964

The electoral outcome of 1964 guaranteed the passage of legislation on medical care for the aged. Not one of the obstacles to Medicare was left standing. In the House, the Democrats gained thirty-two new seats, giving them a more than two-to-one ratio for the first time since the heyday of the New Deal. In addition,

Reprinted from Theodore R. Marmor, *The Politics of Medicare* (Chicago: Aldine, 1973), pp. 59–81. Copyright © 1973 by Theodore R. Marmor. Reprinted by permission of the author and Aldine Publishing Company.

President Johnson's dramatic victory over Goldwater could be read as a popular mandate for Medicare. The President had campaigned on the promise of social reforms—most prominently Medicare and federal aid to education—and the public seemed to have rejected decisively Goldwater's alternatives of state, local, and private initiative.

Within the Congress, immediate action was taken to prevent the use of delaying tactics previously employed against both federal aid to education and medical care bills. Liberal Democratic members changed the House rules so as to reduce the power of Republican-Southern Democratic coalitions on committees to delay legislative proposals. The twenty-one-day rule was reinstated, making it possible to dislodge bills from the House Rules Committee after a maximum delay of three weeks.

At the same time changes affecting the Ways and Means Committee were made which reduced the likelihood of further efforts to delay Medicare legislation. The traditional ratio of three members of the majority party to two of the minority party was abandoned for a ratio reflecting the strength of the parties in the House as a whole (two-to-one). In 1965, that meant the composition of Ways and Means shifted from fifteen Democrats and ten Republicans to seventeen Democrats and eight Republicans, insuring a pro-Medicare majority. A legislative possibility until the election of 1964, the King-Anderson program had become a statutory certainty. The only question remaining was the precise form the health insurance legislation would take.

THE ADMINISTRATION'S PROPOSAL: H.R. 1 AND S. 1

Administration leaders assumed after the election that the Ways and Means Committee would report a bill similar to the one rejected by the conference in 1964. Hence Anderson and King introduced on January 4, 1965, in the Senate and House respectively, the standard Medicare package: coverage of the aged, limited hospitalization and nursing home insurance benefits, and social security financing. The HEW staff prepared a background guide on the bill which continued to emphasize its modest aims. The guide included assurances that the bill's coverage of hospitalization benefits "left a substantial place for private insurance for nonbudgetable health costs, [particularly for] physicians' services." It described H.R. 1 as "Hospital Insurance for the Aged through Social Security," and no doubt would have encouraged the substitution of "Hospicare" for "Medicare" as its popular name, had this been still possible by 1965.

Social security experts within HEW, with a rich history of sponsoring unsuccessful health insurance bills, were doubly cautious now that success seemed so near at hand. Wilbur Cohen, for instance, busied himself, with President Johnson's blessings, convincing the congressional leadership to give Medicare the numerical symbol of highest priority among the President's Great Society proposals: hence Medicare became H.R. 1 and S. 1. Its content, however, remained essentially unchanged. The HEW leaders, like everyone else, could read the newspapers and find criticisms that Medicare's benefits were insufficient, and that the aged mistakenly thought the bill covered physicians' services. The strategists believed, however, that broader benefits —such as coverage of physicians' care—could wait: the reformers' fundamental premise had always been that Medicare was only "a beginning," with increments of change set for the future.

The election of 1964 had a vastly different impact on critics of Medicare than on promoters of the Administration bill, H.R. 1. If the election promoted satisfaction among H.R. 1's backers with their customary position, it provoked significant reactions among its opponents. Both Republican and AMA spokesmen shifted to discussions of what one AMA official, Dr. Ernest Howard, called "more positive programs." These alternatives grew out of the familiar criticisms that the King-Anderson bills had "inadequate" benefits, would be too costly, and made no distinction between the poor and wealthy among the aged. The AMA gave the slogan "Eldercare" to its bill, and had it introduced as H.R. 3737 by Thomas Curtis (R., Mo.) and A. Sydney Herlong (D., Fla.), both Ways and Means members. In comparing its bill and H.R. 1, the AMA earnestly stressed the disappointingly limited benefits of the latter:

Eldercare, implemented by the states would provide a wide spectrum of benefits, including physicians' care, surgical and drug costs, nursing home charges, diagnostic services, x-ray and laboratory fees and other services. Medicare's benefits would be far more limited, covering about one-quarter (25 percent) of the total yearly health care costs of the average person. . . . Medicare would *not* cover physicians' services or surgical charges. Neither would it cover drugs outside the hospital or nursing home, or x-ray or other laboratory services not connected with hospitalization.

Claiming their "program offered more benefits for the elderly at less cost to the taxpayers," the AMA charged, as did some Republicans, that the public had been misled by the connotations of the "Medicare" epithet. Seventy-two percent of those questioned in an AMA-financed survey during the first two months of 1965 agreed that doctors' bills should be insured in a government health plan. Sixty-five percent of the respondents preferred a selective welfare program which would "pay an elderly person's medical bill only if he were in need of financial help" to a universal social security plan which would "pay the medical expenses of everyone over 65 regardless of their income." Armed with these figures, the AMA once again launched a full-scale assault on the King-Anderson bill, hoping to head it off with what amounted to an extension of the Kerr-Mills program.

By February, the issue was once again before the Ways and Means Committee. Pressure groups—medical, labor, hospital and insurance organizations primarily—continued to make public appeals through the mass media and made certain their viewpoints were presented to the committee. Ways and Means had before it three legislative possibilities: the Administration's H.R. 1, the AMA's Eldercare proposal, and a new bill sponsored by the senior Republican committee member, John Byrnes.

THE WAYS AND MEANS COMMITTEE AND THE HOUSE TAKE ACTION: JANUARY–APRIL

For more than a month Ways and Means worked on H.R. 1, calling witnesses, requesting detailed explanation of particular sections, and trying to estimate its costs and benefits. Executive sessions, closed to the press and one mark of serious legislative intent, began in January. The atmosphere was business-like and deliberate; members assumed the Administration bill would pass, perhaps with minor changes, and there was little disposition to argue the broad philosophical issues that had dominated hearings in the preceding decade. When spokesmen for the AMA invoked their fears of socialized medicine, they irritated committee members intent on working out practical matters, and Chairman Mills refused to consult AMA representatives in further sessions of the committee's officially unreported deliberations.

Mills led his committee through practically every session of hearings on the Administration bill, promising to take up the Byrnes bill (H.R. 4351) and the Eldercare bill in turn. By March 1, there had been continued reference to the exclusions and limits of the King-Anderson bill, with the charges of inadequacy coming mostly from the Republicans. On March 2, announcing his concern for finding "some degree of compromise [that] results in the majority of us being together," Mills invited Byrnes to explain his bill to the committee.

The Byrnes bill was ready for discussion because the Republicans on the committee, in the wake of the 1964 election, wanted to prevent the Democrats from taking exclusive credit for a Medicare law. The Republican staff counsel, William Quealy, had explained this point in a confidential memorandum in January, reminding the Republican committeemen that they had to "face political realities." Those realities included the certain passage of health insurance legislation that session and excluded the strategy of substituting an expanded Kerr-Mills program. "Regardless of the intrinsic merits of the Kerr-Mills program," Quealy wrote, "it has not been accepted as adequate . . . particularly by the aged, [and a] liberalization of it will not meet the political problem facing the Republicans in this Congress." That problem was the identification of Republicans with diehard AMA opposition to Medicare, which some Republican leaders thought contributed heavily to their 1964 electoral catastrophe. Hence Byrnes, who had been working since January on a Republican alternative, was anxious to distinguish his efforts from those of the AMA. At the same time, with the AMA spending nearly $900,000 to advertise its Eldercare plan, the criticism of H.R. 1's "inadequacies" was given wide circulation.

Byrnes emphasized that his bill, which proposed benefits similar to those offered in the Aetna Life Insurance Company's health plan for the federal government's employees, would cover the major risks overlooked by H.R. 1, particularly the costs of doctors' services and drugs. He also stressed the voluntary nature of his proposal; the aged would be free to join or not, and their share of the financing would be "scaled to the amounts of the participants' social security cash benefits," while the government's share would be drawn from general revenues. The discussion of the Byrnes bill was spirited and extended; the AMA's Eldercare alternative, not promoted vigorously by even its committee sponsors, was scarcely mentioned.

The Byrnes and King-Anderson bills were presented as mutually exclusive alternatives. HEW officials were exhausted from weeks of questioning and redrafting, and viewed the discussion of the Byrnes bill as a time for restful listening. But Mills, instead of posing a choice between the two bills, unexpectedly suggested a combination which involved extracting Byrnes' benefit plan from his financing proposal. On March 2, Mills turned to HEW's Wilbur Cohen and calmly asked whether such a "combination" were possible. Cohen was "stunned," and initially suspicious that the suggestion was a plot to kill the entire Administration proposal. No mention had even been made of such innovations. Cohen had earlier argued for what he called a "three-layer cake" reform by Ways and Means: H.R. 1's hospital program first, private health insurance for physician's coverage, and an expanded Kerr-Mills program "underneath" for the indigent among the aged. Mills' announcement that the committee appeared to have "gotten to the point where it is possible to come up with a medi-elder-Byrnes bill" posed a surprise possibility for a different kind of combination. That night, in a memorandum to the President, Cohen reflected on Mills' "ingenious plan," explaining that a proposal which put "together in one bill features of all three of the major" alternatives before the committee would make Medicare "unassailable politically from any serious Republican attack." Convinced now that Mills' strategy was not destructive, Cohen was delighted that the Republican charges of inadequacy had been used by Mills to prompt the expansion of H.R. 1.

Byrnes himself was reluctant to approve the dissection of his proposal, humorously referring to his bill as "better-care." Nonetheless, from March 2 to March 23, when the committee finished its hearings, Ways and Means members concentrated on the combination of what had been mutually exclusive solutions to the health and financial problems of the elderly. Mills presided over this hectic process with confident but gracious assurance, asking questions persistently but encouraging from time to time comments from other members, especially from the senior Republican, Byrnes. The Byrnes benefit formula was slightly reduced; the payment for drugs used outside hospitals and nursing homes, for instance, was rejected on the grounds of unpredictable and potentially high costs. After some consideration of financing the separate physicians' insurance through social security, the committee adopted Byrnes' financing suggestion of individual premium payments by elderly beneficiaries, with the remainder drawn from general revenues. But while Byrnes had proposed that such premiums be scaled to social security benefits, the committee prescribed a uniform $3 per month contribution from each participant. The level of premium was itself a matter of extended discussion: HEW actuaries estimated medical insurance would cost about $5 per month, but Mills cautiously insisted that a $6 monthly payment would make certain that expenditures for medical benefits were balanced by contributions.

HEW was of course vitally interested in the uses to which Mills put the Byrnes plan. As one of the chief HEW participants, Irwin Wolkstein, explained,

> Many features of the Byrnes Bill which had been objectionable were changed to be sure to keep administration support although some objections remained—including inadequate protection of beneficiaries against over-charging, absence of quality standards, and carrier responsibility for policy. The issue to the Department was whether the benefit advantages to the aged of SMI [Supplementary Medical Insurance] overweighed the deficiencies, and the answer of the administration was yes.

In its transformation into the "first layer" of the new "legislative cake," H.R. 1 was not radically altered. Levels of particular benefits were changed, reducing, among other things, the length of insured hospital care, and increasing the amount of the hospital deductible and co-insurance payment beneficiaries would have to pay. (Deductibles are the payments patients must make before their insurance takes over, and co-insurance contributions are the proportion of the remaining bill for which patients are responsible.) The continuing debate over these matters illustrated the divergent goals of those involved in reshaping Medicare. High deductibles but no limit on the number of insured hospital days were sought by those anxious to provide protection against chronic and catastrophic illness. Others insisted on co-insurance and deductibles so that patients would be given a stake in avoiding overuse of hospital facilities. But the most contested changes made in H.R. 1 involved the methods of paying hospital-based RAPP specialists (radiologists, anaesthetists, pathologists, and physiatrists) and the level of increase in social security taxes required to pay for the hospitalization plan.

The Johnson Administration recommended that the charges for services like radiology and anaesthesiology be included in hospital bills unless existing hospital-specialist arrangements called for another form of payment. Mills, however, insisted that "no physician service, except those of interns and residents under approved teaching programs, would be paid" under H.R. 1, now Part A of the bill Mills had renumbered H.R. 6675. His provision required changes in the customary billing procedure of most hospitals, and became the subject of bitter disagreement. Such an arrangement, hospital officials quickly reminded the committee, would cause administrative difficulties and upset existing arrangements. But Mills stuck by his suggestion and easily won committee approval. More than any other issue, the method of paying these hospital specialists was to plague efforts in the Senate and conference committee to find a compromise version of the bill Mills steered through the Ways and Means Committee and the House.

Ways and Means also required more cautious financing of the hospital program than the Administration suggested. Social security taxes—and the wage base on which those taxes would be levied—were increased so as to accommodate even extraordinary increases in costs. The final committee report announced with some pride that their estimates of future hospital benefits reflected a "more conservative basis than recommended by the [1964 Social Security] Advisory Council and, in fact, more conservative than those used by the insurance industry in its estimates of proposals of this type. (Mills' penchant for "actuarial soundness" was justified by Medicare's costs during the first year of operation; in 1966 both hospital and physician charges more than doubled their past average rate of yearly increase, thus substantially inflating program costs beyond HEW's initial predictions.)

Throughout March, Mills called on committee members, HEW officials, and interest group representatives to lend their aid in drafting a combination bill. The advice of the Blue Cross and American Hospital Associations was taken frequently on technical questions about hospital benefits. HEW spokesmen were asked to discuss many details with directly interested professional groups and report back their findings. Blood bank organizations, for instance, were consulted on whether Medicare's insurance of blood costs would hamper voluntary blood-giving drives. Their fear that it would prompted the committee to require that Medicare beneficiaries pay for or replace the first three pints of blood used during hospitalization. Throughout, Mills left no doubt that he was first among equals—he acted as the conciliator, the negotiator, the manager of the bill, always willing to praise others, but guiding the "marking up" of H.R. 6675 through persuasion, entreaty, authoritative expertise, and control of the agenda.

The Medicare bill the committee reported to the House on March 29, 1965, had assumed a form which no one had predicted in the post-election certainty that some type of social security health insurance was forthcoming. The new bill included parts of the Administration bill, the Byrnes benefit package, and the AMA suggestion of an expanded Kerr-Mills program. These features were incorporated into two amendments to the Social Security Act: Title 18 and 19. Title 18's first section (Part A) included the hospital insurance program, the revised version of H.R. 1. Part B represented the modified Byrnes proposal of voluntary doctors' insurance. And Title 19 (now known as Medicaid) offered a liberalized Kerr-Mills program that, contrary to AMA intentions, was an addition to rather than a substitution for the other proposals. Essentially, the program provides for the unification of all medical vendor payments under state programs and uniform coverage for recipients. The provision in Title 19 which enables a state at its option to elect to cover individuals (regardless of age) not on public assistance, but whose incomes are close to the public assistance levels, could also extend coverage to a significantly large portion of the poor population.

On the final vote of the committee, the Republicans held their ranks, and H.R. 6675 was reported out on a straight party vote of 17–8. When the House met on April 8 to vote on what had become known as the Mills bill, they gave the Ways and Means chairman a standing ovation. In a masterly explanation of the complicated measure (now 296 pages long), Mills demonstrated the thoroughness with which his committee had done its work. The health insurance program in H.R. 6675, Mills explained, was to cost about $3 billion. Byrnes presented his alternative bill after Mills had finished, and a vote was taken on whether to recommit H.R. 6675 in favor of the Republican alternative. The motion to recommit was defeated by 45 votes; 63 Democrats defected to the Republican measure, and only ten Republicans voted with the Democratic majority. Once it was clear that H.R. 6675 would pass, party lines re-formed and the House sent the Mills bill to the Senate by an overwhelming margin of 315–115.

What had changed Mills from a Medicare obstructionist to an expansion-minded innovator? Critics speculated on whether the shift represented "rationality" or "rationalization," but none doubted Mills' central role in shaping the contents of the new legislative proposal. The puzzle includes two distinct issues: why did Mills seek to expand the Administration's bill, and what explains the form of the expansion he helped to engineer?

By changing from opponent to manager, Mills assured himself control of the content of H.R. 1 at a time when it could have been pushed through the Congress despite him. By encouraging innovation, and incorporating more generous benefits into the legislation, Mills undercut claims that his committee had produced an "inadequate" bill. In both respects, Mills became what Tom Wicker of *The New York Times* termed the "architect of victory for medical care, rather than just another devoted but defeated supporter" of the Kerr-Mills welfare approach. Mills' conception of himself as the active head of an autonomous, technically expert committee helps explain his interest in shaping legislation he could no longer block, and his preoccupation with cautious financing of the social security system made him willing to combine benefit and financing arrangements that had been presented as mutually exclusive alternatives. The use of general revenues and beneficiary premiums in the financing of physicians' service insurance made certain the aged and the federal treasury, not the social security trust funds, would have to finance any benefit changes. In an interview during the summer of 1965, Mills explained that inclusion of medical insurance would "build a fence around the Medicare program" and forestall subsequent demands for liberalization that "might be a burden on the economy and the social security program." What Mills may have meant, as one government official explained off-the-record, was that Ways and Means could avoid "physician coverage in the future under social security by providing it now under the [Supplementary Medical Insurance] approach."

In sharp contrast to Mills' flexibility, HEW cautiously had settled for proposing its familiar King-Anderson plan. In comparison with the committed Medicare advocates, Mills was the more astute in realizing how much the Johnson landslide of 1964 had changed the constraints and incentives facing the 89th Congress. President Johnson, busy with the demands of a massive set of executive proposals, was willing to settle for the hospitalization insurance which the election had guaranteed. Liberal supporters of the Johnson Administration were astounded by Ways and Means' improvement of Medicare and befuddled by its causes. *The New Republic* captured the mood of this public at the time of the House vote, suggesting that the Mills bill could "only be discussed in superlatives":

> Fantastically enough, there was a tendency to expand [the Administration's bill] in the House Committee. Republicans and the American Medical Association complained that Medicare "did not go far enough." Trying to kill the bill they offered an alternative—a voluntary insurance plan covering doctor's fees, drugs, and similar services. What did the House Ways and Means Committee do? It added [these features] to its own bill. Will this pass? We don't know, but some bill will pass.

H.R. 6675 PASSES THE SENATE: APRIL–JULY

There was really no doubt that the expansion of Medicare would be sustained by the more liberal Senate and its Finance Committee. But the precise levels of benefits and form of administration were by no means certain. The Finance Committee Chairman, Russell Long (D., La.), held extended hearings during April and May, and the committee took nearly another month amending the House-passed bill in executive sessions. Two issues stood out in these discussions: whether to accept the payment method for in-hospital specialists on which Mills had insisted, and whether even more comprehensive benefits could be financed by varying the hospital deductible with the income of beneficiaries.

The first issue was taken up, with White House encouragement, by Senator Paul Douglas (D., Ill.). The question of specialist payment brought out in the open a dispute within the medical care industry. The American Hospital Association told the Finance Committee that encouraging hospital specialists to charge patients separately would both "tend to increase the overall cost of care to aged persons" and imperil the hospital as the "central institution in our health service system." HEW's general counsel, Alanson Willcox, prepared a list of supporting arguments which Wilbur Cohen supplied in defense of the Douglas amendment to pay RAPP specialists as specified in the original H.R. 1. "These specialists," Willcox pointed out, "normally enjoy a monopoly of hospital business and yet they seek the 'status of independent practitioners' without the burden of competition to which other practitioners are subject."

The AMA responded with fury to Douglas' revisions. Defending the specialists, the AMA hailed Mills' payment plan as a way to break down the "corporate practice of medicine" which made radiologists, anaesthetists, pathologists, and physiatrists coerced "employees" of hospitals. "Medical care," the AMA told the Finance Committee, "is the responsibility of physicians, not hospitals." Apparently unconvinced, the Senators approved the Douglas amendment in early June.

In mid-June the Finance Committee approved a plan to eliminate time limits on the use of hospitals and nursing homes. The supporters of this amendment were a mixed lot of pro- and anti-Medicare Senators, and it was clear the latter group thought this change might deadlock the entire bill. For those who wanted more adequate protection against financial catastrophe there was the subsequent realization that a well-intentioned mistake had been made. With the White House and HEW insisting on a reconsideration, the committee scrapped the amendment on June 23 by a vote of 10–7. In its place, it provided "120 days of hospital care with $10 a day deductible after 60 days."

The Finance Committee also took up a variety of provisions within the Mills bill which Administration spokesmen considered "important defects." The Medicare sponsor in the Senate, Clinton Anderson, argued that paying physicians their "usual and customary fees" (the Byrnes suggestion) would "significantly and unnecessarily inflate the cost of the program to the tax-payer and to the aged." The House bill had left the determination of what was a "reasonable charge" to the insurance companies, which would act as intermediaries for the medical insurance program, and Anderson saw no reason why these companies would save the government from an "open-ended payment" scheme. Medical spokesmen, however, were so critical of the overall Medicare legislation that fears of a physicians' boycott persuaded Senate reformers not to raise further the sensitive topic of fee schedules for physicians.

The Senate, unlike the House, does not vote on social security bills under a closed rule. This meant further amendments and debate would take place on the Senate floor on the Finance Committee's somewhat altered version of the Mills bill. On July 6 debate was opened and the Senate quickly agreed to accept the recommendation to insure unlimited hospital care with $10 co-insurance payments after 60 days. Three days later, after heated discussion, the Senate finished with its amendments, and passed its version of Medicare by a vote of 68–21. On the crucial but unsuccessful vote to exclude Part A from the insurance program, 18 Republicans and 8 Southern Democrats took the losing side. According to newspaper estimates, the expanded bill passed by the Senate increased the "price tag on Medicare" by $900 million. The conference committee was certain to have a number of financial and administrative differences to work out through compromise.

MEDICARE COMES OUT OF THE CONFERENCE COMMITTEE: JULY 26, 1965

More than 500 differences were resolved in conference between the Senate and House versions of Medicare. Most of the changes were made through the standard bargaining methods of *quid pro quo* and splitting the difference. The most publicized decision was the rejection of the Douglas plan for paying RAPP specialists under the hospital insurance program. Mills' victory on this score was to cause much further alarm in the months to come, when the Social Security Administration began its administrative task of preparing for Medicare's initiation, July 1, 1966.

The bulk of the decisions were compromises between divergent benefit levels. The changes of duration and type of benefit involved either accepting one of the two congressional versions or combining differing provisions. The decisions on the five basic benefits in the hospital plan aptly illustrate these patterns of accommodation:

1. *Benefit duration*—House provided 60 days of hospital care after a deductible of $40. Senate provided unlimited duration but with $10 co-insurance payments for each day in excess of 60. *Conference* provided 60 days with the $40 House deductible, and an additional 30 days with the Senate's $10 co-insurance provision.

2. *Posthospital extended care (skilled nursing home)*—House provided 20 days of such care with 2 additional days for each unused hospital day, but a maximum of 100 days. Senate provided 100 days but imposed a $5 a day co-insurance for each day in excess of 20. *Conference* adopted Senate version.

3. *Posthospital home-health visits*—House authorized 100 visits after hospitalization. Senate increased the number of visits to 175, and deleted requirements of hospitalization. *Conference* adopted House version.

4. *Outpatient diagnostic services*—House imposed a $20 deductible with this amount credited against an inpatient hospital deductible imposed at the same hospital within 20 days. Senate imposed a 20 percent co-insurance on such services, removed the credit against the inpatient hospital deductible but allowed a credit for the deductible as an incurred expense under the voluntary supplementary program (for deductible and reimbursement purposes). *Conference* adopted Senate version.

5. *Psychiatric facilities*—House provided for 60 days of hospital care with a 180-day lifetime limit in the voluntary supplementary program. Senate moved these services over into basic hospital insurance and increased the lifetime limit to 210 days. *Conference* accepted the Senate version but reduced the lifetime limit to 190 days.

None of these compromises satisfied the pro-Medicare pressure groups which had been anxious to make the law administratively less complicated. By late July, the conference committee had finished its report. On July 27, the House passed the revised bill by a margin of 307–116 and the Senate followed suit two days later with a 70–24 vote. On July 30, 1965, President Johnson signed the Medicare bill into Public Law 89–97, at a ceremony in Independence, Missouri.

THE OUTCOME OF 1965: EXPLANATION AND ISSUES

One of the most important lessons of Medicare's enactment is that the events surrounding its passage were atypical. The massive Democratic electoral victories in 1964 created a solid majority in Congress for the President's social welfare bills, including federal aid to education, Medicare, and the doubling of the "war on poverty" effort. To find the most recent precedent, we must go back almost 30 years, to Franklin Roosevelt's New Deal Congresses. In the intervening years, we find a different pattern. Democratic majorities in the Congress have not been uncommon, but normally the partisan margins have been sufficiently close on many issues to give the balance of power to minority groups within the party. Under these circumstances, states' rights Southern congressmen in coalition with Republicans have often been successful in blocking or delaying bills which entail the expansion of federal control.

The fragmentation of authority in the Congress compounds the opportunities for minorities to block legislation; bills must be subjected to committees, sub-committees, procedural formalities, and conference groups. To be sure, overwhelming majority support for a given bill can ensure that it will emerge, more or less intact, as law, even though it may pass under the jurisdiction of hostile congressmen in the process. However, it is extraordinarily difficult to create a congressional majority committed to an issue out of Democratic congressional partisans. President Kennedy, in 1961, avoided a major confrontation over Medicare because it was uncertain whether the bill could pass a House vote and because he needed the support of Ways and Means members for his other programs. Congressmen must frequently make similar decisions; for example, many representatives who supported Medicare before 1965 were nonetheless unwilling to launch a major drive to extract it from Ways and Means. Like the President, they often needed the support of Medicare opponents for other legislation which they believed was more important or had a better chance for successful enactment.

Within this context, backers of controversial legislation generally adopt a strategy which looks to the gradual accretion of support. They frame the issue so that opponents will find them difficult to attack, then set out to accumulate both mass public support and the necessary congressional votes. Particular attention is given to crucial committee bottlenecks. The Executive relies heavily on the influence of the House and Senate leadership in this effort, and acts on the assumption that although it is seldom possible to change the mind of a congressman on the merits of an issue, it is sometimes possible to change his vote. While the congressional leaders lack formal means for enforcing party discipline, they have a variety of other resources. Their personal influence with the regional caucuses who selected Ways and Means committeemen, for example, allowed them to deny assignments to Medicare opponents and thereby to alter gradually the voting margin on the committee.

By 1964, the use of this accretionist strategy by Medicare supporters seemed on the verge of success; and had the elections of that year resulted in the usual relatively close partisan margins in the Congress, the Medicare Act of 1965 would have been much narrower in scope, and its passage would stand as a vindication of the incrementalist strategy. In fact, the 1964 elections returned a Congress in which many of the usual patterns of bargaining were less relevant. The Medicare bill which finally emerged as law must be analyzed in terms of the various responses to the highly unusual circumstances in that Congress.

In seeking answers as to why the legislative outcome differed so markedly from the Administration's input, three separable issues are involved. Why did the traditional hospitalization insurance proposal pass as one part of the composite legislation? The congressional re-alignment after the elections of 1964 provides the ready answer. Why the legislation took the composite form it did is partly answerable in this way as well. The certainty that some Medicare bill would be enacted changed the incentives and disincentives facing former Medicare opponents. Suggesting a physicians' insurance alternative offered an opportunity for Republicans to cut their losses in the face of certain Democratic victory and to counteract public identification of Republican opposition with intransigent AMA hostility to Medicare. Wilbur Mills' motives are fully comprehensible only in the context of congressional conventions, especially the relationship of the Ways and Means Committee to the House, and the committee's tradition of restrained, consensual bargaining among its partisan blocs. However, if the political needs of the minority party and the Ways and Means members account for the Republican alternative bill and the committee's expansion of Medicare, the limits of that expansion require further explanation.

The context of the debate over government health insurance sharply delimited the range of alternatives open to innovators. That long debate—focused on the aged as the problem group, social security vs. general revenues as financing mechanisms, and partial vs. comprehensive benefits for either all the aged or only the very poor amongst the aged—structured the content of the innovations. The political circumstances of 1965 account for why innovation by Republicans and conservative Democrats was a sensible strategy. The character of more than a decade of dispute over health insurance programs for the aged explains the programmatic features of the combination that Wilbur Mills engineered, President Johnson took credit for, and the Republicans and American Medical Association inadvertently helped to ensure.

The outcome of 1965 was, to be sure, a model of unintended consequences. The final legislative package incorporated features which no one had fully foreseen, and aligned supporters and opponents in ways which surprised many of the leading actors. Yet the eleventh hour expansion of Medicare should not draw one's attention away from the constricting parameters of change. Were a European to reflect upon this episode of social policy making in America, his attention would be directed to the narrow range within which government health proposals operated. He would emphasize that no European nation restricted its health insurance programs to one age group; and he would point out that special health "assistance" programs, like that incorporated in Title 19, had been superceded in European countries for more than a generation. The European perspective is useful, if only to highlight those features of the 1965 Medicare legislation which were *not* changed.

Although the new law was broader than the King-Anderson bill in benefit structure, it did not provide payment for all medical expenses. P.L. 89–97 continued to reflect an "insurance" as opposed to a "prepayment" philosophy of medical-care financing. The former assumes that paying substantial portions of any insured cost is sufficient; the problem to which such a program addresses itself is avoidance of unbudgetable financial strain. The latter view seeks to separate financing from medical considerations. Its advocates are not satisfied with programs which pay 40 percent of the aged's expected medical expenses (one rough estimate of Medicare's effects); only full payment and the total removal of financial barriers to access to health services will satisfy them. In Medicare's range of deductibles, exclusions, and co-insurance provisions, the "insurance" approach was followed, illustrating the continuity between the first Ewing proposals in 1952 of 60 days of hospital care and the much-expanded benefits of the 1965 legislation.

Nor were major changes made in the group designated as beneficiaries under the insurance program. The Administration had single-mindedly focused on the aged and the legislation provided that "every person who has attained the age of 65" was entitled to hospital benefits. Though this coverage represented an expansion over the limitation to social security eligibles in bills of the 1950s and early 1960s, the legislation provided that, by 1968, the beneficiaries under Part A would be narrowed again to include only social security participants. (This provision "applied only to persons first attaining age 65 in 1968 and after—only a very small fraction of the current aged—and the test of social security eligibility is less strict than is the test for cash benefits.") The persistent efforts to provide Medicare benefits as a matter of "earned right" had prompted this focus on social security and, as a result, on the aged. While the social security system was not the only way to convey a sense of entitlement (payroll taxes in the Truman plans were included for the same purpose), the politics of more than a decade of incremental efforts had effectively undercut the broad coverage of the Truman proposals.

Title 19, establishing the medical assistance program popularly known as "Medicaid," made exception to the age restrictions. This bottom layer of the "legislative cake" authorized comprehensive coverage for all those, regardless of age, who qualified for public assistance and for those whose medical expenses threatened to produce future indigency. As in the Kerr-Mills bill which it succeeded, financing was to be shared by federal government general revenues and state funds. The Medicaid program, too, owed much to the past debates, growing as it did out of the welfare public assistance approach to social problems. Its attraction to the expansionists in 1965 did not rest on its charitable features alone. In the eyes of Wilbur Mills, it was yet another means of "building a fence" around Medicare, by undercutting future demands to expand the social security insurance program to cover all income groups.

The voluntary insurance scheme for physicians' services, Part B of Title 18, represented a return to the breadth of benefits suggested in the Truman plans (although, unlike the Truman proposals, it was neither compulsory nor available to all age groups). Since the adoption of an accretionist strategy in the wake of the Truman health insurance defeats, coverage of physicians' costs had been largely dropped from proposals. Throughout the 1950s reformers had focused on rising hospital costs and the role which the federal government should play in meeting those costs. Except for the Forand bills, proposals for health insurance between 1952 and 1964 fastidiously avoided the sensitive issue of covering doctors' care. Even when the election of 1964 eradicated the close congressional margin which had prompted the accretionist strategy in the first place, the Administration continued to follow it. It was Wilbur Mills, and not the presidential advisers, who most fully appreciated the changed possibilities. Once again acting to build a fence around the program and insure against later expansion of the social security program to include physicians' coverage, he pre-empted the Byrnes proposal with a general revenue-individual contribution payment scheme.

For a decade and more, the American Medical Association had been able to dictate many of the terms of debate, particularly on physicians' coverage. And although the 1964 election revealed how much the alleged power of AMA opposition to block legislation depended on the make-up of Congress, the provisions for paying doctors under Part B of Medicare reflected the legislators' fears that the doctors would act on their repeated threats of non-cooperation in implementing Medicare. To enlist the support of the medical profession, the law avoided prescribing a fee schedule for physicians, and directed instead that the doctors of Medicare patients be paid their "usual and customary fee," providing that the fee was also "reasonable." Moreover, it was not required that the doctor directly charge the insurance company intermediaries who were to handle the government payments; he could bill the patient, who, after paying his debt, would be reimbursed by the insurance company. This left a doctor the option of charging the patient more than the government would be willing to reimburse. But congressional sympathy with the doctors' distaste for government control, and fear that doctors would elect not to treat Medicare patients under more restrictive fee schedules, made "reasonable charges" appear a sensible standard of payment.

The eligibility requirements, benefits, and financing of the Medicare program represent a complex political outcome, a mixture of continuity and surprise not typical of the legislative histories of other social welfare measures. The long process of building support for a hospitalization program covering the aged had not prepared the Johnson Administration for the unpredictable opportunities of 1965. Instead of the King-Anderson bills of the 1960s, HEW had the Mills bill to turn into an operational Medicare program by July, 1966. The politics of congressional bargaining had produced a considerably larger (and many felt a better) bill than the Johnson Administration had proposed in the first weeks of 1965.

part four POLICY IMPLEMENTATION

Most public policies are not self-executing. If, for example, a legislature enacts a law and nothing is done to implement or enforce it, the law in all likelihood will become a nullity. Administrative agencies have the primary responsibility for policy implementation and carry on much of the day-to-day work of government. However, it should be noted that some laws are enforced largely through judicial action, which gives a significant role to the courts. Laws concerning crimes are an obvious example; others include antitrust policy and public school desegregation.

Administrative agencies frequently possess substantial discretion in the execution of public policies. Were it not for this fact, were the implementation of public policy more or less automatic, there would be no need for policy analysts to devote much attention to them. In practice, because agencies have discretion (which can be defined as the opportunity to choose among alternatives), what they do, or do not do, in the way of implementation can importantly affect the content and impact of public policies.

As has been noted, legislative bodies are often unable to formulate and adopt very precise settlements of policy disputes. Many statutes give agencies broad and ambiguous statutory mandates, such as to fix "just and reasonable" railroad rates or to license radio and television broadcasters for the "public convenience and necessity." Such mandates are, in effect, directives to the agencies to get busy and make some more precise policy. Agencies then become the focal point of the struggle to shape public policy, and the legislature, courts, chief executive, pressure groups, communications media, and other agencies as well seek to influence or otherwise affect an agency in the exercise of its discretion. Such, for instance, has been the case with the Federal Power Commission and the regulation of rates paid to the producers of natural gas sold in interstate commerce.

One of the basic American public policies is antitrust, which is designed to prevent monopoly and maintain competition in the economy. To understand antitrust policy one must do more than read the statutes, such as the Sherman Antitrust Act and the Clayton Act. It is also necessary to analyze what the Antitrust Division of the Department of Justice does or does not do to enforce them and how the courts have interpreted and applied the laws in particular cases. Harlan Blake's article on the ITT case of the early 1970s illustrates how political factors may affect the course of antitrust enforcement.

In the development of foreign policy, the President is the predominant actor, drawing upon both his constitutional power and the power delegated to him by congressional legislation, as in the area of international trade. Although some presidential foreign policy decisions may be essentially self-executing, as was President Nixon's decision to extend recognition to the People's Republic of China, most require further implementary action. Some presidential decisions may be precise in nature; others may rather be more general expressions of intention. Whatever the case, presidential decisions may be misunderstood, difficult to carry out, or resisted by other executive branch officials. Morton Halperin discusses some of the problems connected with the implementation of presidential decisions and some of the means by which subordinate officials may resist them.

The ultimate goal of public policies is to secure compliance, to cause those affected to behave in desired ways and not to behave in undesired ways. The basic purpose of a statute prohibiting the sale of unwholesome or diseased meat is not to punish violators but to prevent the sale of such meat. However, prosecution and punishment of some who violate the law may be necessary to help insure compliance with it. Agencies may use a variety of means—education, persuasion, sanctions, propaganda appeals—in an effort to win compliance. Using the perspective provided by cost-benefit analysis, Professors Rodgers and Bullock discuss the factors affecting compliance of citizens and officials with public policy, especially in the area of civil rights.

11. Beyond the ITT Case: The Politics of Antitrust Enforcement

Harlan M. Blake

Dita Beard, the flamboyant Washington lobbyist for the International Telephone and Telegraph Company, opened up into the headlines a situation whose broader implications deserve public attention.

Mrs. Beard's unwilling celebrity resulted from an alleged admission (in conversations with an aide of columnist Jack Anderson) to a political deal between ITT and the Republican party. Supposedly, her cocktail-party conversation with former Attorney General

Reprinted from *Harper's Magazine,* June 1972, pp. 74–78. By permission.

John Mitchell, and an ITT promise to make a hefty contribution, through its Sheraton Hotel subsidiary, to the San Diego Republican party convention, were instrumental in getting ITT's antitrust cases favorably settled. But although it is clear from sources other than Mrs. Beard that getting a favorable antitrust settlement was the subject foremost in the minds of ITT officials during the summer of '71, it is at least an equally plausible hypothesis that the San Diego gift was regarded as a more generalized investment in political goodwill with the Republican party. The fact that Mr. Republican Party happened also to be Attorney General of the U.S. (instead of Postmaster General, once the pattern) was a happy coincidence, for ITT if not for the public interest.

Thus the focus of attention must shift to Richard W. McLaren, Assistant Attorney General in charge of the Antitrust Division of the Justice Department, whose "primary responsibility" it was, to use his own words, to exercise "the broad discretionary authority" to decide whether or not to settle the cases. If McLaren's settlement was a good one from the point of view of public policy, as he claims, and if it is credible that the list of factors he says he took into account is complete, the case for or against improper influence will have to be decided on other evidence. For example, Deputy Attorney General Richard G. Kleindienst's apparent initial attempt to conceal his role in the settlements and ITT's speedy destruction of files may be persuasive to some. If on the other hand McLaren, too, seems to have been less than fully candid, this would point strongly toward pressures, although quite likely subtle ones. It would not, of course, prove that arrangements for the San Diego convention were decisive, although it would seem to suggest that generally ITT's influence in high places is dangerously pervasive.

Since McLaren's earlier honesty and toughness had impressed all observers, it is not pleasant to be forced to conclude that his statement of reasons to the Senate committee was not persuasive. To evaluate the credibility of his testimony it is important to know more about the cases involved and about the recent history of antitrust enforcement policy. To begin, one should note that McLaren *did* change his mind rather abruptly. Briefs on appeal of the ITT cases to the Supreme Court had already been written and filed, and every speech and public pronouncement by Antitrust Division officials in months prior to July

1971 made it clear that the division thought the cases were soundly based and were going to be won.

The legal question involved was whether ITT's acquisitions in 1969 of Automatic Canteen Corporation, the nation's largest food-vending concern; of Grinnell Corporation, the nation's largest supplier of fire prevention (sprinkler) systems; and of Hartford Fire Insurance Company, the nation's second largest fire insurance company, were violations of the antimerger law, Section 7 of the Clayton Act. That statute was amended and strengthened in 1950 by the Celler-Kefauver bill after lengthy Congressional hearings into increasing concentration in the U.S. economy. Before it could be an effective tool in the hands of the Justice Department, however, the language of the new law required definitive interpretation by the Supreme Court. In 1962 this was achieved. The famous *Brown Shoe* case defined strict standards for the legality of horizontal mergers (between competing firms) and for vertical mergers (between a firm and an important supplier or customer).

In short order, thanks to Justice Department enforcement of these rigorous new standards, horizontal and vertical mergers among large companies virtually ceased. But the trend toward increasing concentration in the economy did not subside. During the 1960s the number of mergers rapidly increased. From record levels in 1966, the number of mergers doubled in two years to over 4,000 in 1968. Furthermore, the proportion of large firms acquired by even larger ones increased even more rapidly than the acquisition rate. The total asset value of acquired firms rose from $4 billion in 1966 to $12 billion in 1968; 110 of *Fortune's* 500 largest industrial corporations of 1962 had by 1968 disappeared by merger. The mergers were largely of the "conglomerate" variety, in which there are no important horizontal or vertical relationships between the acquiring and acquired corporations. In a speech delivered shortly after taking office, McLaren noted that "the pace and scale of the current merger trend can be ignored only at the risk of serious and perhaps irreversible damage to our competitive economy, to wit, undue economic concentration. . . ."

The most aggressive conglomerate of the past twelve years, and probably of all time, has been ITT. In 1955 ITT was a firm whose considerable size was concentrated primarily in overseas communications systems. It ranked as the eightieth U.S. industrial corporation, but its $500 million in annual sales were largely outside the domestic market. By 1971 ITT had soared to ninth in rank, with sales of $5.5 billion, largely in domestic markets. This growth within the United States was accomplished not through adding to the productive capacity or employment levels of the economy by new investment or building new plants. It was accomplished almost entirely by buying up existing businesses. Since the arrival of Harold S. Geneen as ITT's president in 1959, the company acquired 110 or more domestic companies (as well as fifty-five foreign firms), by trading its highly leveraged common and convertible preferred shares for those of the acquired firm.

Among its better known acquisitions were Continental Baking Co., Sheraton Hotels, Avis Corporation, Levitt & Sons, and Rayonier. At a meeting early in 1969, the ITT Board authorized acquisition of an additional twenty-two domestic corporations and eleven foreign corporations. Geneen had established himself as the industrial empire builder *par excellence*—a man whose scale of operations challenged that of the legendary John D. Rockefeller, Sr., and surely surpassed any other figure of the era of the "robber barons," whose operations frightened Congress into enactment of the original antitrust law, the Sherman Act, in 1890.

Geneen's development as master *conglomerateur* was helped along by the coincidence that between 1965 and 1968 the Antitrust Division was headed by a Harvard law professor, Donald F. Turner, who took the position, based on his earlier writings, that conglomerate mergers should be dealt with, if at all, by special legislation rather than by antitrust enforcement. Turner neither sought legislation nor filed complaints in conglomerate cases, although he did help divert Geneen's attempted takeover of the American Broadcasting Company.

The day Richard McLaren emerged from Chicago antitrust law practice to take his oath as antitrust chief for the Justice Department, things changed. McLaren had no doubt that Congress had intended that the antitrust laws should be applied to all classes of mergers, including conglomerates, and he was convinced that the Supreme Court would agree if it were provided the opportunity. He promptly gave Attorney General Mitchell a speech to deliver that contained the following warning:

The danger that super-concentration poses to our economic, political and social structure cannot be overestimated. . . . The Department of Justice may very well oppose any merger among the top 200 manufacturing firms . . . [or] by one of the top 200 manufacturing firms of any leading producer in any concentrated industry.

Since ITT ranked ninth among manufacturing firms, and had made itself the nation's star "super-conglomerate" through acquisitions, it seemed clear that if Mitchell meant what he said, ITT's days of empire-building were numbered. Within weeks of taking office, McLaren faced a situation that put this policy to the test. ITT had announced plans to acquire Automatic Canteen, the nation's largest food vendor. McLaren decided to bring suit in Chicago to secure an injunction against the merger. However, Kleindienst—acting for Mitchell, since an ITT division had been one of Mitchell's clients in his law practice—refused to approve the filing of the suit. According to a report of Ralph Nader's antitrust investigators, Kleindienst responded to White House intervention following a lobbying campaign directed at "White House staff close to Nixon" by "ITT, aided by New York investment houses which would greatly profit if the merger were completed. . . ." The Nader report concludes that the suit was filed later, after the merger was consummated, only because McLaren had gone to the White House to make clear the strength of his conviction that the suit should be brought.

The Nader evaluation seems plausible since, shortly before the announcement of the ITT-Automatic Canteen merger, McLaren had filed suit, with no reported difficulty, against Ling-Temco-Vought's proposed acquisition of Jones & Laughlin Steel. Since LTV ranked below ITT on the *Fortune* list and J&L ranked sixth among steel producers, compared to Automatic Canteen's dominant first position in its industry, the ITT acquisition would seem to have been even more clearly exposed to attack. Mr. Ling, a Texas friend of Lyndon Johnson, might have done better if political history had been written differently.

Having won this important victory, McLaren filed a series of conglomerate suits. The most important were two more filed against ITT in August 1969, when temporary injunctions were sought in the District Court for Connecticut to prevent its acquisition of Grinnell

Corporation and Hartford Fire Insurance Company. Geneen was not to be dissuaded by only one lawsuit against the Automatic Canteen acquisition—and the reason soon became clear. Although Grinnell was expendable—indeed, Grinnell, conveniently found in the same (Connecticut) judicial district as Hartford, may have been sought by ITT partly with the thought of later relinquishing it in plea-bargaining negotiations with the Antitrust Division—the billion-dollar annual cash flow of the insurance company would be an important factor in ITT's financing of past and future acquisitions.

As it almost always does in merger cases, the government lost the initial rounds with ITT in the trial courts. Still, its prospect of eventual victory was excellent. Even ITT attorney Lawrence G. Walsh was reported to have advised his client that it was probable that the Antitrust Division's appeals would succeed in the Supreme Court. There was good reason for his prophecy: in *each* of seven merger cases after *Brown Shoe,* the Supreme Court had found it necessary to reverse a district court's decision adverse to the government. The Antitrust Division had never lost a merger case in the Supreme Court since the Celler-Kefauver amendment in 1950. Neither had the Federal Trade Commission, which had litigated two conglomerate cases there. In the one merger appeal decided since Nixon's appointment of Justices Burger and Blackmun, they too joined a unanimous court in deciding for the government; as usual, the district court was reversed.

There are reasons for this pattern. District court judges are accustomed to dealing in the "hard" facts of mail fraud, drug distribution, damage claims, and the like. They find it difficult to "find" so nebulous a fact as that a merger causes a "probability of injury to competition," the criterion of the merger law. The Supreme Court, more attuned to questions of public policy, has no such difficulties. Furthermore, lawyers representing defendant corporations in the trial court are the best in the locality, and even in the country, often well known to and respected by local judges. Frequently, in terms of sheer manpower they outnumber the antitrust staff many times. Too, district court judges, often chosen from among successful local attorneys, are likely to share a similarity of outlook on business matters with their former colleagues.

These facts, and close study of the district court decisions in the three ITT cases, reveal no basis for Solicitor General Erwin Griswold's reckless statement before the Senate Judiciary Committee that the government would probably not have won the cases if the appeals had been taken. This was clearly not the view entertained by McLaren at the time, it was not the view of government lawyers handling the Grinnell and Hartford cases, and it is not a view likely to be shared by a careful student of the Supreme Court's handling of merger cases, which Griswold, it is fair to add, did not claim to be.

THE CHANGE OF MIND

It is against this background that we must evaluate McLaren's statement regarding his change of mind about the desirability of going forward with the cases. Keep in mind that McLaren's decision to move strongly against conglomerates was far and away the most important decision and accomplishment of his entire term of office. He had fought and won permission to bring the cases. For two years or more he had consistently pressed them all the way through trial. None of the other conglomerate cases he had brought remained a suitable vehicle for appeal to the Supreme Court. On two of the three ITT cases, however, the Supreme Court was ready to hear argument. The badly needed clarification of the law that its opinions probably would have provided almost certainly would have embodied Richard McLaren's most important contribution in public service.

The reasons given by McLaren to the Judiciary Committee for changing his mind about settlement of the litigation were (1) that ITT's financial condition—its debt capacity and credit rating—would be jeopardized if it were denied access to the $1 billion annual cash flow of Hartford; (2) that the adverse effect on the stock market, and on the owners of ITT and Hartford shares, might be severe; and (3) that the effect on the international balance of payments might be adverse. None of these reasons, as McLaren presumably knew, could be taken seriously.

First, the twelve-page report in which these arguments were made, prepared in two or three days for a reported fee of $242 by Richard J. Ramsden, a financial analyst recommended to McLaren by the White House's ambassador-at-large to Wall Street, Peter Flanigan, was not—in content, in sponsorship, or in circumstances of author-ship—objectively persuasive.* Most of it reads like the kind of re-search report on a company put out every day by the major brokerage houses. In addition, these are the kinds of arguments that every antitrust lawyer knows by heart and makes in desperation when his arguments "on the merits" are not strong enough to prevail. They are likely to be effective only with men who lack experience in the ways of the world, or who are looking for an excuse to be persuaded.

1. The possibility of an adverse effect on access to the capital market is not a factor that can be taken into account since it is present in every antitrust suit worth prosecuting; monopoly profits or cartel gains, at the expense of consumers, always improve the looks of financial statements and reduce credit risks. Was ITT's elaborate financial structure so shaky during the summer of '71 that it would have been "crippled financially," as McLaren said he feared, if it had been required eventually to divest itself of Hartford? If so, it was surely the best-kept secret in the history of corporate finance. During 1971, in spite of the pending appeals and McLaren's known opposi-tion to settlement, ITT shares were much stronger than they had been a year earlier. A number of Wall Street's most respected investment houses and brokerage firms were acquiring ITT shares or recommend-ing them to clients. It is difficult to conceive of data that would be persuasive to any sophisticated observer in the face of this contrary evidence provided by the attitudes of the financial community ex-pressed in the most sensitive and best-informed marketplace in the world. The worry about a stock-market debacle thus was a red her-ring, and it is not credible that McLaren was persuaded by it.

What seemed to worry McLaren most was ITT's assertion that it had paid a $500 million "premium" for the Hartford stock but took Hartford's assets onto its books at book value. To sell Hartford stock would result in a loss, and ITT would incur capital-gain tax liabilities.

As to this argument, one may note that it has been standard practice in conglomerate takeovers for the acquiring firms to pay a substantial "premium" for the acquired, in that shares selling (or

---

*On April 17 Ramsden testified to the Committee that the Justice Department had made too much of his report.

convertible to shares selling) at twenty-five times earnings (like ITT's) were exchanged for shares selling at fifteen times earnings (like Hartford's). This reduces the former's price/earnings ratio on paper by adding to its earnings account more proportionately than to the number of new shares issued in the exchange. Thus everybody gets rich without adding anything to the real productivity of the economy. This was the kind of empire Geneen was building (for which services, at $812,000 per year, he was surely the best-paid executive in the nation). But if this kind of defense is accepted by the Antitrust Division and the courts, there will seldom be a conglomerate case in which relief can be obtained, except where the government is fortunate enough to secure a temporary injunction to prevent the transaction in the first place.

2. The Ramsden report was equally weak in arguing excessive injury to stockholders. First, this argument is faulty in the same respects as the prior one. No shareholder has any vested right to stock values arising from anticompetitive circumstances. Furthermore, most of the risk to ordinary investors had been absorbed by arbitrage buying and selling during the previous year by sophisticated speculators betting, in effect, on the outcome of the litigation.

Most important, in the event that Hartford were to be ordered divested two or three years hence, the courts have plenty of discretion in choosing plans that prevent injury to the innocent (for instance, by spreading small public offerings over a period of time). Such a plan was developed in 1961, when duPont and its shareholders were ordered to divest themselves of sixty-three million shares of General Motors stock, 23 per cent of the total. Counsel for duPont predicted calamity on Wall Street and enormous losses for defendant shareholders—none of which, of course, came to pass. The Supreme Court warned in that case, however, that "adverse tax and market consequence" arguments could not be decisive:

> Those who violate the [antimerger] Act may not reap the benefit of their violations and avoid an undoing of their unlawful project on the plea of hardship or convenience.

3. Even less is it credible that the Treasury Department offered a balance of payments argument that could have been persuasive. First,

the Treasury now states that its report to McLaren was only informal and casual. Second, such a report could not have been seriously made without the most detailed analysis of ITT's financial structure and its relationship with, and the condition of, several dozen important overseas subsidiaries. No one claims that this was done.

Finally, the balance of payments argument is the reddest and smelliest herring in the entire weaponry of businessmen seeking special treatment in antitrust matters. Even Ramsden's report described the possibility only as "some indirect . . . effect." (The argument is now being trotted out again by Flanigan in the cause of legislation, now being pushed by the Wall Street wing of the Administration, that would exempt export cartels generally from antitrust surveillance.)

TIRED TRUSTBUSTER

As an antitrust lawyer, McLaren must have known well that even if somehow troubled by one or more of these arguments, he could not accept them without violating every tenet of antitrust policy. The U.S. economy is not a planned economy; it is based on the assumption of markets working freely and well enough without extensive government regulation and controls. That is the central policy and objective of the antitrust laws and their administration. The Supreme Court has made it clear that the antitrust rules presume that neither the courts nor the prosecutor shall sit in continuing surveillance over justifications for every price decision in every industry. Neither does Congress presume to make the Justice Department the ultimate arbiter of issues of domestic and international economic policy. The courts must ultimately define the content of the law on the books, subject to supervening legislative change. If Congress decides to move from a relatively free market economy toward a more highly planned system, and finds the antitrust laws inappropriate or inconsistent with that approach, legislative redress may of course be undertaken. Until that day, any Attorney General, or Deputy, or Assistant, who becomes convinced by the economic theories of John Kenneth Galbraith, or Herbert Spencer, or Joseph Schumpeter, or Karl Marx, or Richard Ramsden, in deciding about the impact of antitrust proceedings on balance of payments, stock-market activity, unemployment, or patterns of sunspots, should be persuaded to resign forthwith. Exotic economic philosophies are not part of the job description.

If we assume that McLaren's real reasons for deciding the ITT questions were not those he has publicly provided, it does not follow that he was responding to specific knowledge of a "deal," nor even to overt pressures. No one has suggested the former, or is likely to. His antagonistic response to decisions by Kleindienst that he regarded as improper was demonstrated at the outset of his campaign against conglomerates—in the ITT-Canteen suit.

Thus it seems quite conceivable that, when the signals of interest in high places concerning the ITT settlement began to appear—Kleindienst's repeated intercession, the indication of White House interest through Flanigan, the communication from ITT's Walsh (also, one almost hesitates to note, chairman of the American Bar Association committee on judicial selection)—McLaren may simply have felt too worn down in the apparently endless battle to keep the antitrust machinery functioning in such highly politicized surroundings. Rather than fight yet another round, possibly exhausting completely his presumably already depleted supply of goodwill, and perhaps placing in jeopardy the budgetary well-being of the Antitrust Division and its career staff, he may have persuaded himself that the Ramsden and Treasury "reports" were more credible and relevant than they would have appeared to another observer. That he was, indeed, understandably disillusioned and weary of battle at this stage is borne out by his retirement six months later to accept a hurried appointment to a federal district court judgeship.

The underlying problem is much deeper than the internal politics of the Justice Department, and it is one that should be squarely and promptly faced. During and since World War II there has been growth at an exponential rate of the variety and importance of federal government decisions that vitally affect the profitability of businesses, the power of labor unions, the effectiveness of multifarious organized special-interest groups. Their response has been to establish in Washington innumerable special lobbying and favor-seeking organizations. Hundreds, perhaps thousands, of special-interest groups and large corporations, including ITT, maintain offices in Washington—in ITT's case with an extravagant annual budget. Enormous sums are spent to win lobbyists solid favor and influence with legislators and members of the Administration, perhaps from the White House down. Their presence and influence may have become so pervasive that for many public officials—including administrative and law-enforcement agencies and the courts—it has become virtually impossible to make, and then make stick, a decision in the public interest that runs counter to the lobbyists' special interests.

The worst offender and quickest to jump to the bidding of special interests in the antitrust area has unfortunately been Congress. In recent years, after adverse Supreme Court decisions, the banking lobby has twice demanded, and promptly got, special legislation seeking to exempt bank mergers from usual antitrust standards. After successful Antitrust Division proceedings against unnecessarily anticompetitive joint advertising agreements between newspapers, the publishers' association demanded virtually complete exemption from the merger laws, and got legislation providing most of what it wanted. The patent bar has fought hard, and is still hopeful that it will eventually get, special-interest legislation that would greatly weaken antitrust surveillance over restrictive patent licensing. Among special-interest bills currently moving ahead in Congress is one to reverse the results of twelve years of antitrust proceedings, and four Supreme Court decisions, against El Paso Natural Gas Company's anticompetitive acquisition of its major potential competitor in supplying natural gas to California. Another, sponsored by Flanigan and supported by export trade interests, would permit exporters to form cartels, largely exempt from public-interest antitrust surveillance.

With much of the Administration, and especially the Department of Justice, more aggressively politicized than, perhaps, ever before in history, and with richer lobbyists than ever before playing for higher stakes, the public interest may be a lost cause. At any rate, the top-priority item on the agenda of all who are concerned about the integrity of government should be how to reverse the trend of which the ITT settlement is only a small evidence.

12. Implementing Presidential Foreign Policy Decisions: Limitations and Resistance

Morton H. Halperin

PRESIDENTIAL DECISIONS

Presidential decisions vary in specificity. They are often conveyed only in policy statements expressing a sentiment or intention. The statements may indicate in general that certain kinds of actions should be taken but not say who should take them. Even if they do specify the actor, they seldom indicate when the

Reprinted from Morton H. Halperin, with the assistance of Priscilla Clapp and Arnold Kanter, *Bureaucratic Politics and Foreign Policy* (Washington, D.C.: The Brookings Institution, 1974), pp. 235–60. Copyright © 1974 by The Brookings Institution. Reprinted by permission of the publisher.

action should be taken or the details of how it should be done. In fact the instructions are often so vague as to leave all the actors free to continue behaving as they have in the past.

Even if a decision results from a long struggle among his advisers —indeed, especially when it results from such a struggle—the President tends to delay decisions and then decide as little as possible. Furthermore, the President seldom makes a single comprehensive decision covering a wide range of interrelated issues. More often he decides a series of questions discretely, each one on its own merits, adding up to a series of diffuse and, on some occasions, contradictory guidelines to the bureaucracy about what should be done.

There are a number of reasons why a President may not want to state definitely what should be done to implement his decision. In many cases, the consensus which has been built for the decision may in fact depend on the vagueness of what the President decides. In the case of the ABM, Secretary of Defense McNamara was prepared to go along with a limited deployment provided he could announce it as anti-Chinese and express strong opposition to erecting any large system supposedly designed to counter a Russian missile attack. At the same time, the Joint Chiefs of Staff and Senate leaders, such as Chairman of the Senate Armed Services Committee Richard Russell, were prepared to go along with limited initial deployment provided they could describe it as the first step toward a large anti-Russian system. In order to keep this "coalition" together the President's decision had to be vague enough so that participants on each side could believe that he had decided in their favor (and in any case so that participants on each side were free to describe the decision as they chose). President Truman was confronted with a similar problem of differing views about whether or not the United States should begin the development of a hydrogen bomb. With Atomic Energy Commission Chairman David Lilienthal against any deployment, with the military in favor of proceeding with a deployment, and with the State Department in favor of exploring the options, Truman settled on a tentative and minimal decision which kept everybody on board by giving Lilienthal no target to shoot at but the military enough of a move in their direction that they were prepared to acquiesce.

Often reinforcing the desire to maintain a semblance of harmony by expressing his decision in vague terms is a presidential desire not to be committed to the details of a decision. Presidents typically confront an issue on a very general and theoretical level without much discussion of the details of the best way to implement a decision. When he has not spent time on details and has not looked into the possible problems buried in one kind of decision or another, the President prefers to express only a general desire to move in a particular direction and leave it to a battle among his subordinates to fill out the details. He is likely to assume that important issues will be brought back to him for further decision.

In many cases, a President, after making a decision, wishes it to be kept secret for a while in order to head off attacks on the decision before actions are under way. He recognizes that the further down in the bureaucracy a piece of paper gets which specifies that the President has decided something, the more likely the piece of paper will be leaked. In Washington what the President decides is news, and low-level officials are eager either to show that they know what the President wants or to undercut a policy which they oppose.

In addition, the President may feel that his time must not be squandered in providing specific instructions. Robert Cutler, at one time Assistant to the President for National Security Affairs, reports that this was Eisenhower's view:

> Eisenhower believed that policy decisions at the apex of Government should afford general direction, principle, and guidance, but should not be spelled out in detail. The Council dealt with strategy, not tactics. A Supreme Commander's orders are directed to Army groups and armies; they do not deal with battalions and companies. The last throw of Ludendorff in 1944 [sic] failed, in part, because his orders meddled with the battle movement of small elements. President Eisenhower was as impatient with too much detail as he was with lack of clarity in stating general policy.[1]

Whether or not he considers attention to "details" appropriate, a President when he is new in office tends to assume that faithful subordinates all down the line will labor to put into practice the policies he

---

[1]Robert Cutler, *No Time For Rest* (Boston: Little, Brown, 1965), p. 300.

outlines. One of President Eisenhower's speech writers commented on Eisenhower's initial faith of this kind: "Nowhere did the lack of civilian experience so betray itself as in this system's cheerful assumption that, once the Chief Executive had pointed in a certain political direction, the full force of government would move in that direction, in concert as precise and as massive as battalions and divisions wheeling through field maneuvers."[2]

Even when he comes to understand that specification of detail is necessary if one wishes to have faithful implementation, a President will not have on tap at the White House experts to draft decisions in specific terms in all areas. Nor does the White House staff, whatever its own expertise, have time to prepare detailed instructions on many issues.

Because presidential decisions are seldom formulated in a way that conveys in detail what should be done and because the President himself is seldom the actor to carry out the decision, it is true only in very special cases that presidential decisions are self-executing. Usually, in fact, they begin a process. The President often announces a policy decision in conversation with senior officials who head the organizations which will be responsible for implementing his decisions. On their understanding or recollection of what was said depend the first steps toward concrete action. In other cases, the President decides alone or in the company of White House officials, and the decision is then conveyed (sometimes orally) to the heads of the departments concerned or to a subordinate official who is believed responsible for supervising the required actions. They in turn issue instructions to those who, according to the rules of procedure, are responsible for actually carrying out the decision. Frequently this involves not only distributing directives to subordinates in Washington but also sending out cables to American ambassadors and military commanders in the field. This is not a trivial matter. Turning the sketchy language of a presidential decision into precise terms which can be understood and acted on in the field is extraordinarily difficult and may have to be done at high speed. During the opening days of

---

[2]Emmet John Hughes, *The Ordeal of Power: A Political Memoir of the Eisenhower Years* (New York: Atheneum, 1963), p. 153.

the Korean War, for example, the senior civilian and military officials, after meeting with the President and getting his oral instructions, would move to the Pentagon or the State Department and improvise written instructions to the field.

Once orders are written and sent to the individuals who should act, one might at last expect faithful implementation of the presidential decision, but this does not occur either. Why it does not is our next subject.

LIMITS ON FAITHFUL IMPLEMENTATION

There are three basic causes for failure to comply with presidential or other directives: (1) officials at the operations level may not know what it is that senior officials want them to do; (2) they may be unable to do what they believe they have been ordered to do; (3) they may resist doing what they have been ordered to do. Each of these is discussed in turn.

Uncertainty about Orders

In approaching the question of why presidential orders may not be obeyed, it is important to keep in mind the vast size and diversity of the federal government. Few officials see the President at all. Even fewer see him often enough to have a good feel for his approach to problems. Many of those who have to implement decisions are not privy to conversations between the President and his principal advisers or between those advisers and their subordinates. The orders which they receive in writing or orally are not only very general but are often the only clues they have. Thus the ambassador or first secretary in the field, the commander of a bomber squadron, an assistant secretary in Washington, a Treasury official visiting a foreign government—all may have little information on which to determine what it is the President wants them to do.

In some cases, officials at the operations level may not even know that the President has issued orders in a particular area. After an American U-2 was shot down over the Soviet Union, a public affairs officer in the National Aeronautics and Space Agency held a press conference at which he asserted that the plane had accidentally drifted

212

over Russian territory. This happened long after President Eisenhower and his senior advisers had decided that only the State Department would make any comment. Senior officials, too, may sometimes be unaware of the President's plans. For example, Secretary of Defense Melvin Laird, while visiting Japan, made a number of statements which led to press reports that the United States favored a Japanese nuclear capability. Unknown to Laird, these statements were made at precisely the time that presidential assistant Henry Kissinger was in Peking negotiating with Chou En-lai about the possibility of a trip by Nixon to China. It is believed these comments by Laird greatly complicated Kissinger's mission. Laird was not disobeying orders. He was simply uninformed about Nixon's approach to China and therefore unaware of the fact that what he was saying might halt or at least complicate implementation.

Misunderstanding about what a subordinate is ordered to do crops up. The most dramatic case on record of a pure misunderstanding resulted in President Eisenhower's invitation to Soviet Premier Nikita Khrushchev to visit the United States. Eisenhower had decided that he would be prepared to invite Khrushchev to the United States *only if* there was progress at the ongoing foreign ministers' meeting which would justify the convening of a four-power summit conference. The invitation to the Russians was to be conveyed by Under Secretary of State Robert Murphy, who was to meet Soviet Deputy Prime Minister Koslav during the latter's visit to the United States. Murphy's instructions were given him directly by the President but were oral. Evidently, even this direct communication could not prevent misunderstanding. Murphy conveyed through Koslav an unconditional invitation to Premier Khrushchev, rather than the one that the President wished transmitted (contingent upon progress in the four-power talks). Confronted by this misunderstanding, Eisenhower felt obliged to honor the invitation.

More often, it is not that the official is totally uninformed or that he completely misunderstands his orders. Rather, he has no way of grasping the nuances behind decisions, no guidance as to exactly why he is told to do what he has been told to do. This makes it very difficult for him to implement the policy, to make the day-to-day implementing decisions in conformity with the President's desires. George Kennan explains:

In the execution of policy, we see the same phenomenon. Anyone who has ever had anything to do with the conduct of foreign relations knows that policies can be correctly and effectively implemented only by people who understand the entire philosophy and world of thought of the person or persons who took the original decision. But senior officials are constantly forced to realize that in a governmental apparatus so vast, so impersonal, and lacking in any sort of ideological indoctrination and discipline, they cannot count on any great portion of the apparatus to understand entirely what they mean. The people in question here are in large part people they do not know personally and cannot hope to know in this way. Considerations of security alone would make it difficult, in many instances, to initiate into the reasons of action all those who might be involved if one were to use the regular channels. The expansion of the governmental apparatus has led to a steady inflation of titles roughly matching that of the growth of the apparatus itself.[3]

The problem has gotten even more acute since Kennan wrote. An examination of the State Department prepared by a group of Foreign Service officers in 1970 related this problem to the Nixon National Security Council system:

Specific decisions are generally communicated promptly and clearly to the implementing units. On occasion, however, the implementing unit is not specified precisely, and the system suffers. More often, the specific decision is transmitted without reference to the broader objectives which should guide the action office in carrying it out. Action offices thus must rely on rather rough and ready guidance of their own making, extrapolating from the specific decision and the very broad-brush generalizations contained in public pronouncements by the President and the Secretary. The result can be either inconsistency in implementation or excessive caution. One reason for this lack of guidance is that Departmental inputs to NSSM's [National Security Study Memoranda] are often not framed in such a way as to

---

[3]George Kennan, "America's Administrative Response to Its World Problems," *Daedalus,* Vol. 87 (Spring 1958), p. 19.

produce it. Also the Department usually does not participate in drafting NSDM's [National Security Decision Memoranda] it is required to implement.[4]

The problem of determining what one is supposed to do is further complicated by the fact that no official receives just one order. The directive comes as an item in a flow of paper across an official's desk. He is receiving instructions to do things because other officials have made decisions. He is receiving requests from his subordinates for authority to take actions within existing directives. He is receiving reports of ongoing activities. Whatever effort he makes to implement a particular directive must be within the context of his attempt to implement other directives which have come to him before. He may see a conflict between two very specific directives—a conflict of which senior officials may not be aware. He may perceive a contradiction between a specific directive and a more general policy statement which is received in writing or which he gleans from public presidential and departmental statements. Such a conflict accounts in part for the failure of the State Department to remove missiles from Turkey in 1961. President Kennedy had ordered American missiles removed from Turkey. But he had also ordered the State Department to invigorate the NATO alliance, and, indeed, one of his campaign pledges had been that he would bolster NATO. At the same time, his Secretary of Defense, Robert McNamara, was engaged in an effort to persuade the NATO countries to take conventional military options more seriously. The State Department officials concerned were well aware of the fact that this effort was causing great difficulties within the alliance. The officials who received the directive to remove the missiles from Turkey also felt themselves to be operating under a more general presidential directive to strengthen the troubled alliance. They did not believe that the order to remove the missiles from Turkey was meant

---

[4]William B. Macomber, Jr., *Diplomacy for the 70's: A Program of Management Reform for the Department of State* (Washington: Government Printing Office, 1970), pp. 556–57.

to contradict the order to strengthen NATO. They raised the issue in a tentative way with the Turkish government. When that government registered strong objections, they held off obeying the order to remove the missiles.

Whereas missiles remained in Turkey because of conflicting directives from the President, in other cases uncertainty arises from the fact that an official receives conflicting orders from two or more of his superiors. The President may in effect tell him to do one thing. The Secretary of the Navy or the Chief of Naval Operations seemingly tell him to do another. In such cases, the official often makes his own judgment about which orders have higher priority.

The Difficulty of Implementation

Some orders direct an official to gain a certain outcome but do not specify any particular action. For example, an official may be told to secure ratification of a nonproliferation-of-weapons treaty by a particular government, or he may be told to persuade a certain country to increase its military forces. In such cases, the implementation of the order depends on the cooperation or at least the yielding of a foreign government. In other cases, implementation may depend on the cooperation of Congress or other groups outside the executive branch and beyond the control of the official being given the order. Under those circumstances he may find it impossible to comply.

In still other cases, limits of compliance come from the fact that most presidential orders need to be carried out by large complex organizations. Some presidential decisions can be carried out by a relatively small number of presidential advisers without regard to the capability of large organizations. When President Nixon decided he wished to establish contact with the People's Republic of China, he was able to dispatch Henry Kissinger, his Assistant for National Security Affairs, to Peking. Kissinger could carry on discussions in China without reference to the standard operating procedures of the Department of State. However, when the action to be carried out requires the cooperation of large numbers of people in the major organizations of the American government, what the President can order done is much more limited. For example, when North Korean forces attacked South Korea in June of 1950, President Truman could only order into the fight those forces which already existed and which could reach the battlefield; these were the occupation forces in Japan under General Douglas MacArthur. When President Kennedy in 1961 wished to step up the number of American "advisers" in Vietnam, he could only send those "counterinsurgency" specialists who had already been trained by the government, either in the CIA or in the armed services.

The organization designated to carry out an action will use its standard operating procedures (SOPs) to do so. These procedures are routine methods which permit coordinated and concerted actions by large numbers of individuals. The rules for this purpose need to be simple in order to facilitate easy learning and unambiguous application. Clusters of standard procedures comprise a program for dealing with a particular situation. A set of programs related to a particular type of activity constitute an organization's repertoire. The number of programs in a repertoire is always quite limited. Thus activity according to standard operating procedures and programs does not constitute a farsighted, flexible adaptation to the decision made by the President. Rather, detailed implementation of actions by organizations is determined predominantly by organizational routines. Since the programs cannot be tailored to the specific situation, the organization, when striving to obey presidential decisions, will use whatever program in the existing repertoire seems most appropriate, given its limited understanding of the purposes of the decision.

Again we can cite Kennedy's experience with Vietnam. When he increased the number of American military personnel in Vietnam from 685 in 1961 to 10,000 in 1962, one observer noted that "there was no change in the advice provided by the advisor; there were just more advisors."[5] In general, the American troops later sent to Vietnam performed very much as they would if sent to fight a large-scale military battle on the plains of central Europe—toward which most of their training had been directed. The State Department, AID, and USIA missions likewise performed in accordance with their standard procedures.

---

[5]Corson, *The Betrayal* (New York: Norton, 1968), pp. 45–46.

Large organizations find it extremely difficult to develop new plans quickly or to implement plans developed for a different purpose. When the Soviet Union constructed the Berlin Wall in 1961, Kennedy found that he was offered no suggested choices of action by his advisers. All the contingency planning had been directed to other possible provocations such as a closing of the access routes between West Berlin and West Germany. Routine behavior will be followed even when it appears foolish to an outsider. During the Cuban missile crisis, for example, intelligence officers reported that Russian and Cuban planes were inexplicably lined up wingtip to wingtip on Cuban air fields, making perfect targets. Kennedy, recognizing this as a standard military practice, had a U-2 fly over the American air fields in Florida and discovered that American planes were similarly lined up.

When a senior official gives an order to an organization to carry out an action, he is likely to have an idealized picture of what will then occur. He assumes that the organization will quickly grasp what he is trying to accomplish and adapt its behavior creatively to the particular purpose. The truth is, however, that action, when it involves large numbers, may turn into something quite different from what the official had in mind. One such episode occurred during the summit meeting of 1960. Secretary of Defense Thomas Gates, who had accompanied Eisenhower to Paris, learned that Khrushchev was making rather strong demands and became convinced that the summit conference was about to end in disagreement. He therefore decided on Sunday night to order a worldwide alert of American military forces, feeling that it would be prudent to have local commanders alerted at battle stations all over the globe. He sent a message to the Pentagon calling for a "quiet" alert on a "minimum need to know basis." The Secretary, however, was not familiar with the set of alert patterns that had been developed and did not specify which alert, among alternatives numbered one to five, he wished to have implemented. The Joint Chiefs, feeling the pressure of time and having to guess what Gates wished to accomplish, concluded that alert number three was in order but adhered to Gates's injunction about restricting information. Gates evidently had not visualized that there would be any movement of weapons or troops, but the Pentagon announced that both the continental air defense command and SAC had conducted "limited routine air alert activities." The alert quickly became visible throughout the country and undoubtedly was visible as well to the Soviet Union, sending a signal far different from Gates's simple desire to have the military ready in case the situation should deteriorate.

RESISTANCE

Thus far we have explored why presidential decisions may not be obeyed even though implementers seek faithfully to do what the President or his principal associates have ordered them to do. For that reason, the discussion has been somewhat artificial, for in fact those who are assigned to implement presidential decisions often do not feel obliged to execute their orders. Neither career officials nor political appointees necessarily feel that a presidential decision settles the matter. Participants still have different interests and still see different faces of an issue and have different stakes. They may believe that their conception of what is in the national interest is still correct, and they will resist efforts to do things which they feel are contrary to the national interest or to their own organizational or personal interest even if they have been directed by the President. Henry Kissinger explained the problem to a journalist after serving for several years as President Nixon's Assistant for National Security Affairs:

> The outsider believes a Presidential order is consistently followed out. Nonsense. I have to spend considerable time seeing that it is carried out and in the spirit the President intended. Inevitably, in the nature of bureaucracy, departments become pressure groups for a point of view. If the President decides against them, they are convinced some evil influence worked on the President: if only he knew all the facts, he would have decided their way.
>
> The nightmare of the modern state is the hugeness of the bureaucracy, and the problem is how to get coherence and design in it.[6]

---

[6]Saul Pett, "Henry A. Kissinger: Loyal Retainer or Nixon's Svengali," *Washington Post,* August 23, 1970, p. B-3.

This problem is not a new one. It has confronted every American President in the modern period, and they have reacted either by seeking to concentrate power in the White House or by trying to get the departments under control. Truman in his memoirs revealed his strong feelings on the subject:

The difficulty with many career officials in the government is that they regard themselves as the men who really make policy and run the government. They look upon the elected officials as just temporary occupants. Every President in our history has been faced with this problem: how to prevent career men from circumventing presidential policy. Too often career men seek to impose their own views instead of carrying out the established policy of the administration. Sometimes they achieve this by influencing the key men appointed by the President to put his policies into operation. It has often happened in the War and Navy Departments that the generals and the admirals, instead of working for and under the Secretaries, succeeded in having the Secretaries act for and under them. And it has happened in the Department of State.

Some Presidents have handled this situation by setting up what amounted to a little State Department of their own. President Roosevelt did this and carried on direct communications with Churchill and Stalin. I did not feel that I wanted to follow this method, because the State Department is set up for the purpose of handling foreign policy operations, and the State Department ought to take care of them. But I wanted to make it plain that the President of the United States, and not the second or third echelon in the State Department, is responsible for making foreign policy, and, furthermore, that no one in any department can sabotage the President's policy. The civil servant, the general or admiral, the foreign service officer has no authority to make policy. They act only as servants of the government, and therefore they must remain in line with the government policy that is established by those who have been chosen by the people to set that policy.

In the Palestine situation, as Secretary Lovett said to me after the announcement of the recognition of Israel, "They almost put it over on you."[7]

---

[7]Harry S. Truman, *Memoirs.* Vol. II: *Years of Trial and Hope* (New York: Doubleday, 1956), p. 165.

This view that one knows what is best for national security affects not only career officials but also political appointees even when they clearly understand the President's own perspective. When at the first meeting of the Eisenhower Cabinet, even before inauguration, General Eisenhower expressed his strong support for increased trade with the Soviet Union, Secretary of Defense Charles Wilson said, "I am a little old fashioned. I don't like to sell firearms to the Indians." Eisenhower then explained in detail why he thought that such trade was good. Obviously, however, he failed to convince Wilson to go along, for the discussion concluded with Wilson saying, "I am going to be on the tough side of this one."[8]

One of the reasons the President is overwhelmingly busy is that so many officials maneuver to line him up on their side of an issue. Then, precisely because of the heavy demands made on his time, in part by them, Cabinet members and staff officers get away with ignoring his orders. One observer has commented succinctly on the game of outwaiting the President:

> Half of a President's suggestions, which theoretically carry the weight of orders, can be safely forgotten by a Cabinet member. And if the President asks about a suggestion a second time, he can be told that it is being investigated. If he asks a third time, a wise Cabinet officer will give him at least part of what he suggests. But only occasionally, except about the most important matters, do Presidents ever get around to asking three times.[9]

As a President discovers that his decisions are being resisted, he tends more and more to keep the bureaucracy in the dark and work through outside channels. This further reduces loyalty as well as contributing to inadvertent disobedience, which in turn reinforces presidential inclinations toward secrecy. Henry Kissinger, writing before he became an assistant to President Nixon, described the vicious circle that results:

---

[8]Sherman Adams, *Firsthand Report: The Story of the Eisenhower Administration* (New York: Harper & Brothers, 1961), p. 68. See also Hughes, *The Ordeal of Power*, p. 76.

[9]Jonathan Daniels, *Frontier on the Potomac* (New York: Macmillan, 1946), pp. 31–32.

Because management of the bureaucracy takes so much energy and precisely because changing course is so difficult, many of the most important decisions are taken by extra-bureaucratic means. Some of the key decisions are kept to a very small circle while the bureaucracy happily continues working away in ignorance of the fact that decisions are being made, or the fact that a decision is being made in a particular area. One reason for keeping the decisions to small groups is that when bureaucracies are so unwieldy and when their internal morale becomes a serious problem, an unpopular decision may be fought by brutal means, such as leaks to the press or to congressional committees. Thus, the only way secrecy can be kept is to exclude from the making of the decision all those who are theoretically charged with carrying it out. There is, thus, small wonder for the many allegations of deliberate sabotage of certain American efforts, or of great cynicism of American efforts because of inconsistent actions. In the majority of cases this was due to the ignorance of certain parts of the bureaucracy, rather than to malevolent intent. Another result is that the relevant part of the bureaucracy, because it is being excluded from the making of a particular decision, continues with great intensity sending out cables, thereby distorting the effort with the best intentions in the world. You cannot stop them from doing this because you do not tell them what is going on.[10]

THE STRUGGLE OVER IMPLEMENTATION

What we have said thus far should explain why a presidential decision simply opens a new round of maneuvers rather than settling the question of what is to be done. The process which occurs after a presidential decision goes along in much the same way as the efforts to get a presidential decision. Indeed, in many areas the two processes overlap, since there may be some presidential decisions and a simultaneous struggle over the implementation of them and of the drafting of new decisions. The participants are often the same as those who were involved in framing the decision, although many more lower-

---

[10]Henry Kissinger, "Bureaucracy and Policy Making," in Morton H. Halperin and Arnold Kanter (eds.), *Readings in American Foreign Policy: A Bureaucratic Perspective* (Boston: Little, Brown, 1973), p. 89.

level officials may be involved among those responsible for actual implementation, and senior officials are likely to devote less attention. The participants involved will bring to the process the same range of conceptions of what is in the national interest; they will tend to see different faces of the issue, have different stakes, and fight for different kinds of action. Participants have to decide again whether or not to get involved in the process, and some will develop strategies designed to secure the implementation of the President's decision if they favor it or to resist implementation if that is their position. They are constrained by rules of the game which determine who has the responsibility for implementing the decision, whose concurrence will be needed in any orders given, and who will have the right or responsibility to monitor compliance with the decision. If they favor the action, officials charged with implementation are likely to be able to proceed despite the opposition of other groups. If they resist, then the problem of securing implementation is much more difficult. However, the President's problem is difficult even if officials at the operations level favor his policy.

Overzealous Implementation

When the President approves a decision urged on him by those who will be responsible for its implementation, they often feel that he has not gone far enough, or they may choose to interpret the President's decision as giving them more license than he intended. They are then likely to act in a way which looks from the President's point of view to be overzealous implementation. Truman recalled how this happened to him in connection with his agreement to terminate lend-lease to America's European allies following the surrender of Germany:

> Leo Crowley, Foreign Economic Administrator, and Joseph C. Grew, Acting Secretary of State, came into my office after the Cabinet meeting on May 8 and said that they had an important order in connection with Lend-Lease which President Roosevelt had approved but not signed. It was an order authorizing the FEA and the State Department to take joint action to cut back the volume of Lend-Lease

supplies when Germany surrendered. What they told me made good sense to me; with Germany out of the war, Lend-Lease should be reduced. They asked me to sign it. I reached for my pen and, without reading the document, I signed it.

The storm broke almost at once. The manner in which the order was executed was unfortunate. Crowley interpreted the order literally and placed an embargo on all shipments to Russia and to other European nations, even to the extent of having some of the ships turned around and brought back to American ports for unloading. The British were hardest hit, but the Russians interpreted the move as especially aimed at them. Because we were furnishing Russia with immense quantities of food, clothing, arms, and ammunition, this sudden and abrupt interruption of Lend-Lease aid naturally stirred up a hornets' nest in that country. The Russians complained about our unfriendly attitude. We had unwittingly given Stalin a point of contention which he would undoubtedly bring up every chance he had. Other European governments complained about being cut off too abruptly. The result was that I rescinded the order.[11]

President Kennedy was confronted with an example of overzealous implementation in the case of a proposed multilateral force. A group of officials in the State Department favored the creation of a jointly manned and jointly owned nuclear force of surface ships to be operated by the NATO alliance. Upon securing from Kennedy a decision to ask the European allies of the United States whether they favored such a force, the advocates took this as an indication that the President wished them to seek to persuade others to join the force. Their own reasoning was that the President knew that "nothing happened" in Europe unless the United States forcefully advocated it. Therefore, from their perspective, simply asking the Europeans whether they were interested guaranteed that nothing would happen. Kennedy, on the other hand, apparently assumed that he had authorized only quiet exploration and was surprised to discover the Europeans believed that he was pressing hard for the multilateral force.

---

[11]Harry S. Truman, *Memoirs*. Vol. I: *Years of Decisions* (New York: Doubleday, 1955), pp. 227–28.

Disregarding Orders

As noted above, officials find ways to overlook, twist, or resist orders. Franklin Roosevelt once gave a classic description of how this is done in general:

> The Treasury is so large and far-flung and ingrained in its practices that I find it is almost impossible to get the action and results I want —even with Henry [Morgenthau] there. But the Treasury is not to be compared with the State Department. You should go through the experience of trying to get any changes in the thinking, policy, and action of the career diplomats, and then you'd know what a real problem was. But the Treasury and the State Department put together are nothing compared with the Na-a-vy. The admirals are really something to cope with—and I should know. To change anything in the Na-a-vy is like punching a feather bed. You punch it with your right and you punch it with your left until you are finally exhausted, and then you find the damn bed just as it was before you started punching.[12]

Orders are often disregarded more or less openly. Participants make no effort to disguise the fact that they do not favor the presidential decision and will do what they can to thwart it. For this purpose they set in motion one or more of the following maneuvers.

1. *Do not pass on orders.* One technique available to senior participants is not to pass on to those who actually have to carry out the directive the order received from the President. "Forgetting" and "overriding circumstances" serve as excuses. During the preparations for the Bay of Pigs invasion, for example, President Kennedy directed that if the invading forces were failing to establish a beachhead, they should move quickly to the mountains and become a guerrilla force. However, the CIA did not pass this instruction on to the leader of the brigade. CIA officials later explained that they felt that to do so might weaken the brigade's resolve to fight and that the brigade might choose the alternative plan when the going got rough, even though the

---

[12]Marriner S. Eccles, *Beckoning Frontiers* (New York: Knopf, 1951), p. 336.

invasion still had a chance of success. More than once a Secretary of Defense has kept a presidential directive to himself in the belief that to pass it on would greatly complicate the problem of dealing with the Joint Chiefs of Staff. Both Secretary of Defense Charles Wilson under Eisenhower and Secretary of Defense James Forrestal under Truman failed to deliver presidential directives establishing ceilings on force levels.

2. *Change "cosmetics" but not reality.* A second technique is to change the formal procedures regarding what is to be done but make it clear to subordinates that the reality is to remain the same. Eisenhower during the course of his presidency became increasingly aware of the limited authority of "unified" military commanders who were supposed to be in charge of all of the American forces in overseas areas such as Europe or the Far East. He therefore devoted considerable energy to persuading the services to accept and Congress to enact a change in procedure which would strengthen the area commander's authority. In presenting the 1958 defense reorganization act to the Congress, Eisenhower stated that "each Unified Commander must have unquestioned authority over all units of his command. . . . The commander's authority over these component commands is short of the full command required for maximum efficiency.[13] At the time that Eisenhower sent his message to Congress, the authority of area commanders was known as "Operational Control." The 1958 act invested in the area commander "full operational command," indicating an intent on the part of the Congress to overcome the deficiency pointed out by Eisenhower. However, as a Blue Ribbon Defense Panel subsequently concluded, "[With respect to] Unified Action Armed Forces (JCS Pub. 2) which sets forth principles, doctrines, and functions governing the activities and performance of Forces assigned to Unified Commands, the JCS now define 'Operational Command' as being synonymous with 'Operational Control.'" According to the panel, the command arrangements remained "substantially unchanged," and "the net result is an organizational structure in which 'unification' of either command or of the forces is more cosmetic than substan-

---

[13]Cited in Blue Ribbon Defense Panel, *Report to the President and the Secretary of Defense by the Blue Ribbon Defense Panel* (Washington: Government Printing Office, 1970), p. 50.

tive."[14] Thus there was a change in wording but no change in the reality, despite a clear presidential and congressional directive.

3. *Do something else.* A more blatant form of disobedience is to simply ignore a directive and do something else which either runs contrary to what the President ordered or simply does not take into account what the President sought. On August 15, 1945, for example, Truman sent a formal memorandum to the Secretaries of State, War, and Navy, to the Joint Chiefs of Staff, and to the Director of the Office of Scientific Research and Development. In that memorandum he directed that they "take such steps as are necessary to prevent the release of any information in regard to the development, design, or production of the atomic bomb."[15] Soon thereafter, these agencies released the so-called Smyth Report which contained considerable information about the design and production of the atomic bomb!

Truman was confronted with similar disobedience from the State Department during his efforts to take charge of American policy toward Israel. Truman had directed that the United States should support partition of Palestine. The American delegate to the UN, Warren Austin, despite the fact that he was aware of this presidential directive, declared in public at the United Nations that the United States was no longer for partition. This step was taken with the concurrence of the State Department but without Truman being informed. Nor was Truman the only President treated in this way by his subordinates. Eisenhower relates one episode when Secretary of State John Foster Dulles, who on the whole bent over backward to follow specific presidential directives, probably ignored one:

In the period between the Summit Conference and the Foreign Ministers' meeting, I became ill. Before Foster left to attend the meeting he came to Denver so that we could confer in my hospital room. He had prepared a draft of a reply to Mr. Bulganin, who had asked us for a further explanation of my July proposal for exchanging "blueprints" of military establishments. *Inadvertently,* Foster had omitted my statement to the Soviet delegation at Geneva that if they would accept an aerial inspection system, I was quite ready to accept

[14]Ibid., p. 50.
[15]Truman, *Years of Decisions,* p. 524.

their proposition for ground teams. With this correction made, I signed the letter to Bulganin.[16]

It is difficult to believe that the omission was in fact inadvertent.

4. *Delay*. Another technique to avoid the implementation of a presidential decision is simply to delay, either not taking the action that the President has directed or moving very slowly toward implementing it. A view of this technique at work in a specific setting is offered by a former high official of the CIA who reports on CIA resistance to a presidential directive:

Despite that, shortly thereafter a National Security Council directive ordered the Agency to implement certain of the recommendations. I remember having lunch with Najeeb Halaby and discussing the report and directive. Jeeb Halaby, who later became nationally known as the administrator of the Federal Aviation Administration, was then serving in the office of the Secretary of Defense on matters that later were organized under the assistant secretary for International Security Affairs. He had considerable dealings with the CIA and was anxious to see it develop into a strong agency. I recall the conversation vividly because we both agreed that the report and directive were an important step forward, but I predicted that they would not be implemented at that time. Halaby expressed incredulity, noting that it was a Presidential Directive, but I maintained that bureaucracy grinds exceeding slow and if a directive was unpopular with the bosses it could grind even slower.

Such proved to be the case. When General Smith arrived in Washington in October 1950, nearly a year later, to take over from Hillenkoetter, who had gone on to another naval assignment, little had been done to implement the report.[17]

5. *Obey the letter but not the spirit of the orders.* Because orders are expressed in generalities and the implementing instructions themselves tend not to be very precise, officials at the operations level frequently have leeway to implement the decisions as they choose.

---

[16]Dwight D. Eisenhower, *The White House Years.* Vol. I: *Mandate for Change* (New York: Doubleday, 1963), p. 527 (italics added).

[17]Lyman B. Kirkpatrick, Jr., *The Real CIA* (New York: Macmillan, 1968), p. 89.

They often do this in ways which follow the letter of what they are told to do but not the spirit of what the President had in mind, even insofar as they understand that spirit.

This sort of behavior occurred on March 31, 1968, when the American military officers, in planning the first bombing of North Vietnam after President Johnson's speech announcing a cutback of the bombing, chose to obey the letter of their instructions rather than the spirit of the President's address. Johnson had publicly declared:

> I am taking the first step to de-escalate the conflict. We are reducing— substantially reducing—the present level of hostilities . . . unilaterally and at once. Tonight, I have ordered our aircraft and our naval vessels to make no attacks on North Vietnam, except in the area north of the Demilitarized Zone where the continuing enemy buildup directly threatens allied forward positions. . . .[18]

The unmistakable implication of what he said was that the remaining bombing would be related to tactical targets in order to provide protection for U.S. ground forces immediately below the Demilitarized Zone. Later press reports made it clear that the orders to the field directed the military simply to cease all bombing north of 20 degrees, but presumably the text of the President's speech was also available, at least informally, to those planning bombing raids. Nevertheless, much of the weight of the first bombing raids on April 1, 1968, was directed at the only large city below 20 degrees in North Vietnam. The ultimate "message" conveyed not only to the North Vietnamese but also to the American people was one of selected devastation rather than de-escalation. Thus the credibility gap widened even though the commander-in-chief of U.S. forces in the Pacific, who directed the bombing raids against North Vietnam, was acting fully within his orders in carrying out the strikes on North Vietnam.

Whereas the military can generally stretch orders involving combat operations, the State Department often has this flexibility in drafting cables. Elizabeth Drew describes one episode in a fight by the State

---

[18] *New York Times,* April 1, 1968.

Department to resist White House orders to step up American economic aid to the secessionist province of Biafra in Nigeria:

> When Biafra fell, the White House announced that the President had placed on alert, for relief purposes, transport planes and helicopters, and was donating $10 million. This was done on White House initiative. . . .
>
> This difference was fought out, as such issues usually are, in seemingly minor bureaucratic skirmishes over such things as the wording of cables, and the tone of statements to the press. State, for example, drafted a cable instructing our representatives in Lagos to emphasize that the helicopters and planes were only on standby, and that the $10 million had only been made available because British Prime Minister Harold Wilson had told President Nixon that there was concern over the relief effort. The White House rewrote the cable, deleting the apologetic tone and emphasizing the President's concern that the Nigerians speed relief. It is in such ways that the United States government's posture in a crisis can be determined.[19]

Changing Decisions

The maneuvers that we have discussed so far involve finding ways not to do what one is ordered to do. Different maneuvers exist for resisting a decision by seeking to get it changed by the President or (in spite of the President) by Congress.

1. *Insist on a personal hearing before obeying.* Most often presidential orders have been passed on to other officials either in writing or through a member of the White House staff. When they do not like such orders, senior officials can demand a hearing from the President, insist that, before they will accept his orders, they must be sure that he has heard their side of the argument and that the orders are being transmitted accurately to them. As part of this ploy they are likely to claim that the President may well have been misunderstood; and they may enlist the support of a friendly member of the White House staff.

2. *Suggest reasons for reconsidering.* A related technique which can be used even when one has gotten an order from the President is

---

[19]Elizabeth B. Drew, "Washington," *Atlantic Monthly,* Vol. 225 (June 1970), pp. 6, 10.

to insist upon going back to him to "report unforeseen implications." This technique is easiest to use when the President has turned down a request for permission to do something, but it also can be used when the President very specifically directs that a certain action be carried out. Dean Acheson describes in his memoirs in vivid detail the aftermath of a presidential decision to send a cable to General MacArthur ordering withdrawal of a message that MacArthur planned to make public regarding the terms for peace in Korea:

> For some time the President had had a meeting scheduled with the Secretaries of State, Treasury, and Defense, Harriman, and the Joint Chiefs of Staff for nine-thirty on that morning. When we filed into the oval office, the President, with lips white and compressed, dispensed with the usual greetings. He read the message and then asked each person around the room whether he had had any prior intimation or knowledge of it. No one had. Louis Johnson was directed to order MacArthur from the President to withdraw the message and report that he (MacArthur) had done so. The President himself would send directly to MacArthur a copy of Ambassador Austin's letter to Trygve Lie, from which he would understand why the withdrawal order was necessary. The business for which the meeting was called was hastily dispatched.
>
> When we left the White House, nothing could have been clearer to me than that the President had issued an order to General MacArthur to withdraw the message, but Secretary Johnson soon telephoned to say that this could cause embarrassment and that he (Johnson) thought it better to inform MacArthur that if he issued the statement "we" would reply that it was "only one man's opinion and not the official policy of the Government." I said that the issue seemed to be who was President of the United States. Johnson then asked me an amazing question—whether "we dare send [MacArthur] a message that the President directs him to withdraw his statement?" I saw nothing else to do in view of the President's order.
>
> At Johnson's request, I asked Averell Harriman whether he was clear that the President had issued an order. This shortly resulted in another call from Johnson saying that the President had dictated to him this message to go to MacArthur: "The President of the United States directs that you withdraw your message for National Encampment of Veterans of Foreign Wars, because various features with regard to Formosa are in conflict with the policy of the United States and its position in the United Nations."

Still Johnson doubted the wisdom of sending the order and put forward his prior alternative. Stephen Early, his deputy, came on the telephone to support him, raised the question of General MacArthur's right of free speech, and proposed that the President talk to General MacArthur. At this point I excused myself and ended the conversation, duly reporting it to Harriman, saying that if Johnson wished to reopen the President's decision, he should apply to the President to do so. The President instructed Harriman that he had dictated what he wanted to go and he wanted it to go. It went. MacArthur's message was both withdrawn and unofficially published.[20]

3. *Go to the Hill.* Another way to fight a presidential decision is to bring the matter to Congress, either in open testimony or privately. This maneuver is of course most effective when the presidential decision requires congressional concurrence such as appropriation of funds, approval of a treaty, or the enactment of legislation permitting government reorganization. The channel of communication usually runs between career officials of an organization in the executive branch and staff members of congressional subcommittees. Congressmen often see it as their duty to protect the permanent bureaucracy against encroachments of the President and the Cabinet officers.

The undercutting of the President can be done quite subtly, simply, for example, by not showing the necessary enthusiasm for a proposal to get it through. Sherman Adams, President Eisenhower's principal White House assistant, describes one such episode during Eisenhower's long campaign to get a reorganization of the Defense Department approved by the Congress:

Unfortunately for the President, his Secretary of Defense, Neil McElroy, did not appear to share Eisenhower's spirited dedication to the reorganization plan when he appeared to testify on it before the House committee. In sending his recommendations to Congress, the President had drafted most of the wording of the bill himself. This was a rare procedure. Usually the President left the drafting of a bill to the ranking member of his party on the appropriate committee to work out with the department head concerned. This time, because

---

[20]Dean Acheson, *Present at the Creation: My Years in the State Department* (New York: Norton, 1969), pp. 423–24.

Eisenhower had drafted himself, almost word for word, the legislation that he wanted enacted it was assumed in the House that he was taking an unshakable no-compromise stand on it. But McElroy gave the committee the impression that the administration would be willing to make concessions. He was unable to give the inquiring Congressmen any specific examples of the "outmoded concepts" that Eisenhower had cited as the main reason for the need of unification. He indicated that the terms of the bill were in some respects broader than was necessary, but the President was in some degree responsible for McElroy's comment since he had said that he did not regard the exact language of the bill as necessarily sacrosanct. This weakened the President's case somewhat and gave Uncle Carl Vinson the opening to drive in objections to some of the key provisions.

After McElroy left the door open, the President jumped up fast to close it, but the room was already filled with snow. McElroy admitted to Uncle Carl's committee that the Secretary of Defense did not actually need the sweeping powers to assign and transfer that the bill conferred upon him. The President reversed the Secretary and came back strongly to assert that any retreat from this position of demand for supervisory control would make unified strategy impossible. Eisenhower sent word to Congress that no concessions would be made because they had already been made before the bill was submitted. What they were considering were the bare essentials, he declared.[21]

Military officers more often than others have resorted to Congress —in part because of the automatic support they have found there for their views. Many legislators insist that Congress has a duty to hear the views of career military officers who disagree with the President. The White House naturally opposes this outlook, and over the years efforts have been made to reduce the freedom of the military to testify independently before Congress. Under Truman, military officers had the freedom to volunteer the information that they disagreed with an administration proposal and, after making clear that the administration favored the proposal, to express their personal views against it. Secretary of Defense McNamara in the 1960s sought to impose a much more restrictive rule: that the military reveal differences only

---

[21]Adams, *Firsthand Report,* pp. 418–19.

if pressed and then in admitting the disagreement to give the administration's side of the case as well.

4. *Go public.* One way to alert Congress as well as the public is to provide information to the press. Here the hope is that news of disagreement over a decision will stir up public or congressional opposition forcing the President to back down. In 1961, for example, the Army, concerned about the fact that President Kennedy was forcing on the military a counterguerrilla strategy in Vietnam which would impair the ability of the South Vietnamese forces to resist a conventional invasion from North Vietnam, leaked news of Kennedy's action and the Army's objections to the press.

5. *Go to another government.* If all else fails, those seeking to oppose implementation of a decision can go to another government and try to get them to intervene. Where the action directed was to try to persuade a second government to do something, this can be resisted by quietly urging that government not to go along with the U.S. demands. Averell Harriman believes that this was done during his efforts to negotiate an agreement concerning Laos. He maintains that the head of the right-wing forces, General Phoumi, was advised by some U.S. officials to hold out against U.S. pressures for a compromise settlement.

Resisting Requests for Proposals

Thus far we have considered mainly those cases in which the President gives an order to do something, often something that may affect the behavior of another government. Occasionally, however, the President orders his staff to work up a proposal *for* doing something in a certain area. In such cases, the bureaucracy's ability to ignore presidential demands is probably greater. Among the techniques commonly used are the following.

1. *Do not respond.* Presidents often make such requests for imaginative or new proposals in a particular area. Such requests are often ignored, and then, when the President inquires, he is told the problem is so difficult that a proposal is not yet ready. This technique is particularly convenient when the President insists that he receive a proposal unanimously agreed to by all his advisers. President Eisen-

hower, for example, apparently believed strongly that the United States should put forward more imaginative proposals in the arms control field, and he continuously pressed his advisers to come up with proposals which could be put to him for his approval. But he also expected his advisers to agree with each other, and such proposals were seldom forthcoming. The no-response technique can be used even when the President's request is a relatively simple and straightforward one and he asks not for opinions but simply for a procedural plan to implement a proposal already decided upon. One example is the way the State Department delayed action upon President Kennedy's wish to create the post of Under Secretary of State for Latin American Affairs. As Arthur Schlesinger, Jr., relates the incident:

> The President was more troubled than ever by the organization of Latin American affairs within our own government. Late in October he discussed with Richard Goodwin and me the old problem which Berle had raised in 1961 of an Under Secretaryship of State for Inter-American Affairs, embracing both the Alliance and the political responsibilities of the Assistant Secretary. Kennedy, remarking sharply that he could not get anyone on the seventh floor of the State Department to pay sustained attention to Latin America, dictated a plain-spoken memorandum to Rusk saying that he wanted to create the new Under Secretaryship. "I am familiar," he said, "with the argument that, if we do this for Latin America, other geographical areas must receive equal treatment. But I have come increasingly to feel that this argument, however plausible in the abstract, overlooks the practicalities of the situation." Historically Latin America was an area of primary and distinctive United States interest; currently it was the area of greatest danger to us; and operationally it simply was not receiving the day-to-day, high level attention which our national interest demanded. "Since I am familiar with the arguments against the establishment of this Under Secretaryship," his memorandum to the Secretary concluded somewhat wearily, "I would like this time to have a positive exploration of its possibilities."
>
> He had in mind for the job Sargent Shriver or perhaps Averell Harriman, whom he had just designated to lead the United States delegation to the São Paulo meeting. We later learned that Rusk sent the presidential memorandum to the Assistant Secretary for Administration, who passed it along to some subordinate, and it took Ralph Dungan's intervention to convince the Secretary that this was a

serious matter requiring senior attention. Receiving no response, the President after a fortnight renewed the request.[22]

2. *Not now.* An alternative to no response at all is a plea for postponement. State Department officials often caution the White House that the timing is wrong for a particular initiative because of the delicate political situation. John Foster Dulles was able to use this technique with great effectiveness because of President Eisenhower's feeling that he should defer to Dulles on diplomatic issues. As Eisenhower implied in an interview shortly after leaving office, it was this maneuver that kept the United States from withdrawing any troops from Europe despite the President's strong feelings that they should come out and despite his expertise as a former commander of those forces.

> Though for eight years in the White House I believed and announced to my associates that a reduction of American strength in Europe should be initiated as soon as European economies were restored, the matter was then considered too delicate a political question to raise. I believe the time has now come when we should start withdrawing some of those troops.[23]

3. *Come back with a different proposal.* A further technique for stalling is to come back and present to the President a proposal significantly different from the directive that he has put forward. Often the proposal will take account of the organizational interests of the bureau or department involved. When President Kennedy was preparing to ask General Lucius Clay to go to Berlin as the President's principal adviser, reporting directly to Kennedy and taking overall charge of the situation, the State Department and the Defense Department combined to change the draft so that Clay became simply an adviser with no operational control over the military or diplomatic mission in Berlin.

---

[22]Arthur M. Schlesinger, Jr., *A Thousand Days: John F. Kennedy in the White House* (Boston: Houghton Mifflin, 1965), pp. 1001–2.

[23]Interview with Eisenhower, *Saturday Evening Post,* October 26, 1963, as quoted in Charles H. Percy, "Paying for NATO," *Washington Monthly,* Vol. 2 (July 1970), p. 36.

13. Civil Rights Policies and the Matter of Compliance

Charles S. Bullock, III
Harrell R. Rodgers, Jr.

This article will attempt to isolate some of the factors which determine the various consequences of laws, and thus, their impact on civil rights policy. We shall raise some questions about the conditions under which laws will be obeyed and the conditions under which they will be met with disobedience or even revolt. We believe that such findings are

Reprinted from Charles S. Bullock, III, and Harrell R. Rodgers, Jr., *Law and Social Change* (New York: McGraw-Hill, 1972), pp. 181–209. Copyright © 1972 by McGraw-Hill Book Company and used with their permission.

best summarized in terms of a cost-benefit framework. We begin therefore by defining compliance as the consequence of individual evaluations about the cost and rewards of alternative courses of behavior.

THE UTILITY OF COMPLIANCE

Laws are political decisions (collectively made or otherwise) which can be perceived in a variety of ways by members of the political system. If a law is deemed to benefit all, compliance will probably be the rule. If it is considered to benefit none, it will probably not be obeyed. Typically, however, a law will be seen as a benefit by some, and as a burden by others. The important question is under what circumstances will those who perceive that they are harmed by a law still obey it? One answer is that the individual will maximize his utility by taking that action which entails the least personal cost and the greatest benefits. Evaluations of factors such as the certainty and severity of punishment for deviation, and the value hierarchy of each individual will determine how the costs involved in each compliance situation are perceived. If the individual determines that he stands to suffer a greater loss from obedience than disobedience, he will break the law. If he judges that he will suffer the greater cost by disobedience, he will comply.

The cost-benefit calculus is based on the assumption that the average individual's approach to law is rational. Even though a number of factors mitigate against perfect rationality (e.g., lack of information about the value, consequences, and number of alternatives), we believe that over a period of time the average citizen's behavior does reveal a pattern of rationality.

Our survey of the impact of law on five areas of civil rights policy provides evidence which handily supports the cost-benefit calculus. Repeatedly we noted that the efficacy of law, i.e., the ability of law to produce change is determined in large part by public acceptance. That is, the effectiveness of the civil rights laws has been determined considerably by whether the public and state and local officials evaluated them positively and decided they should be obeyed. Similarly, in the face of recalcitrance, compliance has improved as the cost of noncompliance has been raised.

To find that individual evaluations about the law are important to its efficacy runs counter to some traditional assumptions about democracy and majority rule. According to the norms of democracy a citizen's personal agreement or disagreement with a law should not determine compliance once the law has been promulgated. Society, it is assumed, can function only when most citizens are in the main willing to abide by the rules. We are, it is often said, a nation of laws and not of men, meaning that all men must be willing to accept the restraints of society for the common good. A citizen who disagrees with a particular law has only one legitimate option: to work through the democratic processes to achieve change. Even advocates of civil disobedience frequently argue that anyone who violates the normal pattern of seeking change in law must be willing to accept the sanctions of society.

Law-abidingness then is seen as basic to society. Children are taught from their earliest years, both at home and in school, that a good citizen obeys the law. Studies show that young children firmly hold this belief. Evidence also indicates that even as adults, the vast majority of citizens still believe in the importance of law-abidingness. For example, in one study a sample of adults was asked to react to the statement: "Even though one might strongly disagree with a state law—after it has been passed by the state legislature, one ought to obey it." Only 3 percent of the total sample disagreed.

Despite these findings, we have seen that in the area of civil rights large numbers of citizens and officials do not always obey the law. Can we conclude that the breaking of civil rights laws is exceptional behavior? Obviously not. Common sense and personal experience tell us that every citizen disobeys the law occasionally. Studies show that almost all citizens (91 percent) admit they have broken laws that carried penalties severe enough to send them to jail. What this means is that individual attitudes about law and law-abidingness do not provide a very accurate guide to behavior where specific laws are concerned. Once we descend from the civics books' ideal of law-abidingness and focus on specific laws, the cost-benefit calculus is a much more accurate guide.

Evidence about individual compliance is strongly supportive of the cost-benefit calculus. For example, one study found that when the average citizen evaluates a specific legal problem, he does not use a general societal standard, such as a sense of justice or a concept of law-abidingness, to decide how the dispute should be resolved. Instead the personal attitudes of the individual toward the law or the participants involved in the dispute determine the type of rule application he prefers. The individual, in other words, will favor a decision which maximizes his private utilities (i.e., the most benefits and the least cost). Similarly, if the average citizen is asked whether he thinks a schoolteacher who breaks the law by holding prayer in class should be punished, his decision will most often be based on whether he favors prayers in school. The fact that it is the "Supreme Law of the Land" that school prayers are illegal is less salient than the respondent's subjective evaluation of the situation. Under such circumstances the individual does not reject the norms of democracy; he simply does not see the connection between his abstract attitudes toward law-abidingness and his attitudes toward the application of legal rules in a specific situation. This is very much like the average citizens' attitudes toward individual rights. On the one hand, citizens will say they believe in freedom of speech, but not for communists, atheists, or people with whom they disagree or fear. Converse found a similar lack of constraint in most citizens' attitudes toward political issues. The average citizen, it would seem, does not have the cognitive skills necessary to develop a consistent philosophy toward law, democracy, or political issues; therefore his attitudes and behavior are not as congruent as one might assume.

Our argument does not hold that citizens subject every law that affects them to the cost-benefit calculus. Many laws that the average citizen comes in contact with affect him in such an unimportant way that he merely complies automatically without consideration of the cost-benefits of his behavior. Under these circumstances the law falls into what Chester I. Barnard has called the "zone of indifference." It is when the individual perceives that the law affects him in a meaningful way that he evaluates the utility of compliance.

Although most citizens are prone to be compliant even when they disagree with a law, most employ the cost-benefit calculus at one time or another and decide against obedience. Two types of lawbreaking seem to result. It is safe to say that most citizens engage in a type of lawbreaking that might be called "rule exception," in which they break (make exceptions to) laws they generally support because an immediate benefit of noncompliance is perceived which outweighs the anticipated cost of compliance. For example, most citizens support traffic laws that they occasionally, or even frequently, break. Such behavior is rationalized with familiar excuses: "I was in a hurry," or "There was hardly any traffic." A more dramatic form of lawbreaking might be called "rule rejection," in which the individual breaks the law because he disagrees with it or he questions the right of the government to make such a law. Rule rejection is the type of noncompliance that has occurred so frequently in the area of civil rights. Sanctions play an important role in keeping rule rejection and rule exception from getting out of hand.

Having established our conceptual framework, we turn now to an evaluation of the factors which determine the cost-benefits of civil rights laws and thus their outcome.

THE POLITICAL CONTEXT

Since individual attitudes and behavior are normally shaped by the traditions and mores of the society one lives in, the social, economic, and political characteristics of an environment have a tremendous impact on the success of a law. Dolbeare has found, in fact, that these factors are often more important than the substance of a law in determining what policy changes will take place. Naturally rule rejection and rule exception are facilitated by public approval. A law that runs strongly against the mores of a particular environment has little chance of effecting change unless it is enforced very rigorously. An unpopular law (e.g., prohibition or civil rights laws in some regions) or a law that regulates a type of deviant behavior that many citizens engage in frequently or occasionally (liquor, gambling, or game laws) is very difficult to enforce, the reason being that when the public or one's peers sanction disobedience, the cost of lawbreaking decreases dramatically. The punishment for breaking a law is not decreased; but if the social disapproval associated with an act of lawbreaking is low, the likelihood that the sanction will be invoked is lessened. Thus, in some parts of the country even murder has gone unpunished. Also, under conditions of social approval, even if the lawbreaker is punished, the social stigma associated with the punishment is decreased. In fact, punishment may even enhance one's prestige (e.g., even though George Wallace lost the confrontation with Federal marshals at the University of Alabama, he won the undying loyalty of much of the electorate in the Deep South). When an act of lawbreaking is strongly condemned by society, the cost of disobedience is high both in terms of public (and possibly personal) disapproval and the chances of being punished. In such cases, lawbreaking occurs more rarely.

Frequently we have found local and state officials obligated to uphold civil rights laws with which they and their constituents have disagreed. Reflecting on the subjective orientation of individuals toward law, it is not difficult to understand why many of these officials would choose to violate or ignore the law. The fact that they ostensibly believe in the democratic system does not deter them from noncompliance. When the law violates personal beliefs or cultural mores, the perceived cost of compliance rises. Under these circumstances officials may feel justified in—even obligated to—disobeying the law.

The South, which has remained a subsystem of the United States, naturally finds itself frequently at odds with national laws. Since the South has long prided itself on a refusal to subordinate local practices to national norms, noncompliance with a number of Federal laws has been more frequent in the South. . . .

Perception of the Legitimacy of Law As a Cost Factor

An important factor in determining whether an individual will comply with a specific law is his evaluation of the legitimacy of the law. If the individual rejects the legitimacy of the law, the psychic cost of disobedience is lowered considerably. Legitimacy is related to whether the individual has a positive attitude toward the agent of the law and whether he believes that the agent had the authority to make the law. This evaluation may vary with the subject matter of the law (even when the same agent is involved) and is closely linked to the individual's agreement or disagreement with specific laws. For example, Southerners who reject the right of the Supreme Court to make certain decisions concerning civil rights may be more than willing to uphold its right to make powerful decisions in other areas.

Perceptions of the legitimacy of a law are closely related to the prevailing traditions and mores of a community or region. For example, Murphy and Tanenhaus found that Southerners are much more critical of the United States Supreme Court than are citizens in other parts of the nation. They also found that the public's support for the Court is based, to a large extent, on its agreement with the Court's decisions. Individuals who disagree with the civil rights decisions of the Court are then more likely to reject these laws as being illegitimate and, as a consequence, find the psychic cost of breaking the law to be lower.

The origin of a law can play an important role in conditioning perceptions of legitimacy. The Supreme Court is the most vulnerable branch of the national government when questions of legitimacy are raised because, as surveys show, the public's support for the Court has been moderate to low in recent years and because the public does not perceive the Court as a policy-making agency. The public expects policy to be produced by popularly elected officials such as the Chief Executive or Congress. Consequently, there is less doubt about the legitimacy of a law if Congress or the President is the agent. For example, Congress would have been a much better agent of the policy initiated in the *Brown* decision. In the school desegregation cases the Court was making policy. Public awareness of this fact frequently leads to rejection of the legitimacy of the decisions. Hogan has observed that: "Supreme Court legislation has a great limitation—its effective authority is limited to doing those things which society is ready to do." Wasby concurs, adding that "if the Supreme Court is 'ahead of the times' in its decisions, noncompliance bulks large, but if the Court is 'behind the times' (but not too far), reactions to its decisions will be positive, and they will be both applauded and accepted."

Decision Makers

If the cultural context is the most important determinant of the outcome of a law, decision makers (elites) are the most critical ingredient of this context. Only a handful of studies have been conducted by political scientists on compliance, but they all agree that state and local decision makers exert the most important influence in the compliance equation. Additionally, these studies indicate that the attitudes of the decision makers' constituents may influence how they react, but the most important determinant of their behavior is their own cognitive attitudes. In the area of race relations decision makers usually seem to be able to obey Federal laws if they want to. If local citizens are extremely hostile, the decision makers may have to pave the way for compliance, but this is usually possible.

Undoubtedly civil rights is novel in terms of the amount and intensity of public feelings on the topic. Occasionally the public may be so violently opposed to compliance that decision makers cannot but wait for tempers to cool. In most cases where the public has become violent, however, it has taken its cues from the political leaders. As Dolbeare and Hammond point out, "clearly, compliance rates are linked to the words and action of state officials." The ability of decision makers to set the tone and pace of compliance is revealed by the fact that the least compliance has occurred in those areas in which state and local leaders have been most vocal in their opposition. Let us look at an example. School desegregation has been a topic of intense debate in the South. In the Border states (e.g., Tennessee, Kentucky, Virginia, Texas, and Oklahoma) some progress in desegregation was achieved in the years immediately following *Brown*. In the Deep South states (e.g., Georgia, Mississippi, Louisiana, and Alabama) progress did not begin for many years. In terms of social, economic, and political factors the two areas have much in common. Why then was there so much difference in progress? Officials in the Deep South states would have us believe that the difference resulted from more intense problems in their areas. This may be true in some parts of the Deep South, but it is clearly not the prime factor. The major difference is that many decision makers in the Border states accepted responsibility for seeing that the law was obeyed, while in many areas of the Deep South officials were still holding out. Clearly environmental hostility in the latter region generates some of this reluctance, but equally intense problems were overcome in several of the Border states. Mississippi and Alabama, which have had the most outspoken racist governors in the country, have progressed at a slower pace than Georgia, which had two moderate governors before Lester Maddox took office. As a result of Orville Faubus' reign, Arkansas has progressed more slowly than other Border states. The point is that when decision makers work toward achieving compliance they can produce results, especially when they have 15 years to do the job. When decision makers criticize and defy the law they free, and indeed cast a mantle of legitimacy upon, the most violent and recalcitrant elements in society.

We shall consider some of the factors which determine whether decision makers will consider compliance a benefit or a cost.

Disagreement with the law. An obvious factor is that many decision makers have honestly disagreed with the civil rights laws and have believed that they would be letting themselves and their constituents down by complying. This is not surprising since decision makers usually have more intense political preferences than average citizens. To many decision makers, being on the side of law and order has not been as important as defending what they believe to be the integrity of their state or community. In most instances, of course, racial prejudice has been the motivating factor behind disagreement with the law. Inherited fears about slave revolts and black political takeovers have motivated responses in other instances. Also, stereotypes linking blacks with violence, drunkenness, and immorality have played a negative role.

Demagogism. Many decision makers saw personal benefit to be gained by defying the law. The race issue gave many public officials and would-be officials a means of elevating themselves by playing on the fears and hostilities of the public, e.g., Wallace's campaign in the 1968 presidential race.

Fear of conflict. Many decision makers avoided enforcement of the law for fear that one of the costs of compliance would be serious conflict in their state or community. These leaders probably realized that if they wanted to pave the way for compliance they could, but the path of least resistance was to simply avoid the issue at no risk to their image. In many cases local officials would have had a difficult time enforcing the law without serious conflict in situations in which their state leaders were opposed to the law. As Crain et al. pointed out, to obey the law local officials frequently "must take considerable risk, . . . must be willing to alienate the 'rednecks,' to run the danger of social . . . or even physical attack." Also since citizens opposed to the law were usually more vocal and more organized than citizens in favor of the law, no action resulted in the least conflict.

The need to be liked and to maintain existing relationships. Many decision makers feared that if they defended or implemented the law, they would be shunned by their friends and neighbors. This was a serious cost, one weighing upon even some Southern judges. On the other hand, defiance of the law usually enhanced a decision maker's prestige with the local populace. The need to be liked and accepted is a powerful motivating force in most people, and it is not surprising that many decision makers proved vulnerable.

The need to conform. Similarly, studies show that the need to conform to local patterns and mores is extremely strong. It is the rare person who transcends his culture, for the costs are heavy. To enforce the law or work toward achievement of compliance would be an act of considerable courage in many communities.

The need to be correct. Most individuals likewise have a strong need to be correct. To admit that one has been wrong entails certain personal costs. Public recanting does not come easily. Once decision makers decided not to obey a law or decided a law was invalid, they resisted ever obeying such a law because this would be an admission that their earlier behavior was wrong. Dolbeare and Hammond in a study of compliance with the Court's prayer decisions found that decision makers in their study evinced this need. "Having once committed themselves to inaction, they apparently generated cognitive and perceptual screens against dissonance or role strain."

IF PUSH COMES TO SHOVE: THE ROLE OF COERCION

If decision makers or the public will not comply with the law and the government must take measures to force compliance, a number of factors determine the cost-benefits of compliance and thus the success of the government's efforts. We will examine these factors in terms of: (1) the government's commitment, (2) the nature of the policy involved, and (3) the substance and mechanics of the law.

Before such an analysis we might note some of the pros and cons of using force to gain compliance. On the negative side it is clear that when the government has to force compliance with civil rights laws, extensive delays are in the offing. The first delay takes place while the government provides enough time for voluntary compliance. If voluntary compliance does not take place, a series of negotiations between Federal, state, and local officials occurs, followed either by attempts to enforce the law or another period of grace in which reluctant officials are given another chance to comply voluntarily. This round may produce little progress because officials may still refuse to comply voluntarily or because the law may be too weak to produce much change. More time may then be consumed while the government debates and passes a new law. This series of adventures and misadventures has been most obvious in the areas of voting rights, school desegregation, and employment. All of these activities require a large number of personnel, considerable finances, and a great deal of time.

Fear of other negative consequences has frequently been behind the government's failure to vigorously enforce civil rights laws. The government's reticence seems to be based on two things: (1) a belief that results will be more satisfactory if state and local officials recognize the legitimacy of the law by complying voluntarily; and (2) a fear that forcing large numbers of individuals to obey the law may have negative consequences. For example, unrelieved force may alienate large groups of citizens from the party in office or even from the political system. The Supreme Court is as reluctant as Congress and the executive branch to coerce compliance with its decisions. The Court realizes that its authority is derived from the public (or at least elites) and that this authority cannot be based on coercion alone. Consequently the Court, like the other branches of the Federal government, usually tries patiently to persuade recalcitrant officials to comply with the law by emphasizing the legitimacy of the law and the obligation to comply.

Another negative consequence of coercion is that it may not work. In many instances even rather vigorous attempts to force compliance by public officers have not been successful because it is almost impossible to write laws without loopholes through which determined decision makers can escape. Hundreds of evasive actions can typically be used to flaunt the law. In many instances truly exceptional creativity produced new ways of avoiding the law. One need only consider the efforts made by white Southerners to keep black Americans from exercising the franchise to understand this point. An acceptance of the rules of the game by all the parties involved is extremely important for the law to function.

Regardless of the disadvantages of coercion, it is critical to the cost-benefit equation. Even when citizens agree with specific laws and support the rules of the game, coercion is necessary to insure compliance. As Malcolm Freeley has pointed out, "the coercive provisions of law are . . . the 'cost factors' in the calculus of decisions affecting behavior governed by legal rules." If the law is to be effective, there are conditions when coercion must be used. In civil rights policy the government has generally overlooked the functional nature of coercion, and this has greatly impeded progress. We might consider some of the conditions under which force is functional. First, the use of sanctions can show that the government is serious about its responsibility for achieving a certain policy. Second, if the government is steadfast in its position and demonstrates a determination to see the law enforced, the cost of compliance may be lowered for some decision makers. For example, if decision makers under considerable pressure from constituents not to obey the law are faced with penalties for noncompliance, they can obey the law and defer local sanctions by saying they had no choice. This works best if the alternatives for resistance are cut off and a consistent policy is applied to all communities. Local decision makers are put on the spot if their community goes further in obeying the law than neighboring communities. In many instances the government has failed to give local officials the support needed.

Additionally, it is well known that once an individual is influenced to go partway toward a goal, it is easier to get him to go all the way. By taking action toward a goal, the individual has accepted, in part, its legitimacy. This is referred to by social psychologists as the "foot-in-the-door technique." If the government had forced officials to make a good faith start toward obeying the civil rights laws earlier, progress would have been much more dramatic. Similarly, when the government passes a law which calls for some benefit to be allocated to black Americans, and this law is successfully ignored or defied, it is harder to gain compliance later. The lesson is simple: if the government allows any part of the public to flaunt a law, a subsequent decision to enforce the law is more difficult to achieve. This has happened repeatedly in civil rights. The government continuously set up standards and regulations and then failed to enforce them. This failure led recalcitrant whites to believe that such laws could be safely ignored. Once decision makers decided they could ignore the law, the cost of changing their position and obeying the law went up drastically and continued to increase every time they successfully evaded new efforts at enforcement.

The Commitment of the National Government

The strength of the government's commitment to achieving compliance in a given policy area is very important in determining the costs of noncompliance. There should be no mistake that if the government wants compliance with its civil rights policy it can achieve it—possibly not immediately but certainly through persistent efforts. A law that is completely anachronistic (e.g., hanging horse thieves) or one opposed by a large part of the citizenry throughout the nation (e.g., Prohibition) might well be impossible to enforce. Polls, however, show that only a small percentage of the American public still favors strict segregation. Recalcitrant groups can hold out for substantial periods, but ultimately the law can be enforced if the government makes the cost of resistance high.

The national government's commitment to gaining compliance with civil rights laws has typically been neither strong nor consistent. It has normally moved into areas of civil rights gingerly, even timidly. Early efforts, which are usually symbolic, recognize certain rights, develop limited machinery for enforcement, and provide rather weak penalties for noncompliance which are but laxly levied. If the law only calls for an end to discrimination, considerable voluntary compliance may take place. If, however, the law calls for some positive effort to overcome discrimination, compliance is much lower. Attention is usually centered on those individuals, communities, or states which will not obey the law at all. This has been the signal for new efforts to enforce the law which normally fail because the law is not strong enough to conquer a determined foe. A new law is now passed which is more encompassing and powerful. The cycle may be repeated; every time the government has to go back to the well, the law becomes more forceful, and more compliance is achieved.

The government's efforts to insure the right of all Americans to vote is a good example of this process. When the Fifteenth Amendment, the 1957, 1960, and 1964 civil rights acts, and several Supreme Court decisions proved unsuccessful in extending the franchise to all black Americans, the government redoubled its efforts with the 1965 act. The result was a takeover of some traditional functions of the states. In some areas Federal officials registered black voters, protected their right to vote, and verified the ballot count. This is an example of the government going all the way to insure compliance.

The government's commitment in the area of employment and housing has been very limited. In the area of school desegregation the government's commitment has been inconsistent and never very strong. Since the government has always tried to win the civil rights struggle with limited personnel and finances, its priorities determine in large part how much incursion the law will attain. Once the right of all Americans to vote was judged top priority, the government made sure the right was extended. This is, of course, simply another way of saying that the better organized, equipped, and persistent are efforts toward compliance, the more success is obtained in the face of resistance.

Differences in Policy Areas

Progress in civil rights has differed considerably in the various policy areas studied. Compliance has been more thorough in public accommodations and voting rights than in housing, school desegregation, and employment. The differences in progress are directly related to the cost-benefit of compliance. In the area of voting rights the government has made the cost of noncompliance very high. Compliance with public accommodations requirements contained a benefit to those responsible for implementing the law. The cost of noncompliance has increased in school desegregation and employment, and as the cost has risen compliance has been more widespread. Only in the area of housing has the cost of noncompliance remained very low, with progress minimal.

The function of the cost-benefit calculus becomes clearer if we compare progress in two policy areas, voting rights and public accommodations. Two reasons seem to explain why compliance with public accommodations has been considered by many to contain only a marginal cost. First, businessmen have been primarily responsible for desegregating public accommodations, and where profit is concerned the conscience is more easily rested. Businessmen have always appreciated the profit to be made from black citizens. Even in the Deep South businessmen usually coveted black patronage so long as it did not alienate white customers. If the business involved personal mingling of the races, special efforts were made to reduce contact. Many eating establishments had separate takeout counters or gave service from a rear door. Only the few businesses that could not achieve this state of separateness, e.g., taxi services, wholly excluded black patrons. Once the law was unambiguous and businessmen could claim to see no way out, they were usually willing or even happy to obey the law.

Second, the cost of compliance was lowered by the fact that most people did not feel as strongly about maintaining racial segregation in this area. The difference in the public's attitude related to the amount and type of contact between the races and the public's perception of the importance of this victory for black Americans. In the area of public accommodations the amount of contact is minimal, impersonal, and transient. In the contrary situations, such as schools, employment, and housing, white hostility goes up measurably. Also, the blacks that whites encounter in areas of public accommodations are more likely to be middle or upper-middle class. As such they do not conform to the stereotyped black (half Stepin Fetchit and half Sporting Life) who conjures up the most fear and hostility in whites.

The cost of compliance with voting rights was, despite the foregoing, considered to be very high by many Southerners. The right to vote increased contact between the races very little but was perceived to be an important victory with potential status and material benefits—a victory that could spell the end of dominant white rule in parts of the South.

The various policy areas differ also in terms of how hard it is to raise the cost of noncompliance in an effort to gain compliance. We turn to a number of these factors.

First, it is more difficult to detect disobedience in some areas than others, which influences efforts to increase the cost of noncompliance. Feedback, in other words, is better in some areas than others. Failure to serve a black or refusal to allow him to vote or enroll in a school is much easier to detect than refusal to sell a house or employ an individual because of race. Employers can simply say that the applicant did not have the right qualifications. A homeowner is more restricted but he can simply refuse to honor appointments or stall a black potential buyer until he has found a white buyer. In many instances the difficulty of detection is based on whether an official or a private act is involved. It is much harder to regulate private discrimination (e.g., housing and employment) than official discrimination.

Second, if compliance necessitates changes in public behavior and attitudes, rather than simply official compliance, the law is harder to enforce. Extension of voting rights, like reapportionment, necessitated only action by public officials. A major difference in these two areas, however, is that the constituents (especially in the South) are concerned about black voting but largely indifferent to the size of their state senate district. Public acceptance can be important even when any official compliance is required because of fear of public hostility, both real and potential. In all areas of civil rights, public acceptance of the law is important, and this has slowed compliance. In several areas (e.g., employment and housing) progress is dependent on changes in private behavior.

Third, it is harder to raise the cost of noncompliance where there are larger numbers of decision makers to be supervised. Imagine the number of school boards in the South, and it will be obvious how difficult it is to force all these individuals to obey the law. On the other hand, in an area like reapportionment the Supreme Court could hold a handful of individuals in each state responsible for seeing that its decisions were obeyed. In civil rights the number of individuals who have to cooperate with the law is usually vast. Even within civil rights, however, there are some obvious differences. Voting registrars are much less numerous than private employers or individual homeowners and landlords.

Finally, the ability of authorities to raise the cost of noncompliance is also conditioned by the visibility of those individuals responsible for implementing a decision. It is easier to supervise a highly visible decision maker such as the attorney general of a state than school board members, and the latter are more visible than private employers. Individuals responsible for implementing civil rights are usually low in visibility.

The Substance and Mechanics of a Law

The substance and mechanics of a law are important in determining whether obeying it will be considered a cost or a benefit and whether the government can raise the cost for noncompliance to unattractive levels. Important here are at least seven factors.

1. Dolbeare and Hammond have pointed out that the amount of change called for by a law affects public perceptions about the cost of compliance. They argue that an incremental change *usually* entails less cost than a drastic one. This would seem to be especially true in civil rights. Many times an incremental approach, say in school desegregation or employment, has allowed whites to adjust to new situations.

An equally important point discussed earlier, however, should be recalled, i.e., too much incrementalism can be extremely bad. For the law to be effective, the time allowed for adjustment must be controlled very carefully with the deadline fixed and with enforcement perceived as swift and sure. In civil rights excessive delays have often encouraged obstinate whites to believe that the law could be circumvented. The point, then, is that the law should allow only limited and legitimate delays; evasion should be swiftly and consistently penalized.

2. The way a law is written makes a considerable difference in individual calculations about the cost-benefits of compliance. For example, if a law is too ambiguous or contains loopholes, the cost of noncompliance is lowered greatly. As noted earlier, most civil rights laws have in their early stages been ambiguous and weak. The *Brown* decision is a good example. Calling for desegregation "with all deliberate speed" is too indefinite to bring about meaningful change. Ambiguity always lends itself to individualized perceptions, and naturally an individual will interpret the law in a way that is most favorable to him (i.e., the most benefit and the least costs). Civil rights laws have frequently been so ambiguous as to be ludicrous. If traffic laws only required drivers to act "in a safe manner" one can imagine how many interpretations there would be—one for every driver. In civil rights, efforts have frequently been made to regulate recalcitrant officials with similarly broad language, which the courts and Congress refuse to define more precisely. For example, government agencies have been extremely reluctant to define the requirement that employers execut-

ing Federal contracts take "affirmative action" to insure equality in employment. It is easy to doubt the seriousness of the government's efforts under these circumstances.

Vague laws have frequently allowed officials to claim that they were obedient when in fact they had changed their behavior very little. Ironically, some foot-dragging decision makers have claimed that they could not obey the law because they could not understand what it required.

Law is most effective when it carefully defines the type and amount of compliance required and cuts off all unacceptable alternatives. If the law allows too many options, disobedient officials will surely take the alternative that produces the least change. For example, in the area of school desegregation obstructionist school boards are allowed to continue receiving funds if they take any of a number of actions. Experience showed that submitting to a final court order produced the least change, so school boards naturally chose this alternative that did not produce desirable levels of compliance. Such evasive routes should be terminated. In sum, the clearer the legal standard, the greater is the movement toward compliance. Progress in the area of school desegregation, for example, increased dramatically when HEW laid down specific administrative standards for determining compliance. When public officials were left to determine for themselves what action should be taken, change was minimal.

3. The law is more effective if it is clear that an offender will be punished for his disobedience. Just as a law cannot be effective if it rests solely on punishment, a law that can be broken with impunity will be frequently ignored. Many times public officials have failed to act in accord with civil rights laws because they knew that there would be no punishment for defiance. The government's threats of sanction frequently lacked credibility. Studies have found that the certainty of punishment for noncompliance is at least as important as formal sanctions in deterring deviance. Probably the whole pace of the civil rights effort would have been accelerated if a few public officials had received jail sentences for defying the law. School board members have been some of the most guilty. Every school board member takes an oath to uphold the United States Constitution, yet thousands have disobeyed the law for considerable periods of time with impunity.

Several governors have obstructed the law and have suffered no sanction. Civil rights leaders who have violated racially motivated laws know the insides of jails well.

Not only must sanctions be employed for noncompliance, but these sanctions must be stringent enough to make noncompliance unappealing. Studies by social psychologists have revealed that in a compliance situation sanctions are of no value unless they are credible and severe enough to outweigh the benefits of noncompliance. If the cost-benefits of a law are equally balanced, individuals who disagree with the law may decide against compliance for the reward of defying authority. Sanctions have infrequently been levied against those who trample upon the civil rights of blacks and, when assessed, penalties have been comparatively mild.

4. The law is more successful when it centers responsibility for compliance on specific individuals or agencies. If the law does not specify who shall be held accountable for insuring its execution, the cost of noncompliance will be reduced since the law will most likely not be enforced. For example, in most states no one is answerable for carrying out open housing laws.

5. Similarly, the cost of noncompliance can be raised if a specific agent or agency is created to enforce the law. Civil rights laws in three areas surveyed provided such agencies, but they are badly understaffed and underfinanced. Thus, in 1968 HEW tried to supervise school desegregation with only 48 enforcement officers. This is typical of other government agencies.

6. The cost of noncompliance is also affected by the availability of remedies for gaining compliance. In the areas of civil rights surveyed, it has been extremely difficult for black Americans to force obdurate whites to obey the law. Enforcement has been difficult in terms of money, time, and courage. Usually black citizens could not obtain justice except by hiring an attorney, if they could find one brave enough to represent them. This process required too much on the part of those whose rights have been so long discriminated against.

In recent years the government has improved the means of gaining compliance, usually by authorizing the attorney general to institute suits on behalf of citizens. Voting rights and school desegregation remedies have been improved considerably; but housing and employment remedies are still not viable. Even where the remedies have been made more accessible, the amount of time that may lapse before any action is taken can be extremely discouraging to those seeking relief. In the area of employment as much as a year may pass before a complainant even hears from the Equal Employment Opportunity Commission, and then the commission does not always have the power or the personnel to see that an obvious act of bias is corrected. The law quite simply has had limited impact in many instances because it has been too difficult for complainants to seek its protection and because too often the law has had no teeth.

7. The availability of remedies and the ability to make the cost of noncompliance high is also related to the power of the agent who originally formulated a civil rights law. For example, the Supreme Court has proved to be a less effective agent of civil rights policy on a day-to-day basis than the other branches of the national government. This is true for a number of reasons. Both Congress and the executive have more resources and personnel to implement their decisions. Congress can appropriate money and hire the personnel it needs. The President can, and has, used the Army and National Guard to back up his decisions. The Supreme Court has limited resources, limited personnel, and only enforcement powers—the injunction and contempt proceedings—that it has obviously considered too drastic for frequent use. Additionally, the Court lacks subordinates to carry out its decisions who can be supervised as easily as those employed by Congress and the President. The Supreme Court most frequently has to rely on district judges to implement its orders. It is well known that district judges do not always follow the Court's decisions. The Supreme Court can overrule district courts, but the process is slow and expensive.

Courts, in general, are also less effective agents of change because they function very slowly. The adversary process is by design slow and deliberative. Since court dockets are usually overcrowded, considerable delay usually occurs even before a court can consider a case. Also cases handed down by the court are frequently limited to the specific situation before the court, thus no uniform standards are produced. Congress and the Executive are much better equipped to produce uniform standards.

SUMMARY AND CONCLUSIONS

We have defined compliance as the consequence of individual evaluations about the cost-benefits of alternative courses of behavior. The evidence supporting the subjectivity of individual law-abidingness and the cost-benefit calculus is substantial. By analyzing the impact of law on five areas of civil rights we have been able to isolate a large number of factors which determine the cost-benefits of various laws and, consequently, their policy impact.

An obvious conclusion is that law "is better understood as a catalyst of change rather than a singular effector of change." To paraphrase James Levine, the ability of law to produce social change is probabilistic, contingent, and sequential. If a law is enacted it is probable that certain changes will follow; but the degree of change is contingent on certain circumstances prevailing. Law, in other words, is no talisman. It is not self-executing. The cost-benefit calculus provides insight into the factors that will determine the amount of change a law will produce and reveals that the probabilities of each law are different.

Law is sequential to the extent that it must precede certain desired changes, but because a large number of factors influence progress, the time lag is not obvious. The gap between cause and effect may, in fact, be considerable. Additionally, a number of factors other than the law may have an effect on change in a particular area (i.e., urbanization on school desegregation, economic expansion on black employment), which means that the cause and effect relationship between law and change is very difficult to identify.

part five POLICY EVALUATION

The last stage of the policy process when it is conceptualized in sequential functional terms is the evaluation of policy. Policy evaluation can be briefly defined as the appraisal or assessment of policy, including its content, implementation, and impact. As a functional activity, policy evaluation does not only take place following the adoption of and efforts to implement policy. Rather it may occur throughout the policy process; those involved in the formulation of policy alternatives, for instance, will be concerned with estimating their possible impact on the problem at which they are directed. Moreover, it should be kept in mind that evaluation may restart the policy process. That is, evaluation may lead to efforts to alter or eliminate a particular policy.

Policy analysis has been around as long as policy itself. Legislators, administrators, and others have always made judgments concerning the merits or worth of particular policies, projects, and programs, both preceding and following their adoption. Such evaluations have often been impressionist in style and based on fragmentary, anecdotal, or "soft" evidence at best. This sort of evaluation is discussed by Ralph Huitt in the selection on "Political Feasibility." Those concerned with the formulation and adoption of policy are not only concerned with whether it will "work" but also with whether they can win approval for it. Politics, as the old cliché has it, is the "art of the possible." Whether a proposed policy can be adopted, whether it is politically feasible, is one criterion for its evaluation.

Another variety of policy evaluation has focused on the administration or operation of particular policies and programs. Here answers may be sought to such questions as: Who receives the benefits provided by the program? Is the program honestly run? What are its financial costs? Could the distribution of services or benefits be made more effective? Evaluations conducted along these lines can help tell us whether programs are honestly or efficiently operated. They will tell us relatively little, however, concerning the societal effects of a program or whether it is achieving its objectives.

A third type of policy evaluation is concerned with the systematic and objective evaluation of policies and programs in order to determine their societal effects and whether they are accomplishing their objectives. Also involved here is a comparison of programs either to assess their relative benefit for society or to determine which of two or more programs can best achieve a particular goal. This form of evaluation has been undertaken with increasing frequency in recent years, and many national administrative agencies now have regular policy evaluation staffs.

Systematic policy evaluation is a complex and difficult task. There may be a lack of agreement on the goals or objectives of a program. Or, even if there is such agreement, it may be difficult to acquire statistical and other data concerning the actual impact of a program. Moreover, impacts of a program may be diffuse, that is, for example, a program may have unintended impacts or affect groups other than those it is supposed to affect. In "What Does the Most Good?" Alice Rivlin discusses some of the problems in policy evaluation, especially the use of the technique of cost-benefit analysis.

Anyone who deals with the subject of policy evaluation for very long becomes quite aware of the fact that it is a political as well as a scientific or objective enterprise. Those who seek to be objective evaluators of policy, notwithstanding their good intentions, often soon find themselves involved in, or even the center of, political controversy. Agency and program officials, for example, may resist policy evaluation, particularly if it appears that the result of the evaluation might be adversely critical of their program, as this could jeopardize their positions, their program, or their agency. Or given a critical program evaluation, agency officials and their supporters may attack the way the evaluation was done (for example, how the data were collected) or contend that some of the program's benefits were ignored. Williams and Evans provide us with a case study of the political controversy surrounding an evaluation of the Head Start Program. Carol Weiss moves beyond the case-study approach and provides a general discussion of "The Politicization of Evaluation Research." Since politics is concerned with the distribution of advantages and disadvantages (or with "who gets what, when, how"), and since evaluations may affect such distributions, it should not be surprising that evaluation frequently becomes a matter for political struggle.

14. Political Feasibility

Ralph K. Huitt

If politics is the "art of the possible," as it is often said to be, and the study of it is concerned with "who gets what, when, and how," the question of what is politically feasible would seem to come close to the heart of the matter. But perhaps the empiricism and practicality implicit in these and like definitions suggest why there is little systematic work to suggest what "political feasibility" *is;*

Reprinted from Austin Ranney, ed., *Political Science and Public Policy* (Chicago: Rand McNally, 1968), pp. 263–75. Used by permission of the author.

it remains the province of the operator, not the theoretician. Pragmatic judgments in politics, as in other human endeavors, nevertheless are based on calculations about how people will behave in certain stable institutional situations, what problems they face, and what resources they can bring to bear on them. If these are largely unconscious and institutional on the part of the operator, they need not be for the student.

It may be that there are certain elements common to "political feasibility" in all political situations, but searching for them would hardly seem to be the way to begin. At first glance it would appear that what is feasible would vary with the enterprise at hand, with the arena in which action must be mounted, in the goals one has in mind, and with the political actor who is deciding what is feasible. The relatively single-minded business of getting elected President of the United States furnishes an example. It clearly is one thing to win primaries, another to capture a national convention—unless, of course, the first is done so successfully that the second is converted into a ratifying device. Mr. Kefauver was eminently proficient at the first but not at the second; Mr. Kennedy and Mr. Goldwater were nominees virtually before their conventions met. Mr. Dewey and his cohorts demonstrated that it is possible to be masters of convention strategy and tactics and still lose two national elections—one when the prospects were poor, it is true, but the other apparently unlosable. This is to say that each stage of the process presents a different "arena," or institutional setting, with its own peculiar requirements of resources, skills, and sense of timing. These differences may make it fairly easy for a candidate and his coterie to succeed at one and impossible to win at another. But even when the auguries are good at each level, it is still possible—to cite the unfortunate Mr. Dewey once more—to bungle the job somewhere.

The two houses of Congress obviously present similar arenas that differ markedly from Presidential electoral arenas. (Perhaps it is not so obvious; more than one gifted senator has failed to recognize it.) The legislative leader learns the mood and rhythm of his house, the kinds of combinations that can be put together on various categories of issues, and the timing necessary to the success of good strategies. It is well established that men who move from state to national legislature, or from House to Senate in Congress, usually are well prepared and content in their new assignments, while former governors often are not. The move from legislator to chief executive surely must entail similar readjustment and socialization, though it probably helps that the incumbent wanted to make the change and probably considers it an advancement.

The question of feasibility in politics also turns upon the goals under consideration. The election of a man to an office is one thing; a change in the drift of national policy clearly is quite another. One is relatively simple, the other enormously complex, requiring skills and good judgment in many arenas. Again, there is the question whether what is wanted is an immediate victory—say, the passage of a bill—or a major change over time. Political education is part of the legislative process, and a succession of defeats may be necessary to prepare the way for an ultimate victory that in retrospect seems inevitable. President Johnson's choice of Independence, Missouri, as the place to sign the Medicare Act, in the presence of Mr. Truman, was acknowledgment that his predecessor had taken the first step toward Medicare when he fought a losing battle for a more sweeping measure almost twenty years earlier. Again, a plan of action which no practical politician would touch might change the climate in which an issue is joined, making feasible what hitherto would have been deemed impossible. The sit-downs in segregated places staged by well-mannered young Negro students a few years ago are a case in point. Much that came later flowed from these simple expressions of courage and dignity, the political feasibility of which at the time could not have been calculated because they were without precedent and because so much depended on the way they were carried out.

A decentralized political system like our own multiplies the actors whose judgments of feasibility significantly affect a policy decision. It would be too much to expect the President and a member of Congress of his party to strike the same balance on an issue affecting their political futures quite differently. A requisite of responsible party government, after all, is to put leaders and rank-and-file as nearly as possible in the same boat. The calculations of the political price to be paid for a course of action, a basic element in a judgment of political feasibility, likewise would vary widely. Two senators otherwise similarly situated, for example, might compute cost quite differently if one aspired to the White House and the other did not.

The purpose of this study is to state some of the conditions of political feasibility which seem to be operative in the making of national policy through the executive and legislative branches and the groups associated with them. The courts, active partners though they are, will not be included because they are somewhat isolated, their reaction is delayed, and the behavior appropriate to them is quite different, and because we shall have trouble enough without them. Moreover, it is policy-making in the here and now that we shall be talking about, not the slow evolution of major change.

THE PROBLEM

There are Americans who believe that almost any social problem that can be solved with money is within the competence of the U.S. government if only the attack on the problem is sufficiently massive. Indeed, there are many who seem to believe that *all* social problems could be tackled at once with adequate scope, if only the country would withdraw from Vietnam. Even a casual attention to what went on in congressional committees early in 1966 will bear this out. Again and again members decried attempts to hold down expenditures on this or that problem with the simple contention: But more is needed! And so it was. But the first point to be made is this: that for all its affluence, the American system cannot deal adequately with its acknowledged needs; that this is a system in which an allocation of scarce resources must indeed be made, with all the pain that inevitably entails.

No attempt will be made to catalogue the needs. Anyone can make a list in a few minutes which would overtax resources for years to come. Some samples will suffice. Water-pollution control, which has barely begun, could use $100 billion without wasting a cent. Hospital modernization, to replace 260,000 obsolete beds (and the 13,000 annual increment) would take at least $8 billion. Building 375,000 classrooms in the next five years would cost $15 billion. Building really modern urban transportation, re-creating core cities, breaking the poverty cycle of families by using all the health, education, and welfare resources in a coordinated way—each of these would cost immense sums. Put more accurately, each would call for trained manpower and other resources, which already are in short supply, far beyond any present capacity to meet the demand.

This catalogue of needs, some of them almost catastrophic in proportion, is all the more remarkable in the light of the efforts that have been made. The budget of the Public Health Service, for example, increased in twelve years from $250 million to $2.4 billion in fiscal 1967. The Office of Education spent only $539 million in 1961; in fiscal 1967 its budget was about $3.5 billion. Three sessions of Congress (1963–65) enacted twenty pieces of landmark legislation in health, nineteen in welfare.

The requirement that resources be allocated among needs that cannot be met poses the problem of priorities. Which is more important to society, intensive care for high-risk infants (40 percent of children who die in their first year die in their first day) or artificial kidneys to keep productive adults alive (there are facilities now for continuous treatment of 200 to 300 patients of a possible 10,000 who might be saved)? Head-start programs for disadvantaged preschoolers or basic education for disadvantaged adults? The problem is even harder when the claims of cancer research, say, are compared with the desirability of getting to the moon.

This is an academic discussion of little interest until one is forced by experience to realize that decisions on questions like these actually *do* have to be made and actually *are* being made. What happens to various segments of the population next year depends on these decisions. But what really is appalling is to know upon what flimsy data and partial information these choices often are made. It is perfectly possible, for instance, that it may be decided to increase the funds for adult basic education by a certain amount without the slightest notion of how many people have been taught to read, say, under the existing program. This is not said in criticism of anybody; the men who set the priorities feel their burdens heavily and they get the best help they can. The policy system simply is not geared to let them do better.

What considerations enter into the selection of priorities and the specific program designed to meet them? One, inevitably, is "political feasibility." Will it "go" on the Hill? Will the public buy it? Does it have political "sex appeal"? What "can't be done" is likely to get low priority. An administration bill must be passed if possible, and the men who bear the responsibility for that shrink from taking on one that may discredit them. Political columns like to run a Presidential "box score," and there is no place on it for the bill no one expected to pass, the bill that was introduced as part of the educational process necessary to enact the legislation later on. The "box score" mentality is likely to permeate the discussions of men charged with preparing the President's program. What determines political feasibility therefore is a matter of urgent concern.

Political feasibility as a consideration in national policy-making is, so far as I know, a term of art. It is a seat-of-the-pants judgment, based on the experience of the person making it. It may be shrewd indeed, or appear so, if the men pooling their experience are shrewd and artful men. It may be simply a repetition of some long-accepted and untested cliché about what public or politicians will do. For nearly two decades, for instance, many members of Congress have said in private conversations, "I favor recognizing Red China (or admitting her to the UN), but I wouldn't dare say it. It would be political suicide." How did they know? Again, it may be based on what representatives of interest groups have said, probably in all honesty, but from a remoteness from the currents that run in the country which only a man who spends twenty years in Washington can have. Political feasibility as a target will not track. Any consideration of it that gets anywhere must start from some assumptions and limit the task that is undertaken.

Let us begin therefore by assuming that it is possible to confront the policy system with a set of proposals that actually do maximize the benefits the American people can get from the expenditure of a given amount of appropriations—that is, an ideal allocation of scarce resources. As a matter of fact, a process designed to do just that already has been set in motion, a major innovation in the executive branch called Planning-Programming-Budgeting System (PPBS). This system sets out to bring to the conference table where decisions are made an analysis based on the program goals of the government, and the relative success of various programs in achieving them, which will give the decision-makers the materials they need.

PPBS in the federal government originated in the Pentagon, where Secretary McNamara abandoned the old practice of considering a budget for each military service, with the traditional outlays for personnel, operations, equipment, and the like, in favor of a budget based on nine major defense missions. The weapons that could be assigned to each mission were listed without regard to the service that nominally claimed them. All costs of developing, procuring, and operating a weapon were assigned to it and the measure of defense provided by each system was determined. With this kind of information, choices among weapons and systems in terms of their costs and relative effectiveness could be made.

Because the goals of the Defense Department are relatively simple and consistent—deterrence of war, defense of the country, victory in war—PPBS encounters fewer problems there than in departments with many, perhaps conflicting, goals. Nevertheless, in the summer of 1965 President Johnson ordered more than eighty agencies comprising the executive branch to set up staffs capable of establishing the new system. Each agency is to set up broad program goals, with more specific subcategories. All operating programs with similar goals are to be placed in the appropriate category, regardless of the organizational units to which they are attached. If a program goal is stated as "Breaking the Poverty Cycle," for instance, it might require a grouping of programs in education, health, welfare, vocational rehabilitation, poverty, and perhaps others.

The costs of various programs could be established then and measured against specific benefits. The budget would be stated, not in terms of "inputs"—items for personnel, research, planning, etc.—but in the amount of reduction in delinquency, improvement in health or education, and so forth. Thus it would be possible to estimate which programs did more to achieve the goal per dollar expended.

PPBS aims ultimately to do more than help determine which programs contribute most to the same goal. The system would aim in time at measuring one goal against another, so that priorities could be set on the basis of knowledge of comparative benefits.

I have not attempted to explain PPBS in any detail, but rather to set forth its basic assumptions and suggest how it will work. I wish to accept the most extreme claims that could be made for it—to assume that it could produce clear proof that one goal is socially preferable to another, and one way to reach it better than another; that a budget can be drawn which demonstrably gets the most benefits for the resources expended—as a basis for examining some of the structural arrangements in the political system which would have to be taken into account in putting its findings into effect. Of course, it is not necessary for PPBS to achieve anything like these extreme claims to be a highly useful tool of analysis, capable of introducing more rationality in decision-making. Neither is it necessary to postulate a successful PPBS to pose the problem: if pure social intelligence confronted the system with a program, could the system accept it and put it into effect? In a word, would the program be politically feasible?

THE EXECUTIVE BRANCH

The classic solution to decentralized national power is more power concentrated in the President. He is the one official elected by the people. He is the one person charged with, and capable of, thinking about the national interest. It would seem therefore that the social intelligence made available by a perfected PPBS would inevitably strengthen his hand. Perhaps it would. Nevertheless, a few more studies that concentrated on the President himself as a political man, trying to survive and have his way (like Neustadt's *Presidential Power*), studies whose authors are not hypnotized by the many hats he wears, might suggest some difficulties the President will have if and when he is confronted by the national program he (or his predecessor) has caused to be made. I have not made such a study and probably never will, but perhaps I can suggest a couple of places a student might look for the answers such a study would provide.

One is the peculiarly vulnerable political position of the President. He is the one American politician who cannot hide. He must be prepared at all times for whatever ill wind may blow. Moreover, his power depends to some extent at least on never surrendering the initiative for very long—or so it must seem to him. When a competitor threatens to propose something good, the temptation is strong for the President to occupy the field first, or to deluge it with something Presidential in scope if he cannot. If there is a carefully constructed legislative proposal at hand, so much the better. If there is not, something may very well be proposed anyway. If he finds himself in congenial company, he, like other men, may suggest what the country needs. Once it has been said, however casually, the machinery works inexorably. Furthermore, the bill that goes up must be passed if possible. Failure catches on much more quickly than success. (Exceptions might occur in election years, when a proposal that cannot pass might make a good campaign issue.) Finally, it is reasonable to doubt whether a President can be the good shepherd of a program someone else has made, even though it be made by his own people and the very best computers. The drama of leadership, of his awful isolation, of his lonely decisions, is the great weapon in his armory.

The second area worth the student's investigation would be the network of executive staff which can truly be called Presidential. This might be stretched to include the Presidential appointees in the agencies, whose loyalty to him usually is dependable, though their lack of intimate knowledge of much of his business reduces their direct usefulness to him almost to the vanishing point. It certainly would not include the bureaucracy, the source of information both branches perforce rely upon, but which in its multitudinous bureaus, divisions, and offices is no more certainly allied to him than to congressional committees or interest groups—or to nobody. Those that remain—the tiny White House staff and the Bureau of the Budget (an effective staff arm whose political judgment often is affected, alas, by its preoccupation with the budget)—are not really a match for the bureaucracy. They are in the sense that they speak for the President and so may have the last word. They are not in the sense of information and expertise. In having the last word, which they must if the President is to have his way, they often overrule the work of months with judgments made in haste and under pressure. Like Congress, they can deal really effectively with the bureaucracy's expertise only by constructing a bureaucracy of their own. If to the weight of experience and expertise which they now bring to the table the bureaucracy could add the authority of PPBS, what then would the President's people do? It must be remembered, after all, that each agency has its own PPBS. Obviously, it is crucial that the ultimate formulations of PPBS would have to be brought under the President's control, with all the very human intrusions on computerized rationality that implies.

The heart of the matter probably is that no intellectual system—and certainly not PPBS—is designed to produce a single right policy, but rather to present policy alternatives, with analyses of the costs and benefits of each. The President would have the advice of his agency heads based on their choices. In all likelihood he would also have his own staff of professional program specialists who would work with agency counterparts and assist him with his own decisions, as members of the Bureau of the Budget staff do now in their own fields. If their advice sometimes reflected their own policy biases, they would be no more guilty of human frailty than are the agency planners. In a word, there are no insurmountable difficulties in the way of getting to the President the kind of advice PPBS can give; the problem would be to get for PPBS the kind of political respectability and acceptance that would cause the President to heed it against the other influences that bear upon him.

The character of the bureaucracy presents problems for unified policy, some of which appear, at least, to be insoluble. First there is the inescapable question of the basis upon which an agency should be organized. By function—health, education, welfare—which augments professionalization and promises a high quality of service? By clientele—labor, farmers, commerce—which has a kind of built-in coherence? By ecological unit—the core city, the river basin for water-pollution control—which encompasses a broad array of related problems? By problem—poverty, crime—which calls for the application and coordination of many services? Each has its justification and all are actually used, of course. No single organizational structure will do for all, nor is it judicious to try to apply logical consistency to their division of labor. If all education were to be placed in the Office of Education, for instance, more than fifty agencies would have to surrender programs to it. The Office of Education would have to administer the three military service academies, the Department of State's foreign service school, Agriculture's graduate school, and the in-service training programs of all the agencies of the federal government —to name only a few. It is safe to say that if any large department tried to claim all the programs that might logically be assigned to it, the federal executive branch would grind to a stop.

Needless to say, overlapping and duplication of effort are inevitable, inspiring the continuous demand for "coordination." But coordination is more easily subscribed to than accomplished. Agencies perforce are parochial; they think in terms of their own statutory authority, operating structure, and clientele. Even plans they make for coordination tend to have agency perimeters. One proposal that has won a high degree of acceptance from all the relevant agencies, to give an example, is the so-called "multipurpose" (or "one-stop") neighborhood center, containing under one roof all the services that a family is likely to need. But when agencies submit concrete plans, they usually are *single-agency* "multipurpose" centers.

The problem of parochialism is exaggerated by the occupational immobility of the civil service. It is not uncommon for careers to be spent wholly in one department, perhaps in a single bureau. Transfers within the bureaucracy threaten status and a way of life; when they take employees outside the civil service, even to Capitol Hill, they disturb and may temporarily destroy retirement rights, to mention only one of a host of disabilities. But clearly, if the flexibility and innovation implicit in PPBS are to be exploited, it must be possible to reduce, perhaps eliminate, some organizational entities. This is incredibly difficult where employees have a justifiable vested interest in their jobs, which they are quick to protect. When a thirty-year man in the bureaucracy takes his grievance to Congress (where occupational immobility is perhaps the supreme value), he is sure of a sympathetic hearing from members he has worked with for years. There is much talk about occupational mobility among officials in the bureaucracy, but little more than talk. What is needed, if PPBS or something like it is to succeed, is a genuine career line in the civil service (not in a particular agency) with easy transferability from one agency to another. More than that, genuine mobility requires an easy flow into and out of private employment, with vested rights in retirement and all the other elements of job security. This would seem to be relatively simple with professionals, whose central loyalty tends to be to their own disciplines, but probably very difficult to achieve with nonprofessionals, whose loyalties and habits are agency-oriented.

To the political people who man the President's program, the relationship of civil servants to Congress is perennially troubling. At one extreme, bureaucrats may resist *all* political considerations, rejecting job applications tainted with congressional recommendations, ignoring legislative intent in administering the laws, and refusing to consider the effect of political reactions on the success of their own legislative and appropriation bills. On the other hand, bureaucrats who know full well the transience of their political superiors may build up mutually advantageous relationships with relevant committees which defy the wishes and will of the President himself. In between are the political "volunteers" who gratuitously help with the legislative process, threatening delicate relationships with sadly misplaced self-confidence. Needless to say, each in his way will obstruct or dilute any coherent Presidential program.

THE LEGISLATIVE BRANCH

When a programmatic approach to national policy is mentioned, any student of American government with adequate reflexes is bound to say "Congress." The inability of Congress to consider, at any stage of the legislative process, the whole sweep of a program sponsored by the President is notorious, and a fair number of political scientists have made a respectable living emphasizing it. The outlines hardly need repeating. The party leadership is weak. The committee chairmen, selected by seniority, are strong. The result is a kind of confederation of little legislatures, some of them fragmented even further into subcommittees with specialized jurisdictions which have managed to become small feudalities in their own right. This is the system that baffles the champions of responsible party government, and it is this system that has kept Congress strong. One by one, other national legislatures subservient to party leadership (for which read "executive") have been turned into passive partisans whose hope of sharing power depends upon their climbing into the executive themselves. Not so Congress. Committee chairmen often care about the President's wishes, even when he belongs to the other party. They usually take an administration bill seriously—even if only as a point of departure, which it often is when the President's party is in a minority on the committee. But they cannot be forced by party leadership in either branch. Indeed, when administration spokesmen go as a matter of courtesy to discuss their programs with congressional party leaders, the latter are polite but not much interested. They know that their work begins after the committee has reported a bill.

The organization of Congress around specialized concerns shapes the entire system that makes legislation. It is fashionable to speak of a "legislative system," which includes Congress, the interest groups that serve and influence it, the executive agencies that must deal with it, the press that writes about it, and the constituencies that reward and punish and occasionally know what is going on. It is more accurate, I think, to begin with the committees and speak of the *policy system,* which is focused about each pair of committees that shares similar, if not identical, jurisdiction. There are interest groups that have commitments ranging across a broad sweep of the legislative spectrum, and there are executive departments with similarly large responsibilities. Just the same, none is likely to deal regularly with more than four or five committees in either house, and then there probably is specialization on their legislative staffs. Large newspapers are likely also to develop subject-matter experts on their staffs. More common than the giants by far are the groups with a single interest (albeit a broad one, like higher education), and the executive agency with one or a handful of bills, all of whose business is done with a single committee in each house. The term "constituency" likewise begins to make sense when it signifies numerous specialized interests that are likely to get involved only when those interests are touched. The concept of the mass constituency is hardly more useful analytically than the notion of a mass public.

Two points perhaps should be stressed. The first is the relative isolation that develops around each of these policy systems. They are like planes that cut each other only at points of decision-making, such as the roll-call vote on the floor. One reason for the unresponsiveness of Congress to Presidential pleas for economy in 1966 (in the early days of the session, at least) undoubtedly was the submersion of each committee and its associates in their own work, which they knew to be vitally important. The President was right, of course, but he certainly must have been talking about somebody else. Only after heroic efforts on the President's part did the message begin to sink in that he was talking about, and to, everybody. The sense of isolation is less stark in the Senate, where each member belongs to more than one committee and several subcommittees. But the result ultimately is the same, or worse. The burden of many assignments requires the members to rely heavily on committee staff. Needless to say, these persons are experts if they can be, their fierce specialization unrelieved by the varied life of chamber and constituency which tends to liberate the minds of their principals.

The second point to be emphasized is the very large measure of control over the business in their charge by each of these policy systems. This too may be demonstrated many times over in the second session of the 89th Congress. After unprecedented success with a huge legislative program the year before, President Johnson decided, because of the Vietnam war and threats of inflation, to make only modest increases in most programs and actual cuts in some. One of the latter was aid to school districts that bore the impact of federal installations, in which he proposed a sharp reduction on the ground that the large sums available under new federal education programs justified it. Roughly 315 congressional districts were affected. The two education committees agreed with the powerful impacted-area lobby that it was not worth discussing—and they did not discuss it. The Secretary of Health, Education, and Welfare was not asked a single question about it in either house. In their own good time the committees increased the authorization.

An incident equally revealing concerned the President's proposal to convert the direct loans to students under the National Defense Education Act to private loans guaranteed by the government. The education subcommittee in the House believed the colleges needed to know what they could count on for the next year, whereupon by a simple unanimous vote in executive session they eliminated that title from the bill. It is significant that the colleges could not know what they could count on then unless they had complete confidence the subcommittee action would stand. The subcommittee never doubted they would have that confidence, and they did.

COMMENTS ON POLITICAL FEASIBILITY

If the foregoing sketch of the policy systems that pool their respective programs to make the national policy is reasonably correct, it should be possible now to make some suggestions about political feasibility at the national level.

What is least feasible is what requires serious, responsible consideration of some unitary conception of national need. Congress does not manage it, does not try to do so, and with its present power structure is virtually incapable of trying. With the President the case is not so clear. He does indeed present his "program" in the early months of the year, in successive unveilings marked by messages to Congress. Viewed uncharitably, they represent an agglomeration of most of the programs the policy systems would have insisted on anyway. Nevertheless, they bear his imprint. The President—in the institutional sense at least and, in what matters most, personally—has considered them all and supplied emphasis. Moreover, his notions of relative weights are expressed in his budget, the only genuinely unitary policy instrument in national life. Congress, it may be said in passing, cannot even pretend to look at national policy whole until it develops an institutional capacity to cope with the concept of a budget. Needless to say, once the budget is delivered to Congress and dismembered among its subcommittees, the President too virtually abandons the unitary view and plays the congressional game: he fights for his bills.

Low feasibility also must be attached to whatever is genuinely new or innovative, especially if it can be successfully labeled as such, and more especially if it rubs an ideological nerve. What is most feasible is what is purely incremental, or can be made to appear so. Paradoxically, it is politically attractive to tout a proposal as "new" so long as it is generally recognized that it is not new at all, but a variation on a familiar theme. But the political art can make feasible what is not feasible by finding halfway houses (what the lawyers might call "quasis") which supply at least part of what is needed under the guise of doing something else. Halfway houses may become so numerous and large they occupy the field; nevertheless, a simple declaration that this is so may cause bitter controversy.

Examples are legion. President Hoover's misfortunes demonstrated for those who could learn that the President must accept, or have thrust upon him, responsibility for the health of the economy. President Roosevelt demonstrated that he had learned the lesson well; his twelve years in the White House were studded with attempts to mend the health and even the structure of the economy. Just the same, a watered-down policy statement of national responsibility for employment had real trouble in Congress as late as 1946. Again, the federal government had been the most important influence in the housing market long before a bill plainly marked "housing" could pass finally in 1949. In education, the three furies—federal interference, racial strife, church and state—never sleep, but they doze; they can be stepped around. Veterans can be helped, federally impacted areas aided, education for national defense fostered, disadvantaged children succored. All this so long as the dread concepts are not invoked by name.

The halfway-house approach comes at a high price, it must be admitted. It cannot face a whole problem frankly and try to do what needs to be done, and usually it cannot deal equitably among respective claimants for federal benefits. Moreover, what is accomplished this way becomes imbedded in law. Beneficiaries may support broader, better laws when the climate is propitious, but they will not let go what they have. The legislative halfway house tends to be as permanent as a temporary government building.

It follows that what is most feasible is what is incremental, what can be made to seem a comfortable next step under a program that has already received the good-conduct medal. Nothing is better than an amendment. A once hated housing law becomes an annual invitation to try to get something else under a respected umbrella, where it may take shelter forevermore. A higher education bill that was killed in conference in 1962 by a telegram and passed with great exertion in 1963 was renewed and extended by the House of Representatives in 1966 under suspension of the rules, without a recorded vote. No one fears the familiar; nothing succeeds like success: in politics the bromides are the best guides.

All of this is not meant to say that the approach to policy represented by PPBS is doomed to futility. Far from it. Even if it is only modestly successful in the kind of analysis it will attempt, its weight in the policy process should not be discounted. Who would deny that the unitary approach represented by the budget has had a real, if incalculable, influence on the conduct of the national government? It is without doubt the most formidable policy tool the President has. So could it be with systematic program planning: a President who can support his values with the authority of science will be a formidable competitor indeed. Rationality is respected, sometimes irrationally, in a democratic society.

The history of the national budget may provide an answer to our original question: if social intelligence could confront the policy system with a program that would maximize the benefits to be received from the exertions of the federal government, could that program ever be made politically feasible? The budget experience suggests it could. The budget was adopted because it had to be; the fiscal system could no longer afford the luxury of irresponsibility. The decentralized policy structure with its many policy systems which has evolved here under our constitutional separation of institutions has many virtues: diversity of skills, creativeness within appointed bounds, easy public access to a multiplicity of decision points, openness in the conduct of public business, hospitality to ideas, continuous political education for those who pay attention, and the enormous stimulation that comes with the opportunity to fashion great careers. Nevertheless, the sheer weight of items on the national agenda will require that choices be made, which in turn could force changes in process and structure to make possible a more coherent approach to the needs of the system.

15. What Does the Most Good?

Alice M. Rivlin

The advances in measuring the distribution of social problems or needs and in identifying who could win and who would lose from particular social action programs have led to better-informed decisions on welfare, higher education, and other social action programs.

The big difficulty, however, is that there are so many social problems. Action could be taken in so many fields—from preschool to

Reprinted from Alice M. Rivlin, *Systematic Thinking for Social Action* (Washington, D.C.: The Brookings Institution, 1971), pp. 46–62. Copyright © 1971 by The Brookings Institution and reprinted with permission.

graduate education, from training welders to feeding infants, from biochemical research to welfare payments. It is not possible to do everything at once. The problem facing decision makers is the classic economic problem of allocating scarce resources among competing ends. What would do the most good? What do the analysts have to say about the *comparative* value of social action programs?

To be useful in answering these questions, the analysts must do two things. The first is to identify the objectives of education, health, and other social action programs and to develop measures of progress toward these objectives. The second step is to find a way of comparing the benefits to the union of moving toward these various objectives.

IDENTIFYING THE OBJECTIVES

Social action programs are sometimes described as "soft," in contrast with the "hard" programs like defense and space. The implication is that a major impediment to decision making in the social action area is lack of definable and measurable objectives.

Despite appearances, however, I believe there is a wide measure of agreement in the nation, if not about final goals, at least about desirable directions of change. The bitter argument that rages among the radical right, the middle, and the new and old left over social action programs is not primarily about the objectives themselves. The real issues are the relative importance of these and other objectives (curing poverty versus preserving self-reliance, for example) and the means of reaching them. Almost all the participants in the argument genuinely want healthier, better-educated citizens, and less poverty. These are not empty slogans. They suggest indicators—a set of measurements —that most people would accept at least with respect to the desirable direction of change. Most people believe infant mortality rates should go down, reading levels should go up, and the number of people with low incomes should decline. They are not agreed on what they would give up to achieve these changes, how to achieve them, or which ones are most important.

A number of social scientists have recently advocated the development of a comprehensive set of indicators to show social progress or retrogression, and the preparation of an annual "social report" that would attempt to assess the social health of the nation, much as the

President's Economic Report assesses its economic health. Toward the end of the last administration, the Department of Health, Education, and Welfare (HEW) explored the feasibility of social reporting and produced a document modestly (and appropriately) entitled, *Toward a Social Report*. The exploration revealed monstrous gaps in available information. It did not, however, reveal much disagreement on what would be desirable indicators of progress or retrogression in health, education, and income status.

Almost everyone, for example, can accept, at least conceptually, a common set of measures that would indicate that the nation is getting healthier. Not all of these measures now exist and most of those that are available are negatively oriented. Infant mortality rates, death rates by age and by specific disease, days of bed disability, and indices of crippling and inability to function all measure some aspect of the ill health we are trying to reduce. One can, however, easily imagine a set of positive indicators of health, including physical measures of strength and vigor and attitudinal measures of healthy feelings. Modern survey techniques permit development of such a series, on whose desirable direction of movement most people could agree.

Education presents a more difficult case. One has to be especially careful not to take inputs for outputs: Much of the literature reads as though preventing dropouts and keeping children in school longer were ends in themselves. But even among educators there is a fairly wide measure of agreement on three types of objectives.

The first is improvement in basic intellectual skills—the ability to read, communicate, manipulate numbers, and handle scientific and mechanical concepts. Tests that are now available are, of course, far from perfect measures of how well people handle these skills. Many tests have cultural and linguistic biases that make them insensitive instruments for measuring the skills of minority groups, whose members may communicate skillfully in their own languages but fail tests given in standard English, loaded with middle-class words, and scored by middle-class values. It is surprising that more effort has not been devoted to constructing better tests. It is even more surprising that more effort has not been made to analyze the test data that are now collected. Schools do a great deal of testing and use the results, for better or worse, in the diagnosis and counseling of individual students, but rarely for analytical purposes—to compare the effectiveness of different programs or different schools, or to identify progress or retrogression of the system over time. Seeking an answer to the question, "Is the nation better educated than it used to be?" the authors of *Toward a Social Report* scoured the literature, and found almost nothing worth reporting. The much-disputed National Assessment of Education, a series of tests on various subjects to be administered periodically to a national sample of children and adults, promises at long last to provide some continuing information on the knowledge and basic intellectual skills of a cross-section of Americans.

Besides basic intellectual skills, a second set of objectives in education might loosely be called the "ability to cope." Most people believe that an important objective of education is the development of self-confidence, a positive self-image, and the ability to deal with new situations. The schools have often failed here. The black power and black pride movements are in part a reaction to the dismal failure of schools to help black children feel pride and confidence in themselves. Measures of ability to cope are even more primitive and questionable than test scores, but in principle there seems to be no reason why they could not be developed.

The third set of objectives in education has to do with job skills and future income. There is general agreement that a good education prepares a student either for a good job or for the future education that will lead to one. Here again, surprisingly little effort has been made to measure the extent to which our schools, even our supposedly vocational schools, actually succeed in preparing students for jobs, but in principle their success or failure would not be impossible to measure.

The reduction of poverty also seems to be a generally accepted objective. Definitions of poverty differ, but most people would agree that they want, by some means, to raise the standard of living of the poorest Americans, and that this standard can be at least roughly measured in money income, corrected for price levels and family size. This does not mean that there is agreement on a desirable distribution of income, or on how much the rich should give up to help the poor; it means simply that raising the lowest end of the income distribution is generally thought to be desirable.

To be sure, in important areas of social concern objectives are vague and measures nonexistent. There is concern, for example, about the "alienation" of individuals from society, but little agreement on how to measure it or how much of it is just rugged individualism. Most people would like to see a reduction in individual criminal behavior, but many disagree on whether civil disorder is inherently bad. Are student riots a symptom of alienation and the breakdown of law and order, or are they evidence of social concern among the young and active who desire to make a better world?

Despite these gray areas, we seem to have fairly wide agreement on *some* objectives of social policy. We can at least conceive of ways to measure movement toward objectives for which we know the appropriate sign. The really difficult problems do not arise until we attempt to attach weights to these objectives so that we can allocate scarce resources among them—until we ask, "Which is more important, curing cancer or teaching poor children to read?"

COMPARING THE BENEFITS: CANCER CURE VERSUS READING

How can we compare the merits of a program to find a cure for cancer with those of a program to teach poor children to read? If resources are insufficient to do both, the orthodox answer of the economists is to add up the costs and benefits of each and choose the program with the higher excess of benefits over costs. Of course, it is unlikely to be an either-or decision. Resources can usually be allocated to both programs, and the question is how much to each. In this case, the task is to find out whether additional funds would bring more benefits in one program than in the other.

How helpful is cost-benefit analysis in the real world of social action decisions?

Our ability to estimate the costs of such programs is admittedly weak. The costs of finding a cure for cancer are inherently uncertain; they depend on unforeseeable outcomes of basic and applied research. At best, one could make an informed guess about the probability of success at various levels of funding. Teaching poor children to read, however, seems more amenable to cost estimation. In principle, one could examine successful reading programs, determine which ones showed most success per dollar expended, and estimate the costs of extending them to larger numbers of children. In fact, however, this has not been done. The problem of estimating the costs of alternative types of social action has not received nearly the attention that has been devoted to similar problems involving weapons systems.

Unlike cost analysis, benefit measurement in the social action area has attracted some very good minds. Two conferences sponsored by the Brookings Institution, for example, have been devoted primarily to this subject, and the journal literature is substantial.

In setting values on the benefits of public programs, the economist's first line of attack is market price: How does the market value X relative to Y? But market prices offer almost no help in valuing the outputs of social action programs, since they are not usually sold and thus have no price. If they are sold, it is under conditions of monopoly and great consumer ignorance, so their prices have little meaning. A cure for cancer is not sold because it does not exist. There is no widespread private market for reading instruction.

In the absence of market prices the economist turns to a second probing point: He attempts to estimate what people might be willing, or ought to be willing, to pay for the outputs if they could buy them. Education and health services clearly increase an individual's productivity, and the increases are reflected in his earnings. Educated people usually earn more than uneducated people; healthy people more than sick people; and the living more than the dead. It seems reasonable to look at education and health and other social services as investments, expenditures that serve to improve the nation's productivity and the individual's earnings, which are a measure of his productive contribution. Alternative investments can thus be compared by computing the present value of the income increase that would be attributable to each and determining which promises the highest rate of return on the last dollar invested. Following this line of reasoning, economists have put a good deal of effort into estimating cost-benefit ratios for various social action programs in which the present value of future income changes is used as the measure of program benefit.

Two HEW studies used this approach in analyzing programs for disease control and manpower training. The disease control study focused on several diseases for which remedies were known to be at least partially effective; it did not attempt to evaluate the benefits of research into new remedies. "Disease" was defined broadly to include injuries from motor vehicle accidents, as well as tuberculosis, syphilis, certain cancers, heart disease, and arthritis. Since programs to control each of these diseases were already in operation, the problem was to determine where additional funding would do the most good. Estimates were made of the lives that would be saved and the disabilities that would be prevented as a result of incremental expenditures on each program, and the ratio of the benefits to the costs in each program was computed.

For the killer diseases these calculations showed that, if the assumptions and guesses were right, campaigns to induce drivers to use seat belts produced relatively high ratios of lives saved per dollar expended, while tuberculosis control programs had relatively low ones. This procedure valued all lives equally and ignored differences in the future productivity of the individuals whose lives would be saved.

For diseases, like arthritis, that cripple but do not kill, the problem was to find a way of comparing the benefits of preventing disability with those of preventing death, and eventually with those of other types of human investment. Another set of benefit measures was based on estimates of the present value of additional income that would be realized through prevention of death and disability. Because estimated future income was higher for men than for women, and for those just starting their working lives than for those nearing retirement age, this procedure gave greater weight to men than to women and favored the young over the old.

A second study examined a group of training and education programs, including adult basic education, vocational education and rehabilitation, and the work-experience and training program, which gave individuals education or training that might be expected to enhance their earning capacity. Again the information available on the programs was of such poor quality that it was impossible to make firm estimates of their effects on the recipients. In principle, however, the methodology of the study was straightforward benefit-cost analysis. Estimates of the earnings of recipients after the training program were compared with estimates of what their earnings would have been in its absence. The present value of the difference between the two was used as a measure of benefit in computing the ratios. Not much confidence could be placed in these ratios, but for most programs they did appear to indicate benefits well in excess of costs. Incidentally, the highest ratios of benefit to cost (about 12 or 13 to 1) were found in the program that was believed to have the most reliable data, the program for vocational rehabilitation of handicapped persons.

To bring programs for younger children into this framework of analysis requires considerable ingenuity, since the income increases that might result are far in the future. Program results are usually stated in more immediate terms, such as reading proficiency at the end of the second grade. But analysts have found ways to approach even this problem.

Thomas Ribich, in his book, *Education and Poverty,* developed an ingenious technique for translating achievement test scores in grade school into equivalent additional years of schooling, which he then translated into equivalent income increases. This technique requires a chain of heroic assumptions: that raising a child's achievement level from, say, fifth grade to sixth grade in a short time will "have the same implications for future earnings as do gains in knowledge that result from a continuation of schooling"; that "test score gains recorded in the short run will not expand or erode with the passage of time"; and that the value of additional time spent in school can be inferred from census data on the average earnings of people with differing years of schooling. If these broad but not implausible assumptions are accepted, it is possible to estimate the future income increases attributable to certain school programs and to compare them with increases attributable to health and manpower training programs.

At first glance, then, benefit-cost studies seem to be pioneering efforts in a direction that might prove really useful to decision makers seeking to establish whether it would do more good to cure cancer or teach children to read. Perhaps the analysts are on the right track, and the major problem is to improve the quality and reliability of the data. With time and effort we may hope for better information on the results of reading programs, the extent to which these results hold up as the children get older, and the actual income differences between good and bad readers. We may collect additional information on the earnings of cancer victims whose death or disability would be preventable if a cure were found. One might even expect to develop a better basis for estimating the probability that a given level of research effort on cancer would yield results.

In fact, neither HEW analysts nor any others have made much effort to refine estimates of the present value of income increases attributable to health and education programs. After the initial illustrative studies, little has been done. Are we overlooking an opportunity to improve decision making on social action programs?

WEAKNESS OF BENEFIT-COST ANALYSIS

The declining enthusiasm of the analysts for cross-program benefit-cost comparisons seems to me well founded. In the first place, as noted above, the easiest benefits for analysts to identify and measure are increases in future income. But application of this criterion to social action programs implies the acceptance of an increase in the national income as an overriding goal. It implies that this goal is more important than good health or better education or the elimination of poverty, and that these other goals are legitimate only to the extent that they increase future income. Most of us are less and less willing to accept the primacy of economic growth as an objective. As John R. Coleman, President of Haverford College, has put it:

> It is no longer self-evident that what goes up must win applause. Some costs of growth have become painfully evident: too many people, too much despoiling of the land and the lakes, too much waste left over by a careless and uncaring society. . . . True, the economist never said it would. But the result is still that the growth goal now seems somewhat tarnished and lacking in force.[1]

Analysis based on future income ignores what most people would regard as the most important benefits of health and education. Cancer is a painful and frightening disease. People would want to be free of it even if there were no effect on future income. Reading is essential to culture and communication; it opens the doors of the mind. In their

---

[1]John R. Coleman, "Economic Understanding and Social Values—Can There Be a Consensus Any Longer?" in *Proceedings of a Symposium on Public Policy and Economic Understanding* (American Bankers Association, 1970), p. 63.

complaints about the schools, minority groups now place great emphasis on economic effects. But if such problems as irrelevant training and failure to find a job were solved, the cultural importance of reading and other educational skills would become more obvious.

While the income and economic growth benefits of social action programs will probably become less important and less interesting to decision makers over the next few years, this does not mean that it will be impossible to compare the benefits of social action programs. Ingenious analysts will be able to place shadow prices on the nonincome benefits of social action programs. But these estimates are likely to be shaky and highly judgmental. Once we leave the fairly firm ground of income we move into a kind of never-never land where we must set values on self-reliance, freedom from fear, the joys of outdoor recreation, the pleasures of clean air, and so forth. The result may not be worth the effort.

Even if we could compare the benefits of social action programs in commensurable terms, we would be left with the problem that different programs benefit different people. Social action programs typically produce both private and public benefits. The first accrue to individuals, who are, for example, cured of cancer or taught to read; the second are diffused to others, who suffer less fear of cancer or enjoy the better life a literate society provides.

The private benefits of different types of social action programs may go to entirely different groups of people. People who have cancer are not the people who cannot read. Even if we knew that the benefit-cost ratio was higher for reading programs than for cancer programs, we would not necessarily choose to devote more resources to reading. The decision would depend in part on the values attached to benefiting cancer victims and illiterates.

Although the problem of *who* should be benefited is clearly a political problem, the analyst can still help by indicating the consequences, in benefit-cost terms, of attaching different weights to the benefits flowing to various groups. For example, Thomas Ribich has suggested that, in evaluating poverty programs, greatest weight be given to the very poor. He points out that a program predicated on a single poverty line would define as successful only income increases that move people across it, ignoring the size of the increase. Under these conditions, larger increases that leave families just below the line might be given lower priority. He suggests a method for arriving at a weighting system in which all income increases count, but those for the poorest count most.

Burton Weisbrod has approached the problem from the other end, suggesting that the analysts can at least show the public what implicit weights the political process attaches to benefits for different groups. Where programs with lower benefit-cost ratios are chosen over those with higher ratios but different beneficiaries, Weisbrod suggests a method for estimating and displaying the advantage afforded the favored group. It is a way of saying to the politician and his constituents: "Here is what you are doing. Is this what you really meant to do?" While it seems useful, one needs great faith in the accuracy of the ratios and the identification of the beneficiaries to place much confidence in the implicit weights.

Moreover, one must also deal with the public benefits of social action programs, which are much harder to identify and to measure, though no less important, than the private benefits. Judged in terms of private benefits alone, the Salk vaccine would have been a poor national investment, since polio never attacked more than a minuscule portion of the population. Freeing the whole country from the fear and anguish it caused was clearly worth a lot, but how much? Both cancer research and literacy programs have public benefits, but it is not at all obvious how to value them. Moreover, even if ways are found to estimate these public benefits, they are not shared equally. Some people put a high subjective value on living in a literate society, and some do not. Some prize a cancer-free society, and some do not. Any decision requires weighing individual preferences against each other; while estimated dollar values may clarify the problem, only the political process can resolve it.

It is my hunch that analysts would be wasting time and effort if they gave high priority to making dollar estimates of the benefits of social action programs, for politicians and decision makers are unlikely to pay much attention to them. They and their constituents have strong, intuitive ideas about the relative importance of health, education, and social well-being that are not likely to be shaken by benefit-cost estimates. The ratios are unlikely to sway the choice of a congressman between a reading program and a cancer cure program. He is more apt to be influenced by clear statements of the benefits in physical terms, such as the number of children who will read with specified proficiency or the chances of curing certain types of cancer, and by identification of the probable beneficiaries.

WHEN BENEFIT-COST ANALYSIS IS USEFUL

This discussion should not be construed as a rejection of benefit-cost analysis, nor as an attempt to downgrade the importance of defining and measuring the benefits of social action programs. On the contrary, one of the most important contributions of the analysts to decision making has been the greater precision about what is being bought and for whom. The sensible decision between cancer and reading programs requires knowledge of who will read better, what effect this greater skill might have on their lives, who is likely to escape death and disability from cancer, and what the consequences might be. Moreover, measures of the outputs of social action programs are essential to the analysis of the relative effectiveness of various ways of producing them. Finally, such measurements act to hold the managers of social action programs accountable to their clients and to create incentives for more effective management. If these benefits or outputs can be easily stated in dollars, so much the better. The only thing rejected here is a substantial effort to make the benefits of various social action programs commensurable in dollar terms. Such comparisons seem not only likely to be shaky but unrewarding, since distributional considerations dominate the decision.

Straightforward benefit-cost analysis, and strenuous efforts to place a monetary value on the benefits and compare them, are, however, clearly justified when the programs under consideration are primarily investment programs, designed to increase future income. The justification is especially valid when the decision involves alternative ways of increasing the income of the same people. Two examples of decision problems illustrate the relevance and usefulness of traditional benefit-cost analysis.

The first is a classic decision between alternative dam sites. Here the primary justification for building the dam is investment in the production of cheaper electric power, although other benefits, such as flood control and outdoor recreation, may also accrue. In this instance, evaluation of these other benefits in dollar terms and comparisons of the benefit-cost ratios of the two projects seem helpful. The distributional problem would remain, of course, for the beneficiaries of the two are not the same. The political process may lead to the choice of the project with the lower benefit-cost ratio. But as long as the primary justification of the project is its contribution to economic growth, the ratios are clearly relevant.

In the social action area, benefit-cost analysis aids the choice between income maintenance and various types of human investment as routes out of poverty for the same people. Consider, for example, alternative policies with respect to recipients of aid to dependent children, who are mostly mothers with children, although unemployed fathers are present in some cases. The objective is to provide an adequate income and improve the prospects of productive lives for the children. One policy is straight income maintenance, which might be regarded as paying mothers to look after their own children. Given the number and size of the families and the level of payments, estimating the cost of this policy is fairly straightforward. The alternative policy is to encourage mothers to work by offering them training opportunities, job placement services, and day care for their children. It is much more difficult to estimate what this will cost and what family incomes will result. To develop such estimates requires assumptions about the proportions of mothers who will voluntarily seek training, stick with it, and obtain a job; about their earnings, above the costs incurred by working; about the duration of their employment; and about the costs of day care. With reasonable faith in these assumptions, one can compare the expected incomes of the families and the cost to the government of the alternative approaches.

The choice of one policy over the other, however, should not turn on the relation of future incomes to cost alone. Those who put a high value on self-sufficiency might choose training, work, and day care even if this approach were more costly. The effects of the two policies on the children are also important. The day care experience could have educational benefits for the children that might be reaped in school or later work. Separation from their mothers might also be detrimental, at least to some children. These effects should be estimated, if possible, and weighed in the decision.

16. The Politics of Evaluation: The Case of Head Start

Walter Williams
John W. Evans

A far-reaching controversy has flared over a recent Westinghouse Learning Corporation-Ohio University evaluation study showing that Head Start children now in the first, second, and third grades differed little, on a series of academic achievement and attitudinal measures, from comparable children who did not attend Head Start.

Reprinted from *The Annals* 385 (September 1969): 118–30, of The American Academy of Political and Social Science. Copyright © 1969 by The American Academy of Political and Social Science. Used by permission.

In the heat of the public controversy, there have been some old-fashioned political innuendos based on vile motives, but, in the main, the principal weapons in the battle have been the esoteric paraphernalia of modern statistical analysis. This is appropriate; the methodological validity of the Head Start study is a critical part of the debate. However, the *real battle is not over the methodological purity of this particular study, but, rather, involves fundamental issues of how the federal government will develop large-scale programs and evaluate their results.*

At this deeper level of the debate, what we are seeing is a head-on collision between two sets of ideas developed in the mid-1960's. On the one hand, there was the implicit premise of the early years of the war on poverty that effective programs could be launched *full-scale,* and could yield significant improvements in the lives of the poor. Head Start was the archetype of this hope. Born in late 1964, the program was serving over a half-million children by the end of the following summer. On the other hand, the federal government, during roughly the same period, implemented the Planning, Programming, Budgeting System (PPBS), founded on the premise that rigorous analysis could produce a flow of information that would greatly improve the basis for decision-making. And the notion of evaluating both ongoing programs and new program ideas was fundamental to this type of thinking.

To see the dimensions and ramifications of this clash, it is necessary to return to those halcyon days in which the basic ideas of the war on poverty and PPBS were formulated. Only then can we explore the present Head Start controversy to see what we may learn from it for the future.

THE EARLY DAYS OF THE WAR ON POVERTY

On June 4, 1965, President Johnson said in his Howard University Address, entitled "To Fulfill These Rights":

> To move beyond opportunity to achievement ... I pledge you tonight this will be a chief goal of my administration, and of my program next year, and in years to come. And I hope, and I pray, and I believe, it

will be a part of the program of all America. . . . It is the glorious opportunity of this generation to end the one huge wrong of the American Nation and, in so doing, to find America for ourselves, with the same immense thrill of discovery, which gripped those who first began to realize that here, at last, was a home for freedom.

The speech rang with hope—a call for basic changes that seemed well within our grasp. Viewed from the present, the address marked a distinct watershed. It was the crest of our domestic tranquility, based on the strong belief that black and white could work together in harmony as a nation. The speech also marked the high point of our faith in our ability to bring about significant change. Despite some of the rhetoric of the time to the effect that change would not be easy, it is fair to say that the faith was there that giant steps could be taken quickly. On that June day, there was the strong belief that the concentrated effort of the war on poverty, launched less than a year before, could bind the nation together.

This faith had two dimensions—first, that there could be a redistribution of funds and power toward the disadvantaged and, second, that, with such a redistribution, new programs could bring substantial improvement in the lot of the disadvantaged. The first was both more clearly perceived and more glamorous. To wrest power and money from the entrenched forces was heady stuff. Less clearly perceived was that redistribution was a necessary, but not a sufficient, condition of progress. New programs had to be devised, not just in broad brush strokes, but in the nitty-gritty detail of techniques and organization. Taking young black men from the ghettos to the wilderness of an isolated Job Corps Center was not a solution in itself. One had to worry about such mundane things as curriculum and the morale of these young men in a Spartan, female-absent environment. This atmosphere of confidence and enthusiasm led us to push aside the fact that *we had neither the benefit of experience in such programs nor much realization of the difficulties involved in developing effective techniques.*

Standing in 1969 on the battle-scarred ground of the war on poverty, it is easy to see the naïveté and innocence of that time—scarcely half a decade ago. Events were to crash upon us quickly. Vietnam was to end any hope for large funds. Riots, militancy, and the rise of separatism made the earlier ideas of harmony seem quaint. Those with established power did not yield easily either to moral suasion or to more forceful means. Real power is still a well-guarded commodity.

Most important for this discussion, we have found, over a wide range of social-action programs, both how unyielding the causes of poverty are and how little we really know about workable techniques for helping the disadvantaged. The point is not that we are unable to derive "reasonable" programs from bits and pieces of information and hard thinking. We *can,* we *have.* But our experience seems to point up, over and over again, the almost insurmountable difficulty of bridging the gap between brilliantly conceived programs and those which work in the field. Great pressures exist for new "solutions" to social problems to be rushed into national implementation as soon as they are conceived. But the attempts to go directly from sound ideas to full-scale programs seem so often to end in frustration and disappointment.

THE ORIGINS OF ANALYSIS WITHIN THE GOVERNMENT

In the early 1960's, Secretary Robert McNamara relied on a conceptual framework, formulated at the RAND Corporation, to make analysis a critical factor in the decision-making process of the Department of Defense. In October 1965, drawing on this experience, the Bureau of the Budget issued Bulletin No. 66-3, establishing the Planning, Programming, Budgeting System within all federal departments and agencies. The departments and agencies were instructed to "establish an adequate central staff or staffs for analysis, planning, and programming [with] ... the head of the central analytical staff ... directly responsible to the head of the agency or his deputy." These central offices were to be interposed between the head of the agency and the operating programs and were charged with undertaking analysis that would provide a hard quantitative basis on which to make decisions. For social-action agencies, this was a radical change in the way of doing business.

Before PPBS, not much progress had been made in analyzing social-action programs. Although the broad approach developed at the Department of Defense might be used in such analyses, the relevance of particular methodological tools was less clear. For example, there was little actual experience with the kinds of evaluations which seek to measure the effects of a social-action program on its participants or the external world. And a host of formidable problems existed, such as the lack of good operational definitions for key variables, the shortage of adequate test instruments, and the difficulties of developing valid control groups. Thus, the usefulness of evaluative analysis for social-action programs would have to be proved in particular situations.

Beyond this was the political question of bringing analysis into the agency's policy-making process. As analytical studies were quite new to social-action programs, their results—especially those measuring the effectiveness of ongoing programs—were seen as a threat by those with established decision-making positions. Unfavorable evaluation results have a potential either to restrict a program's funds or to force major changes in the direction of the program. One can hardly assume passive acceptance of such an outcome by the managers and operators of programs.

Thus, one can see how the tiny dark cloud of the Head Start controversy formed at this early date. The push toward new operating programs and the emerging PPBS brought about a role conflict between those who ran programs (and believed in them) and those who analyzed these programs (and whose job it was to be skeptical of them). As former Director of the Bureau of the Budget Charles L. Schultze has observed:

[In the] relationship between the political process and the decision-making process as envisaged by PPB ... I do not believe that there is an irreconcilable conflict. ... But they are different kinds of systems representing different ways of arriving at decisions. The two systems are so closely interrelated that PPB and its associated analytic method can be an effective tool for aiding decisions only when its relationships with the political process have been carefully articulated and the appropriate roles of each defined. ... It may, indeed, be necessary to guard against the naïveté of the systems analyst who ignores *political* constraints and believes that efficiency alone produces virtue. But it is equally necessary to guard against the naïveté of the decision maker who ignores *resource* constraints and believes that virtue alone produces efficiency.[1]

---

[1]Charles L. Schultze, *The Politics and Economics of Public Spending* (Washington, D.C.: Brookings Institution, 1968), pp. 16–17, 76.

Looking in retrospect, at the early **PPBS** vis-à-vis social-action programs, it may be said that: (1) the absolute power of analysis was oversold and (2) the conflicts in the system between the analytical staff and the operators of the programs was underestimated. Hence, the politics of evaluation—in essence, the clash between methodology, political forces, and bureaucracy—looms much larger than was imagined in those early days. At the same time, knowing more today about how difficult it is to develop and operate effective programs, the need for analysis—the need to assess both our current operations and our new ideas—seems even more pressing than in the less troubled days of 1965.

BACKGROUND OF THE HEAD START STUDY

With these general considerations as background, we now need to look briefly at the key elements within OEO: the Head Start program; OEO's analytical office, the Office of Research, Plans, Programs, and Evaluation (RPP&E); and the general state of evaluation of the antipoverty programs prior to the Westinghouse study.

Head Start

The concepts underlying Head Start were based on the thinking of some of the best people in the child-development area and on a variety of research findings (probably relatively rich compared to most other new programs) suggesting a real potential for early childhood training, *but offering few and often conflicting guidelines as to the detailed types of programs to be developed.* In fact, the original concept of Head Start was that it was to be an explicitly experimental program reaching a limited number of children. The idea, however, was too good. It was an ideal symbol for the new war on poverty. It generated immediate national support and produced few political opponents. In this atmosphere, one decision led easily to another, and Head Start was quickly expanded to a $100 million national program serving a half-million children. In the beginning, Head Start consisted mainly of six-to-eight-week summer projects under a variety of sponsors (school systems, churches, and community-action agencies, for example) with a high degree of local autonomy concerning how the project was to be carried out. Later, Head Start funded a significant number of full-year projects with a similar policy of flexibility and local autonomy.

The immense popularity of the early days carried over. Head Start remained OEO's showcase program, supported strongly by the Congress, communities, poor mothers, and a deeply committed band of educators (many with a significant personal involvement in the program).

RPP&E

Analysis came early to OEO because its Office of Research, Plans, Programs, and Evaluation was one of the original independent staff offices reporting directly to the head of the agency. RPP&E predated the *PPBS Bulletin,* but was, in many ways, the epitome of the PPBS analytical staff, in that it was headed by RAND alumni who stressed the power of analysis. RPP&E was both a major developer of analytical data and a key factor in the agency's decision-making process. As one might expect, in this role it had more than once clashed with program-operators.

Evaluation at OEO

Critical to our discussion is the fact that RPP&E did not establish a separate Evaluation Division until the autumn of 1967. Prior to that time, most of the responsibility for evaluation rested with the programs, but RPP&E had had some involvement, particularly in trying to use data developed by the programs to make over-all program assessments.

In the case of Head Start, the program itself had initiated a large number of *individual* project-evaluations, mainly of the summer program. Across a wide range of these projects it was found that, in general, participants who had been given various cognitive and affective tests at the beginning of the Head Start program showed gains when tested again at the end of the program. However, virtually all the follow-up studies found that any differences which had been observed between the Head Start and control groups immediately after the end of Head Start were largely gone by the end of the first year of school. The meaning of this "catch up" by the control group has been and still is subject to considerable debate, ranging from doubts that the immediate post-program gains were anything more than test-retest artifacts, to assertions that the superior Head Start children raise the performance levels of their non-Head Start classmates.

RPP&E had tried fairly early to develop its own national assessments of Head Start, but found little support for such undertakings within the program. Two such studies were developed, but the results were marred by technical and analytical problems. At the time of the establishment of the Evaluation Division, therefore, no good evidence existed as to over-all Head Start effectiveness—a fact that was beginning to concern the agency, the Bureau of the Budget, and some members of Congress.

As one might guess, the program offices hardly greeted the newly created Evaluation Division with enthusiasm—no one was happy with a staff office looking over his shoulder. In a formal division of labor, three types of evaluation were recognized. RPP&E was given primary responsibility for evaluation of the over-all effectiveness of all OEO programs (Type I). The programs retained primary responsibility for both the evaluation of the relative effectiveness of different program strategies and techniques, for example, different curricula in Head Start (Type II) and the on-site monitoring of individual projects (Type III). The basic logic of this division of labor was to ensure that Type I over-all evaluations would be carried out, to locate the responsibility for these evaluations at a staff-office level removed from the programs, and, at the same time, to place the Type II and Type III evaluation-responsibilities at the program level because of the greater need for detailed program-knowledge that these kinds of evaluation require.

This division of labor also matches the type of evaluation with the types of decisions for which different levels within the organization have primary responsibility—the over-all mixture of programs and resource-allocation at the top (Type I), and program design (Type II) and management (Type III) at the program level.

THE WESTINGHOUSE STUDY

Thus, it was out of this total complex of conditions that the Westinghouse evaluation of Head Start originated:

—The explosive expansion of Head Start from what was originally conceived as a limited experimental program to a large national program almost overnight.

—A developing commitment throughout the government to increasing analysis and assessment of all government programs.

—The national popularity of the Head Start program and the widespread equation of this popularity with effectiveness.

—Previous evaluations of Head Start that did not provide adequate information on the program's over-all impact.

—The development of a new staff-level evaluation function at OEO charged with producing timely and policy-relevant evaluations of the over-all impact of all OEO programs.

As one in a series of national evaluations of the major OEO programs, the new RPP&E Evaluation Division proposed for the Head Start program an *ex post facto* study design in which former Head Start children, now in the first, second, and third grades of school, were to be tested on a series of cognitive and affective measures, and their scores compared with those of a control group. Because the program was in its third year and there was, as yet, no useful assessment of its over-all effects, time was an important consideration in deciding on an *ex post facto* design. Such a design would produce results relatively soon (less than a year), as compared with a methodologically more desirable longitudinal study which would take considerably longer.

Within the agency, Head Start administrators opposed the study on a number of grounds, including the inadequacy of the *ex post facto* design, the weakness of available test instruments, and the failure to include other Head Start goals such as health, nutrition, and community involvement. In sum, Head Start contended that this limited study might yield misleading negative results which could shake the morale of those associated with Head Start and bring unwarranted cutbacks in the program. RPP&E evaluators did not deny the multiplicity of goals, but maintained that cognitive improvement was a primary goal of Head Start and, moreover, was an outcome which reflected, indirectly, the success of certain other activities (for example, better health should facilitate better school performance). Further, the study's proponents in RPP&E recognized the risks outlined by Head Start officials, but argued that the need for evaluative evidence in order to improve the decision-making process makes it necessary to run these risks. After much internal debate, the Director of OEO ordered that the study should be done, and a contract was made in June 1968 with the Westinghouse Learning Corporation and Ohio University.

The study proceeded in relative quiet, but as it neared completion, hints came out of its negative findings. Because President Nixon was preparing to make a major address on the poverty program, including a discussion of Head Start, the White House inquired about the study and was alerted to the preliminary negative results. In his Economic Opportunity Message to the Congress on February 19, 1969, President Nixon alluded to the study and noted that "the long-term effect of Head Start appears to be extremely weak."

This teaser caused a flood of requests for a full disclosure of the study's findings. In the Congress, where hearings were being held on OEO legislation, strong claims were made that OEO was holding back the results to protect Head Start. This was not the case, but the demands did present a real dilemma for the agency—particularly RPP&E. For the results at that time were quite preliminary, and Westinghouse was in the process of performing further analysis and verification of the data. Hence, RPP&E, which, in general, was anxious for evaluative analysis to have an impact at the highest levels of government, did not want to suffer the embarrassment of a national debate over tentative results that might change materially in the later analysis. However, after much pressure, an early, incomplete version of the study was released. In June, the final report was published, and it confirmed the preliminary findings.

These background facts are important in order to understand why the controversy rose to such a crescendo, as it ranged over the executive branch and the Congress, with wide coverage in the press. The Westinghouse study is, perhaps unfortunately, an instructive example of public reaction to evaluations of social-action programs. As we turn now to a brief description of the study, its findings, and a discussion of its methodological and conceptual base, this milieu must be kept in mind.

The study and its major conclusions are summarized succinctly in the following statement by the contractor:

The basic question posed by the study was:

To what extent are the children now in the first, second, and third grades who attended Head Start programs different in their intellectual and social-personal development from comparable children who did not attend?

To answer this question, a sample of one hundred and four Head Start centers across the country was chosen. A sample of children from these centers who had gone on to the first, second, and third grades in local area schools and a matched sample of control children from the same grades and schools who had not attended Head Start were administered a series of tests covering various aspects of cognitive and affective development [The Metropolitan Readiness Test, the Illinois Test of Psycholinguistic Abilities, the Stanford Achievement Test, the Children's Self-Concept Index, and the like.] The parents of both the former Head Start enrollees and the control children were interviewed and a broad range of attitudinal, social, and economic data was collected. Directors or other officials of all the centers were interviewed and information was collected on various characteristics of the current local Head Start programs. The primary grade teachers rated both groups of children on achievement motivation and supplied a description of the intellectual and emotional environment of their elementary schools.

Viewed in broad perspective, the major conclusions of the study are:

1. Summer programs appear to be ineffective in producing any gains in cognitive and affective development that persist into the early elementary grades.

2. Full-year programs appear to be ineffective as measured by the tests of affective development used in the study, but are marginally effective in producing gains in cognitive development that could be detected in grades one, two, and three. Programs appeared to be of greater effectiveness for certain subgroups of centers, notably in mainly Negro centers, in scattered programs in the central cities, and in Southeastern centers.

3. Head Start children, whether from summer or from full-year programs, still appear to be considerably below national norms for the standardized tests of language development and scholastic achievement, while performance on school readiness at grade one approaches the national norm.

302

4. Parents of Head Start enrollees voiced strong approval of the program and its influence on their children. They reported substantial participation in the activities of the centers.

In sum, the Head Start children cannot be said to be *appreciably* different from their peers in the elementary grades who did not attend Head Start in most aspects of cognitive and affective development measured in this study, with the exception of the slight, but nonetheless significant, superiority of full-year Head Start children on certain measures of cognitive development.[2]

METHODOLOGICAL ISSUES

We now turn to the methodological and conceptual validity of the study—the *explicit* focal point of the controversy—and this presents difficult problems of exposition. First, both of us are protagonists on one side of the controversy, with Evans being one of the major participants in the debate. Second, a presentation of the methodological questions in sufficient detail to allow the reader to form his own opinions would require an extensive discussion. The final Westinghouse report comprises several hundred pages, with a significant portion of it directed specifically to methodological issues. Under these circumstances, we will summarize the major criticisms that have been made of the study and comment on them briefly in this section. Then, in the next major section, we will set out *our* judgment as to the over-all technical adequacy of the report and its usefulness for decision-making.

Criticisms of the Study

1. The study is too narrow. It focuses only on cognitive and affective outcomes. Head Start is a much broader program which includes health, nutrition, and community objectives, and any proper evaluation must evaluate it on all these objectives.

---

[2] *The Impact of Head Start: An Evaluation of the Effects of Head Start on Children's Cognitive and Affective Development,* Westinghouse Learning Corporation—Ohio University, July 12, 1969, pp. 2, 7–8.

Our experience has been that one of the reasons for the failure of so many evaluations is that they have aspired to do too much. We did not think that it was possible to cover all of the Head Start objectives in the same study: therefore, we purposely limited the study's focus to those which we considered most important. Despite its many other objectives, in the final analysis Head Start should be evaluated mainly on the basis of the extent to which it has affected the life-chances of the children involved. In order to achieve such effects, cognitive and motivational changes seem essential.

2. The study fails to give adequate attention to variations among the Head Start programs. It lumps the programs together into an over-all average and does not explore what variation there may be in effectiveness as a function of differing program styles and characteristics. The study, therefore, fails to give any guidance concerning what detailed changes (for example, types of curricula) should be made in the program.

This is essentially correct. As discussed earlier, the purpose of the evaluation was to measure the over-all effectiveness of the Head Start program in a reasonably short period of time. This in no way denies the need for a study to get at the question of variation among the programs. The fact is that both over-all and detailed information are frequently needed, but the latter generally takes much longer to develop.

3. The sample of full-year centers in the study is too small to provide confidence in the study's findings. Because of such a small sample, the lack of statistically significant differences between the Head Start and control groups is to be expected, and gives a misleading indication that the programs had no effect. With such a small sample, it would take quite large differences to reach a satisfactory level of statistical significance.

The 104 Head Start centers, selected at random, were chosen in order to provide an adequate *total* sample. This was then broken down into an approximate 70–30 division in order to approximate the actual distribution of summer and full-year programs. If we were doing the study over, we would select a larger number of full-year centers. The main advantage, however, would be to allow more analysis of subgroups within the full-year sample. It is very unlikely that the study's principal conclusions about the over-all effectiveness of the program would be altered by a larger sample. A detailed "power of the test" analysis showed that with the present sample size and variance, the statistical tests are capable of detecting differences between the experimental and control groups below the level of what would be practically meaningful. Forgetting the statistical complexities for a minute, the simple fact is that the differences between the Head Start and control-group scores were quite small. Even in the cases in which differences were statistically significant, they were so small as to have little practical importance.

4. The sample is not representative. Many of the original randomly chosen centers had to be eliminated.

The study suffered a loss of some of the centers specified in the original sample because (1) some small rural areas had all their eligible children in the Head Start program (and hence no controls could be found) and (2) some communities prohibited the testing of children in the school system. Centers were substituted randomly, and a comparison of the final chosen sample with the total universe of Head Start centers showed the two to be very similar on a large number of factors (for example, rural-urban location, racial composition, and the like).

5. The test instruments used in this study, and indeed all existing instruments for measuring cognitive and affective states in children, are primitive. They were not developed for disadvantaged populations, and they are probably so gross and insensitive that they are unable to pick up many of the real and important changes that Head Start has produced in children.

It is entirely possible that this is true. However, most of the cognitive measures are the same ones being used by other child-development and Head Start researchers doing work on disadvantaged children. In those cases (relatively few) where previous studies have shown positive changes on these very same measures, they have seldom been questioned or disregarded because of the inadequacy of the instruments. In the affective area, Westinghouse found no appropriate test instruments and had to devise its own. Hence, the results should be viewed as suggestive, but no more. The Westinghouse study used the best instruments available, and with these instruments, few appreciable differences are found between children who had been part of a Head Start program and those who had not.

6. The study is based on an *ex post facto* design which is inherently faulty because it attempts to generate a control group by matching former Head Start children with other non-Head Start children. A vast number of factors, either alone or acting together, could produce a superior non-Head Start group which would obscure the effect of the program.

It is always possible in any *ex post facto* study that failure to achieve adequate matching on all relevant variables (particularly self-selectivity factors) can occur. *Ex post facto* studies, however, are a respected and widely used scientific procedure, although one which does not provide the greater certainty which results from the classic before-after experimental design carried out in controlled laboratory conditions.

In the Westinghouse study, the two groups were matched on age, sex, race, and kindergarten attendance. Any residual differences in socioeconomic status were equated by two different statistical procedures: a random-replication-covariance analysis and a nonparametric matching procedure. Both statistical techniques, which equated the two groups on parent's occupation, education, and per capita income, yielded the same basic results on the cognitive and affective comparisons between Head Start and control-group children.

7. The study tested the children in the first, second, and third grades of elementary school—after they had left Head Start. Its findings merely demonstrate that Head Start achievements do not persist after the children return to poverty homes and ghetto schools. Rather than demonstrating that Head Start does not have appreciable effects, the study merely shows that these effects tend to fade out when the Head Start children return to a poverty environment.

It is possible that poor teachers, impoverished environment, and other similar factors eliminated a significant cognitive advantage gained by Head Start children during the Head Start period. But even if this is true, we must have real doubts about the current course of the program. Unless Head Start *alone* can be improved so as to have positive effects which do not disappear, or unless Follow Through or some other program can be developed to provide subsequent reinforcement that solidifies the gains of Head Start children, the *present* worth of the gains seems negligible. Whatever the cause, the fact that the learning gains are transitory is a most compelling fact for determining future policy.

8. The study's comparison of Head Start with non-Head Start children in the same classrooms fails to take into account secondary or spillover effects from the Head Start children. The children who have had Head Start are likely to infect their non-Head Start peers with their own greater motivation and interest in learning. Their presence in the classroom is also likely to cause the elementary school teacher to upgrade her entire level of teaching or to give more attention to, and therefore produce greater gains in, the less advanced non-Head Start group. Thus, the study minimizes Head Start's effect by comparing the Head Start children with another group of children which has been indirectly improved by the Head Start children themselves.

This is certainly a possibility. However, most of the previous before-after studies of Head Start's cognitive effects have shown, at most, small gains—so small that it is hard to imagine their having such major secondary effect on teachers and peers. Moreover, the first-grade children in the Westinghouse study were tested during the early part of their first-grade year—prior to the time when such secondary influence on teachers or peer children would have had a chance to occur. In results of direct measurements of the children (Metropolitan Readiness Test, Illinois Test of Psycholinguistic Abilities, and the like), there were only marginal differences between the Head Start and control-group children at that time. Also, on the Children's Behavior Inventory, an instrument which obtained teachers' ratings of the children, there were few significant differences between the two groups, indicating that the teachers were not able to perceive any differences between the motivation of the Head Start and non-Head Start children. In the light of these findings, it is hard to see how spillover or secondary effects could have occurred to an extent which contaminated the control group.

AN ASSESSMENT

Our over-all assessment of the study is as follows:

(1) In terms of its methodological and conceptual base, the study is a *relatively* good one. This in no way denies that many of the criticisms made of the study are valid. However, for the most part, they are the kind of criticisms that can be made of most pieces of social science research conducted outside the laboratory, in a real-world setting, with all of the logistical and measurement problems that such studies entail. And these methodological flaws open the door to the more political issues. Thus, one needs not only to examine the methodological substance of the criticisms which have been made of the study, but also to understand the social concern which lies behind them as well. Head Start has elicited national sympathy and has had the support and involvement of the educational profession. It is understandable that so many should rush to the defense of such a popular and humane program. But how many of the concerns over the size of the sample, control-group equivalency, and the appropriateness of covariance analysis, for example, would have been registered if the study had found positive differences in favor of Head Start?

(2) The scope of the study was *limited,* and it therefore failed to provide the answers to many questions which would have been useful in determining what specific changes should be made in the programs.

(3) Longitudinal studies, based on larger samples and covering a broader range of objectives, would be better, and should be undertaken. But until they are instituted, this study provides a useful piece of information that we can fit into a pattern of other reasonable evidence to improve our basis for decision-making. Thus, the Westinghouse study extends our knowledge, but does not fly in the face of past evidence. For the summer program, the study of a national sample shows what smaller studies have indicated—no lasting gain for the Head Start children relative to their peers. This may deflate some myths, but does not affect any hard facts. For the full-year program, the evidence of some limited effect is about as favorable as any we have found to date.

We imagine that this type of positive, but qualified assessment will fit any *relatively* good evaluation for some time to come. For we have never seen a field evaluation of a social-action program that could not be faulted legitimately by good methodologists, and we may never see one. But, if we are willing to accept real-world imperfections, and to use evaluative analysis with prudence, then such analysis can provide a far better basis for decision-making than we have had in the past.

What, then, does the Westinghouse study provide that will help in making decisions? First, the negative findings indicate that the program is failing, on the average, to produce discernible school success for its participants. Put more bluntly, the study shows that along the key cognitive and affective dimension, the program is not working at all well. And from this, one can infer, directly, that we should search hard for, and test, new techniques to make learning gains in the Head Start classroom more permanent and, indirectly, that the years before and after Head Start should also be looked at carefully. Second, the evidence suggests the superiority of the full-year over the summer programs. Most of all, we believe that the value of the study consists in the *credible, validating* evidence which it provides that the honeymoon of the last few years really ought to be over, and that the hard work of finding effective techniques should start in earnest.

Thus, the study pushes policy-makers toward certain decisions, particularly those involving within-program tradeoffs—more experimentation and more full-year projects in place of summer projects. Yet, and this would be true no matter how good the study was, the evidence is not a sufficient condition for major program-decisions. The last statement holds even for the within-program choices (tradeoffs, but not over-all cutbacks) and takes on greater cogency when one seeks implications for decisions concerning the need for more, or fewer, resources. The evaluative evidence must be considered in the light of other pieces of information and various highly important political judgments. For example: How deleterious would a program cutback be for program morale, or for our commitment to increase the outlays going to the disadvantaged for education? Surely, no reasonable person would claim that evaluative evidence alone is sufficient. Rather, such choices ought to be political, in the broad sense of that term, with credible evaluative data—a commodity heretofore in short supply—being considered as one of the inputs in the choice process.

17. The Politicization of Evaluation Research

Carol H. Weiss

Researchers who undertake the evaluation of social action programs are engaged in an enterprise fraught with hazards. They are beset by conceptual and methodological problems, problems of relationship, status, and function, practical problems, and problems of career and reward. To add to the perils of the evaluation career, evaluation is now becoming increasingly political.

Reprinted from *Journal of Social Issues*, Vol. 26, no. 4 (1970): 57–68. Used by permission of The Society for the Psychological Study of Social Issues.

INCREASING VISIBILITY AND SCOPE OF EVALUATION RESEARCH

Evaluation reports are becoming front-page news. Policy decisions sometimes hinge on whether evaluation shows good results from an action program or not. The Westinghouse Learning Corporation-Ohio University evaluation of Head Start made waves at the White House. The Coleman Report has received explicit attention from the President and the Congress, and if its meaning and its implications are still a matter of debate, the study clearly has had an influence on the formation of educational policy. Where once evaluators bemoaned the neglect of their results by policy makers, they are more and more being given an active role in decision making.

Most evaluation studies, of course, are still filed and forgotten. But the case of the exceptional headliner today is likely to be common tomorrow. Increasingly, legislation and administrative regulations require evaluation of social programs, large sums of public monies are being expended, and results are publicized and considered in decision-making councils.

Evaluation has always had explicitly political overtones. It is designed to yield conclusions about the worth of programs and, in so doing, is intended to affect the allocation of resources. The rationale of evaluation research is that it provides evidence on which to base decisions about maintaining, institutionalizing, and expanding successful programs and modifying or abandoning unsuccessful ones. This function as handmaiden to policy is probably the characteristic of evaluation research that has attracted competent researchers, despite all the discontents and disabilities of its practice.

Not so long ago, innovative social action programming and its accompanying evaluation were small-scale enterprises. The greatest effect that evaluation could have would be to encourage further street work with gang youth (by the sponsoring agency and maybe one or two agencies like it) or discouraging individual counseling sessions for clinic patients. The effects tended to be localized, since programs and their evaluations were bounded. Even where similar programs were operated nation-wide, program staffs were so aware of the unique circumstances of their own school or hospital or organization that they saw little carryover of the results on someone else's program to their own operations.

The big change is that both programming and evaluation are now national in scope. Programs may actually be no more standardized in form, content, and structure than they ever were, but they are funded from a common pot and bear a common name: "community action program," "Head Start," "model cities," "legal services," "neighborhood service centers," "Title I of the Elementary and Secondary Education Act," "maternal and child health program," and so forth.

The evaluation, too, is large-scale, not limited as in the past to the "pilot" or "demonstration" program. Evaluation is mandated in much recent legislation in the areas of poverty, manpower, and education—and funds provided. Thus the evaluation of the Work Incentive Program (WIN), sponsored by the Departments of HEW and Labor, is looking at fifty projects in all parts of the country. The NORC study of the impact of community action agencies on local institutions has been expanded from fifty to a hundred communities. The evaluation of multi-service centers sponsored by the Office of Economic Opportunity now includes study of fifty multi-purpose programs, twenty limited-purpose programs, and twenty grass roots organizations. Such extensive coverage is common practice in many recent evaluation endeavors. A recent Urban Institute review of federal evaluation practice explicitly recommends jettisoning the single-project evaluation in favor of multi-project evaluation.

With studies of this scope and concomitant expense, it is not unexpected that some fanfare attends their completion. The evaluator, unaccustomed to the political spotlight, finds old difficulties exacerbated and new problems burgeoning.

Criticisms of methodology. Once evaluation studies are seen as likely to have important political consequences, they become fair game for people whose views are contradicted (or at least unsupported) by the data. A first line of attack is the study's methodology. Critics of every persuasion seem able to locate experts who find flaws in the sampling, design, choice of statistics, measurement procedures, time span, and analytic techniques—even though their real criticisms derive less from methodology than from ideology. Whatever the motivation, a study whose conclusions enter the political arena must be prepared for searching scrutiny of its methods and techniques.

The experimental model remains the ideal in evaluation methodology, with random assignment of subjects to an experimental group which is exposed to the program stimulus or to a control group which is not. An added advantage of experimental design in political terms is that it is scientifically respectable. But the difficulties of applying the experimental model in field studies are legion; in large-scale social programs they are often overwhelming. Control groups with random assignment are rare amenities.

Nor is it clear that the experiment is always the best and most relevant model. Critics have pointed out its customary limitations. Traditional experimental design deals with a stable standardized treatment; it collects before and after measures over a "full cycle" of the program, and uses specified goal criteria. Its results, then, disclose the extent to which a consistent program has reached its stated goals, but rarely *why* the observed results occur, what processes intervene between input and outcome, or what the implications are for improving the effectiveness of the program. For programs whose goals and emphases shift in midcourse, the experiment cannot distinguish the effects of the old from the new, nor will it provide much feedback to programs that need quick help in planning and implementing changes. Most of these limitations are not intrinsic to the experiment —e.g., if interim measures of success are available, short-cycle quick-feedback results are possible—but they are accurate assessments of most experimental evaluation practice.

Quasi-experimental designs free the evaluation from some of the experiment's restrictive conditions, particularly in randomization, and are more compatible with the program environment in which the evaluator works. As a means of ruling out plausible rival explanations (other than the effect of the program) for the outcomes observed, they can be highly effective and useful; additional controls can be added on one at a time to protect against sources of invalidity that the designs leave free. But again the usual—although by no means inevitable—thrust of the study is the degree of change toward the desired goals. Little attention is generally paid to how the program develops, to variations among units, outside events that affect programming and participation, adequacy of program operation, unanticipated consequences, etc.

Interesting developments are taking place in methodology to study the series of events that ensue from the development of a theoretical program strategy through its implementation and short-run and long-term effects. Systems approaches and process-oriented qualitative analyses, for example, are being applied to large-scale programs. But none of these departures, not even the quasi-experiment, has attained the legitimacy of experimental design. When methodology is subject to attack, evaluators are wary of the untried tack. Many apparently prefer to stick unimaginatively to the book, rather than risk the penalties of pioneering.

Relationships with funding bodies. The new-style evaluation money, although larger in amount than ever before, comes ringed around with restrictions. Not only do the government "RFPs" (requests for proposal, the specifications of the research to be done and its scheduling) specify many of the details of objectives, indicators, timing, analysis, and reporting which used to be thought of as the evaluator's bailiwick, but government agencies are requiring increasingly close surveillance during the course of the study. Some are requiring biweekly conferences or monthly reports. The reason is, clearly, the sad experience that many agencies have had with evaluation. Academic evaluators have been known to bend the purposes of the study to suit their own disciplinary interests. (One story, possibly apocryphal, is that one three-year evaluation of public services, because of the investigators' interest, was turned into a study of the speech patterns of local residents.) Their adherence to schedules and deadlines has been characterized by "academic freedom." Commercial investigators, on the other hand, while generally sticking more closely to the intent of the contract, have cut some uncuttable corners, and the credibility of the research has suffered.

Whatever valid reasons gave rise to agencies' current supervisory practices, they inevitably raise questions about the autonomy of the evaluation. Government agencies may seek only to enforce standards of relevance and research quality, but they almost inevitably become suspect of political pressure, pressure to vindicate the program and justify its budget. The agency retains, after all, the authority to cut off the study in the middle if "progress" is poor. The evaluator can be forgiven for uneasiness about the direction of his research.

Relationships with program personnel. Program staff have rarely liked evaluators poking their noses into the operation of programs or measuring outcomes. Whatever soothing explanations are offered about "testing program concepts" or "accountability to taxpayers," the evaluator is a snoop. To the program operator, who knows that his program is doing well, evaluation is at best unnecessary and at worst, if it shows few positive effects, a calumny and a threat to the future of the program, his job, and needed help to clients.

Today, with the visibility of evaluation becoming greater, program staff are increasingly aware of the implications of releasing data. They see the inferences that will be drawn even from service figures (if temporary beds for overflow patients are not included in the hospital's figures on "number of beds," budgetary allotments will be lower), and they are wary of feeding data into the evaluator's "insensitive indicators" of program success. Thus, access to data may be restricted. Occasionally what program staff deem "more relevant" data may be supplied. Even where this is not so, the general atmosphere of uncordiality can dim the evaluator's spirits and his study.

Drawing recommendations. In the increasingly political context of evaluation, the act of drawing implications from study data becomes chancier than ever. Many evaluations are "black box" studies: the evaluator takes "before" measurements on factors relevant to program goals, the subjects are then exposed to the program (an unexamined entity like a black box), and then he records "after" measurements. He concludes that the program has succeeded in achieving its goal(s) to the observed extent.

To go from such data to recommendations requires what Paul Lazarsfeld calls a leap; in many cases, the data do not provide even a jumping-off point. If a job training program doesn't improve the rate of employment, what do you know about future directions? The data aren't informative about the kinds of modifications that should be made. There is a discontinuity between the study and recommendations of a course of action. With large-scale decisions hanging in the balance, evaluators exercise their non-data-based speculatory talents at their own risk.

Null results. Probably the most serious political problem of all is that evaluation results, with dismaying frequency, turn out to be negative. Over the past several years, careful and competent studies have shown few positive effects from such varied programs as psychotherapy, probation services, casework, school desegregation, public housing, and compensatory education. Elinson reviewing the results of ten of the most competent and best known published evaluations found that none of them demonstrated much success. To judge from evaluations, most action programs do not make much change in the behavior of individuals and groups. The evaluator thus is in the position of turning thumbs down on someone's program. The problem is particularly troublesome because old established programs are rarely evaluated. It is the new and innovative program that is subjected to evaluation. The evaluator and his negative findings are gutting the venturesome program and giving aid and comfort to the barbarians.

We say, of course, that null evaluation results need not lead to the abandonment of programs but to their improvement. The Nixon administration, after the poor showing of Head Start in the national evaluation, did after all increase its budget and call for more experimentation in its content. Nevertheless, the proclivity to the negative remains a fact of evaluation life, and there are those who are uneasy about the effects of this saturnine cast. They fear that not only will it lead to premature abandonment of new programs; it may be more likely to lead to the abandonment of evaluation. As an illustration, Ward and Kassebaum, in a paper reporting the null results of group counseling in a correctional institution, report that the state agency's response to the study was to expand the program and close down access to researchers. The next section of this paper discusses alternatives to traditional evaluation procedures with a view to accentuating the positive.

Alternatives

A number of courses are open. One hopeful direction is to place less stress on evaluations of over-all impact, studies that come out with all-or-nothing, go/no-go conclusions. More resources should be allocated to evaluations that compare the effectiveness of variant conditions within programs (differing emphases and components of program, attributes of sponsoring agency structure and operation, characteristics of participants) and begin to explain which elements and sub-elements are associated with more or less success. Such an approach produces data of interest across a wide range of programs and has high utility in pointing direction for further program development.

The Follow Through program has developed an elegant evaluation design to do this kind of study, with several different program strategies being studied in 60 or 70 sites. Some early reports were not hopeful about the possibilities of carrying out the study as designed.

> However, political considerations apparently resulted in complete local choice of strategy, with the result that the planned variations are not present in the design, and the finest evaluation techniques, even if applied to each local program, will not yield very useful information as to which strategies tend to work best in which demographic situations. . . . Finally, the lack of use of comparable pretest and posttest measures over the various Follow Through strategies essentially assures an ultimate lack of comparability.[1]

More recent reports indicate that all is not lost yet. Although communities do select the Follow Through program model that they implement, it is still possible for researchers to compare the results of each model in different sites. (The main problems that the study is having involve the communities' difficulties in implementing the program with sufficient intensity to make a difference in the classroom and their inability or unwillingness to maintain the program strategy as prescribed in the model.)

Comparative study, even without conscious and orderly variation, can have great power. If the evaluator is clever, he can capitalize on variations that occur naturally. Many government programs, as noted above, are not so much unitary programs as a congeries of diverse efforts addressed to the same problem. Within the programs there are different emphases and different content and procedures. The evaluator may be able to identify the different theories that underlie the differing emphases, categorize them—and the program activities—along a number of significant dimensions, and then relate the types of program to program outcomes. Through meticulous specification of program inputs, of participants, and of environmental conditions, evaluation can increasingly locate and identify the factors that make for relative program effectiveness.

---

[1]Light, R. J., "Report Analysis: National Commission on Civil Disorders," *Harvard Educational Review,* Vol. 38 (1968), 765–66.

Another circumstance that evaluators (and people who fund evaluations) would do well to avoid is premature evaluation. Evaluators have been lecturing their program counterparts for a generation on the need to involve them even before the program begins operation. Don't just bring us in on the ground floor, they have said, bring us in to help dig the foundation. That is all to the good, and people in various locations have evidently learned the lesson. But sometimes this has led to evaluation's assessment of results during the start-up period, before the program has learned how to organize itself and put its concepts into practice. When evaluation goes on while the program is still groping for direction, misinterpretations can occur. Lack of success may be attributed to a particular program and program model that never had the chance to see the light of day.

Etzioni has suggested another order of approach, a "system model" rather than a "goal model." Although his original paper was directed at the study of organizations, it is almost equally applicable to evaluation. The system model recognizes that organizations engage in activities other than achievement of their goals. A study, therefore, should not focus exclusively on goal attainment but should look also at measures of the effectiveness of other organizational functions, such as recruiting resources, maintaining the structure, achieving integration into the environment.

A study that adopted the system model for analyzing a delivery organization used three measures to judge effectiveness: organizational productivity (the goal), flexibility in terms of adaptation to change, and relative absence of intraorganizational strain or tension. The latter two characteristics can be conceived as means to the goal and investments in the organization's capability to achieve its goal over the long run.

In evaluation research, the system model might include indicators of such other aspects of program effectiveness as the ability to get grants, recruit qualified staff, gain political support in the community, etc. This would have advantages in assessing the latent functions of programs, as well as in identifying the real and important second-order effects (e.g., providing an organization that speaks for the poor). But over the long run, whatever its other contributions, a program may well be expected to demonstrate some positive results on client outcome measures as well.

Implications of Evaluation: A Radical Critique

In a basic sense, the bent toward the negative that is characteristic of social action evaluations is not something to be masked or shunted aside. To the extent that null results are real and not an artifact of primitive methodology, they betoken serious weaknesses in social programming. The spate of negative results across a whole gamut of programs betokens a series of important shortcomings.

Basic social science. One component is the shortcomings in basic social science. The behavioral sciences do not give many answers to questions on the causes and processes of social ills. Nor do they have much to say about the processes of social change and the conditions necessary to bring desired changes about. Therefore, evaluation may well be revealing the error in the theories and assumptions on which programs are based.

Suchman has stated the issue beautifully:

If a program is unsuccessful, it may be because the program failed to "operationalize" the theory, or because the theory itself was deficient. One may be highly successful in putting a program into operation but, if the theory is incorrect . . . the desired changes may not be forthcoming: i.e., "the operation was a success, but the patient died." Furthermore, in very few cases do action or service programs directly attack the ultimate objective. Rather they attempt to change the intermediate process which is "causally" related to the ultimate objective. Thus, there are two possible sources of failure (1) the inability of the program to influence the "causal" variable, or (2) the invalidity of the theory linking the "causal" variable to the desired objective.[2]

Obviously much remains to be known in order to plan social change efforts wisely. Programs based on intuitive wisdom and extrapolations from past experience are not good enough. Important theoretical and research contributions are due.

---

[2]Suchman, E. A., "Evaluating Educational Programs," *The Urban Review,* Vol. 3 (1969), p. 16.

Program development. Even with basic knowledge at less than adequate levels, we do not put into practice all we know. Instead of profound re-thinking of program services, there is quick adoption of some fashionable prescription which, whatever its other virtues, is likely to attract funding. Instead of innovative approaches to programming, there is tinkering with the mixture as before to give it a shiny new surface but leave the essential ingredients unchanged.

Very few programs are born without roots in the existing order of things. There are ties and obligations to old agency philosophies and ways of work and to the assumptions and methods of traditional professions. The people engaged in program development activities are not likely to come from, or particularly value, the social science frontier. Nor, on their side, are social scientists doing much applied research on the development of programs. Little is done to apply existing theory and knowledge to program development, to study means for securing acceptance of new programs, or to analyze alternative methods for their implementation within bureaucratic structures. On no side does there seem to be encouragement for radical departures from the past.

Management. The administration and management of new programs, particularly the large-scale programs of recent years, have been woefully deficient. In part this has been because of the effort to bring members of new groups (blacks and other minorities) into management when previous experience had been denied them. But much of the problem has no such justification. In fact, a good share of the fault lies in Washington with its shifting rules, perpetual crises and demands, incredibly complicated procedures for funding and re-funding, and political pressures.

Program structure. Certainly a major reason for null evaluation results on social action programs lies in the structure of programs. Fragmentary projects are created to deal with broad-spectrum problems. We know about multiple causality. We realize that a single-stimulus program is hardly likely to make a dent in deep-rooted ills. But the political realities are such that we take what programs can get through Congress (or other sources) when we can get them. Each then becomes elaborated in its own structure. Even when successive programs are legislated that are broader in scope and resources, as in the case of programs to deal with poverty, the early structures survive.

Each continues doing its own thing with sparse recognition of their interrelatedness. The fragmentation of program structures and authority leads to disjointed (and ineffective) services. Competing and conflicting bureaucracies, jockeying for power and prestige, are not apt to make big inroads in the problem.

Today's programs are the result of a series of uncoordinated decisions, disjointed, poorly matched, often working at cross-purposes. They are run by different levels and organs of government—city, county, independent school system, state, special district. They are funded by, and responsive to, different federal agencies with differing purposes and ideologies. Rarely are they responsive directly to the local governmental unit or to the people whom they serve.

The influx of federal programs and federal funds in the social service field has been an attempt to meet needs that local government has largely ignored for generations. But the organizational structures that accompany federal programs and money have complicated an already intolerable fragmentation of services and authority. What is seriously required is basic reform in local governmental institutions, so that services are provided and coordinated at a level meaningful to individuals. No federal patching or categorical funding has been able to coax, bribe, or order this kind of control. The political scientists' prescription—metropolitanization of area services and decentralization of local services to a level responsive to the people—sounds even more important today than it did a generation ago, if no more politically feasible. Local control of government services, which theoretically can bring about coordination on the neighborhood level, has a host of hurdles to surmount before it even gets to tackle the job.

Time for risk-taking. It is time that we recognized the failure of our moderate, piecemeal, cheap solutions to basic social problems. They have been tried, and evaluation research has found them wanting. Bold experiments are called for. It is a fraud to perpetuate variations on outmoded solutions to problems that are rooted in our system of social stratification. If more and more services to the poor do not enable people to move out of poverty, perhaps we have to look to ways of redistributing income so that the poor are no longer poor. Similarly, we may have to question such hardy assumptions as compulsory education to age sixteen, imprisonment of lawbreakers, the private practice of medicine.

Evaluation research may even be able to help chart the new and risky courses if Congress will appropriate funds for small-scale, truly experimental, pilot programs. The programs would be designed for research, not service, and would be under research control to ensure minimal interference with experimental conditions. Although years of melancholy experience with "demonstration" programs should caution against great optimism, it may be possible to develop program-and-evaluation pilots that are neither co-opted, politically pressured, nor ignored.

SUMMARY

In the deepest sense, there is nothing null about recent evaluation research. The newly-visible large-scale evaluations are progressively disclosing the bankruptcy of piecemeal approaches to social programming. Unless society's limited domestic resources are invested more wisely, significant changes are not likely to occur. This is as important a conclusion as evaluation can provide.

Bibliography

ALLISON, GRAHAM T., **Essence of Decision: Explaining the Cuban Missile Crisis** (Boston: Little, Brown, 1971). Examines decision-making on the Cuban missile crisis from the rational actor, organizational process, and governmental politics perspectives.

ART, ROBERT J., **The TFX Decision: McNamara and the Military** (Boston: Little, Brown, 1968). A case study of the controversy over the decision to select a multipurpose aircraft for the military, contrary to its wishes. Insightful on the decision process in the bureaucracy.

BAILEY, STEPHEN K., **Congress Makes a Law** (New York: Columbia University Press, 1950). A classic case study of the legislative process, showing how ideas, interests, individuals, and institutions contributed to the adoption of the Employment Act of 1946.

BALDWIN, SIDNEY, **Poverty and Politics: The Rise and Decline of the Farm Security Administration** (Chapel Hill: University of North Carolina Press, 1968). An administrative history of the Farm Security Administration which is highly insightful on the politics, problems, and pitfalls of the effort to alleviate rural poverty in the 1930s.

BAUER, RAYMOND A., and KENNETH J. GERGEN, eds., **The Study of Policy Formation** (New York: Free Press, 1968). A series of original essays dealing with theoretical and methodological concerns in the study of public policy.

BERNSTEIN, MARUER H., **Regulating Business by Independent Commission** (Princeton, N.J.: Princeton University Press, 1955). A dated but still useful treatment of independent regulatory commissions as policy formulators and implementors.

BOEK, EDWIN A., ed., **Government Regulation of Business: A Casebook** (Englewood Cliffs, N.J.: Prentice-Hall, 1965). Case studies of administrative agencies in regulatory policy formation and implementation.

COBB, ROGER W., and CHARLES D. ELDER, **Participation in American Politics: The Dynamics of Agenda-Building** (Baltimore, Md.: The Johns Hopkins University Press, 1975). Highly useful treatment of how problems get on the systemic and policy agendas in American society.

DAHL, ROBERT A., and CHARLES E. LINDBLOM, **Politics, Economics, and Welfare** (New York: Harper & Row, 1953). Comparison of policy-making by polyarchy, hierarchy, bargaining, and the market system. A classic work.

DAVIES, J. CLARENCE, **The Politics of Pollution** (Indianapolis: Bobbs-Merrill, 1970). On the formation and implementation of pollution control legislation. Especially good on the administrative aspects thereof.

DAVIS, DAVID HOWARD, **Energy Politics** (New York: St. Martins, 1974). An introduction to public policy and politics in the energy area in the United States.

DAVIS, KENNETH C., **Discretionary Justice** (Baton Rouge: Louisiana State University Press, 1970). On the nature, use, and abuse of discretion in policy-making and implementation by administrative agencies and officials. Analytical and disturbing.

DROR, YEHEZKEL, **Public Policymaking Reexamined** (Scranton, Pa.: Chandler, 1968). A comparative treatment of policy-making procedures, with suggestions for reform. Tough reading and general in approach but useful.

DYE, THOMAS R., **Politics, Economics, and the Public: Policy Outcomes in the American States** (Chicago: Rand McNally, 1966). A leading study that compares the effects of political and socioeconomic variables on state policies. Conclusion: Socioeconomic variables are more important.

————, **Understanding Public Policy,** 2d ed. (Englewood Cliffs, N.J.: Prentice-Hall, 1975). Discusses a number of models of policy analysis, illustrates them with case studies, and compares their utility for policy analysis.

ENGLER, ROBERT, **The Politics of Oil** (New York: Macmillan, 1961). An analysis of the impact of the petroleum industry on pertinent public policies. Good background reading for the current "energy crisis."

FREEMAN, J. LEIPER, **The Political Process,** 2d ed. (New York: Random House, 1965). A brief analysis of the role of executive bureau–congressional committee–interest-group subsystems in policy formation.

FRITSCHLER, A. LEE, **Smoking and Politics** (Englewood Cliffs, N.J.: Prentice-Hall, 1975). Focus is on the role of the Federal Trade Commission in the regulations of cigarette advertising. Provides good insight into the administrative process.

FROMAN, LEWIS A., JR., **The Congressional Process** (Boston: Little, Brown, 1967). How congressional procedures can shape policy outputs is one of the concerns of this volume.

GREENBERG, EDWARD S., **Serving the Few: Corporate Capitalism and the Bias of Government Policy** (New York: Wiley, 1974). The author argues that public policy in the United States is designed to serve the interests of big business.

HALPERIN, MORTON H., **Bureaucratic Politics and Foreign Policy** (Washington, D.C.: Brookings Institution, 1974). Analysis of bureaucratic participation and decision-making in American foreign policy in the post-World War II era.

HARDIN, CHARLES M., **Food and Fiber in the Nations Politics** (Washington, D.C.: U.S. Government Printing Office, 1967). An insightful survey of the politics of agricultural policy formation and administration.

JACOB, HERBERT, and KENNETH N. VINES, eds., **Politics in the American States,** 2d ed. (Boston: Little, Brown, 1971). Comparative treatment of policy-making and public policies in the American states.

JAMES, DOROTHY B., **Poverty, Politics, and Change** (Englewood Cliffs, N.J.: Prentice-Hall, 1972.) A critical analysis of public policy toward poverty and how it is shaped by American values.

JONES, CHARLES O., **An Introduction to the Study of Public Policy** (Belmont, Calif.: Wadsworth, 1970). Jones presents a sequential approach to policy analysis, replete with short case studies, in straightforward fashion.

_____, **Clean Air** (Pittsburgh: University of Pittsburgh Press, 1975). A solid treatment of air pollution policy formation and implementation; especially concerned with national, state, and local governmental interaction in the Allegheny County (Pittsburgh) area.

KINGDON, JOHN W., **Congressmen's Voting Decisions** (New York: Harper & Row, 1973). A valuable empirical study of how members of the House of Representatives make decisions and the factors influencing them.

KOHLMEIER, LOUIS J., **The Regulators** (New York: Harper & Row, 1969). A journalist's account of the policy actions of federal administrative agencies.

KRASNOW, ERWIN G., and LAWRENCE D. LONGLEY, **The Politics of Broadcast Regulation** (New York: St. Martins, 1973). An analysis of policy formation by the Federal Communications Commission. Includes a number of case studies of commission action.

LINDBLOM, CHARLES E., **The Intelligence of Democracy** (New York: Free Press, 1965). An examination of bargaining and other forms of mutual adjustment in policy formation.

LOWI, THEODORE J., "American Business, Public Policy, Case Studies, and Political Theory," **World Politics** 16 (July 1964): 667–715. An influential essay that seeks to develop a new framework for policy study. Lowi suggests that the kind of policy (distributive, regulatory, or redistributive) involved in a situation shapes the nature of the policy-making process.

————, **The End of Liberalism** (New York: Norton, 1969). Lowi argues that American public policies no longer are responsive to public needs because they conform to an outworn philosophy, that is, interest-group liberalism.

MAASS, ARTHUR, **Muddy Waters** (Cambridge, Mass.: Harvard University Press, 1951). A good but dated account of the Corps of Army Engineers' role in water policy formation.

MARMOR, THEODORE R., **The Politics of Medicare** (Chicago: Aldine, 1973). A case study of the adoption of medicare legislation in 1965, and preceding events.

McCONNELL, GRANT, **Private Power and American Democracy** (New York: Knopf, 1966). An insightful examination of the role of private groups in policy formation and how pluralism and decentralization have often made them the dominant force.

MOYNIHAN, DANIEL P., **The Politics of a Guaranteed Income** (New York: Random House, 1973). A rambling account by an "insider" of the development of a proposal by the Nixon Administration for a guaranteed annual income and its rejection by Congress.

NADEL, MARK V., **The Politics of Consumer Protection** (Indianapolis: Bobbs-Merrill, 1971). Good analysis of the formation and adoption of consumer protection legislation.

NAGEL, STUART S., ed., **Policy Studies in America and Elsewhere** (Lexington, Mass.: Lexington Books, 1975). An uneven collection of essays on various aspects of policy study. Raises issues, notes developments, and contains much useful bibliographical information.

NEUSTADT, RICHARD, **Presidential Power** (New York: Wiley, 1960). A study of presidential power and leadership in the policy process. A minor classic.

NOLL, ROGER, **Reforming Regulation** (Washington, D.C.: Brookings Institution, 1971). Analysis of the process of economic regulation. Concludes that problems and shortcomings of regulation would not be eliminated by administrative reform.

OPPENHEIMER, BRUCE IAN, **Oil and the Congressional Process** (Lexington, Mass.: Lexington Books, 1974). Analyzes congressional action relating to the petroleum industry on the oil-depletion allowance and water-pollution control. Good substantive treatment.

PEABODY, ROBERT L., et al., **To Enact a Law: Congress and Campaign Financing** (New York: Praeger, 1972). Case study of congressional adoption and presidential veto of the Political Broadcast Act of 1970.

PHILLIPS, ALMARIN, ed., **Promoting Competition in Regulated Markets** (Washington, D.C.: Brookings Institution, 1975). A series of economic studies evaluating government regulation of such industries as airlines, banking, and electric utilities. Their thrust is in the direction of deregulation.

PIERCE, LAWRENCE C., **The Politics of Fiscal Policy Formation** (Pacific Palisades, Calif.: Goodyear, 1971). A political scientist analyzes the process and politics of fiscal policy formation. Especially strong in its treatment of the development of policy proposals by fiscal agencies.

PIVEN, FRANCES FOX, and RICHARD A. CLOWARD, **Regulating the Poor** (New York: Pantheon Books, 1971). A normative evaluation of welfare policies that finds them to be more a means for controlling the poor than for meeting their substantive needs.

RANNEY, AUSTIN, ed., **Political Science and Public Policy** (Chicago: Rand McNally, 1968). An uneven collection of essays on issues, problems, and theoretical concerns in the analysis of policy and policy outcomes.

REDFORD, EMMETTE S., **Democracy in the Administrative State** (New York: Oxford University Press, 1969). An insightful examination of the role of administration in the policy process, together with concern for democratic control of administration.

————, **The Regulatory Process** (Austin: University of Texas Press, 1969). An analysis of the economic regulatory process, with emphasis on administrative agencies and commercial aviation regulation.

RODGERS, HARRELL R., JR., and CHARLES S. BULLOCK III, **Law and Social Change** (New York: McGraw-Hill, 1972). An evaluation of the impact of the civil rights legislation of the 1960s.

Bibliography

ROSENBAUM, WALTER A., **The Politics of Environmental Concern** (New York: Praeger, 1973). Concerned with the formation and implementation of national policies affecting the environment.

ROURKE, FRANCIS E., **Bureaucracy, Politics, and Public Policy** (Boston: Little, Brown, 1969). Focused on the role of administrative agencies in the formation of public policy.

SCHATTSCHNEIDER, E. E., **The Semi-Sovereign People** (New York: Holt, Rinehart and Winston, 1960). A critique of group theory and a discussion of the impact of conflict on political decision-making.

SCHNEIER, EDWARD V., ed., **Policy-Making in American Government** (New York: Basic Books, 1969). An anthology organized under the headings of policy formulation, articulation, mobilization, codification, application, and redefinition.

SHAPIRO, MARTIN, **Law and Politics in the Supreme Court** (New York: Free Press, 1964). Discusses the impact of the Supreme Court on such areas of public policy as labor relations, antitrust, and taxation.

SMITH, T. ALEXANDER, **The Comparative Policy Process** (Santa Barbara, Calif.: ABC-Clio, 1975.) A comparative (cross-national) treatment of public policy formation, using the categories of distribution, sectoral fragmentation, emotive symbolism, and redistribution. A move toward comparative policy theory.

SORENSEN, THEODORE C., **Decision-Making in the White House** (New York: Columbia University Press, 1963). Short analysis of presidential decision-making by the former counsel to President John Kennedy.

SPANIER, JOHN, and ERIC M. USLANER, **How American Foreign Policy Is Made** (New York: Praeger, 1974). An introduction to the structure and process of American foreign policy-making. Considers problems presented by the president's role.

STEINER, GILBERT Y., **Social Insecurity: The Politics of Welfare** (Washington, D.C.: Brookings Institution, 1966). An analysis of welfare policy-making that illustrates the relationship between the nature of the policy process and the substance of policy.

STEVENS, ROBERT, and ROSEMARY STEVENS, **Welfare Medicine in America** (New York: Free Press, 1974). A study of the Medicaid program. It is seen as the product of an incrementalist policy process out of which policy emerges rather than being created.

STEVENSON, GORDON McKAY, JR., **The Politics of Airport Noise** (North Scituate, Mass.: Duxbury Press, 1972). Systematic analysis of the participants in, and process of, the development of noise abatement policies. Good on the details of policy action.

STRAYYER, JOHN A., and ROBERT D. WRINKLE, **American Government, Policy, and Non-Decision** (Columbus, Ohio: Merrill, 1972). Short analysis of the policy process and a number of areas of public policy.

SUNDQUIST, JAMES L., **Politics and Policy: The Eisenhower, Kennedy and Johnson Years** (Washington, D.C.: Brookings Institution, 1968). Highly informative case studies of several major areas of domestic policy are combined with a general explanatory analysis.

THOMAS, NORMAN, **Education in National Politics** (New York: McKay, 1975). A description and analysis of educational policy-making, especially during the Ninetieth Congress (1967–68).

TRUMAN, DAVID B., **The Governmental Process** (New York: Knopf, 1951). A classic treatment of the role of interest groups in the American political process. Indispensable for an understanding of group theory.

WADE, L. L., and R. L. CURRY, JR., **A Logic of Public Policy** (Belmont, Calif.: Wadsworth, 1970). An examination of American public policy from the "new political economy," or public choice, perspective.

WASBY, STEPHEN L., **The Impact of the United States Supreme Court** (Homewood, Ill.: Dorsey, 1970). A nonquantitative analysis of the Court's impact on public policy. Attempts to develop a theory of impact.

WEBER, ARNOLD R., **In Pursuit of Price Stability** (Washington, D.C.: Brookings Institution, 1973). Discussions of the administration of the Nixon Administration's 1971 wage-price freeze by an insider.

WHOLEY, JOSEPH S., et al., **Federal Evaluation Policy** (Washington, D.C.: Urban Institute, 1970). A survey and assessment of the extent and quality of social policy evaluation by federal administrative agencies.

WILLIAM, WALTER L., **Social Policy Analyses and Research** (New York: American Elsvier, 1971). A solid introduction to the systematic evaluation of social policies.

WOLMAN, HAROLD, **Politics of Federal Housing** (New York: Dodd, Mead, 1971). A succinct analysis of the formation and implementation of public housing policies.